SLAVE

...*on Magazine*. Formerly
...*lm Guide* and series editor of
...widely on film and the arts.

...Wood is Artistic Director: Film at HOME and Visiting
...ssor at Manchester School of Art. He is the author of *The*
...*Book of Mexican Cinema* and is also the editor of *Nick*
...*field: Adventures in the Documentary Trade*.

New British Cinema from *Submarine* to *12 Years a Slave*

The Resurgence of British Film-making

JASON WOOD

AND

IAN HAYDN SMITH

FABER & FABER

First published in 2015
by Faber & Faber Ltd
Bloomsbury House
74–77 Great Russell Street
London WC1B 3DA

Typeset by Faber & Faber Ltd
Printed in England by CPI (UK) Group Ltd, Croydon CR0 4YY

Text of the interviews with Andrew Kötting and Peter Strickland
is taken from *Last Words* by Jason Wood © Columbia University
Press, 2014. Reprinted with permission of the publisher.

The right of Jason Wood and Ian Haydn Smith to be identified as
authors of this work has been asserted in accordance with Section
77 of the Copyright, Designs and Patents Act 1988

Every effort has been made to contact all copyright holders. The
publishers would be pleased to rectify at the earliest opportunity
any omissions or errors brought to their notice.

A CIP record for this book is available from the British Library

ISBN 978-0-571-31516-1

FSC
www.fsc.org
MIX
Paper from
responsible sources
FSC® C101712

2 4 6 8 10 9 7 5 3 1

Contents

Preface

Each and every year in the UK, around the time of a major film festival such as Berlin, Cannes, Venice or Toronto, British arts correspondents feel compelled to take the pulse of our national cinema. The number of British films selected for these cultural Nurembergs, as J. G. Ballard described Cannes, is monitored and assessed. If there is a crop of home-grown titles, it is because British cinema is in rude health; if there are only a few, it is ailing.

An article by Tom Lamont in the *Observer* ('British Film on the Crest of a New Wave', 15 September 2013) highlighted the apparent sense of woe when only two films out of seventy-plus features were selected for Cannes 2013. However, Lamont noted that the tone changed when Clio Barnard's *The Selfish Giant* and Paul Wright's debut feature *For Those in Peril* were among the most celebrated films presented. Barnard's follow-up to *The Arbor* proved to be one of the best reviewed films of the year and also garnered significant UK audiences, achieving the feat of marrying critical acclaim with commercial success. Jonathan Glazer's *Under the Skin*, an arresting look at Britain through alien eyes, was booed in Venice but received a kinder reception in Toronto. A genuinely significant artistic vision, it is a bold and striking work. Toronto also welcomed Richard Ayoade's *The Double*, a Dostoevsky adaptation which couples Terry Gilliam with Aki Kaurismäki via Franz Kafka to impressive effect.

It is important for the press to write about the success of UK-produced films at these festivals, since it is not only an opportunity for British cinema to enjoy the international spotlight but also helps export sales. Articles like Lamont's tacitly enforce the unpalatable truth that while film is an art it is also a business that needs to compete commercially. Andrew Pulver's *Guardian* article 'British Cinema's Golden Age Is Now' (13 October 2011) suggested that British cinema's strength lies in the depth and variety of its offering (something this book is keen to support), but also made the point that box-office success is what enables the British film industry to profit in economic and aesthetic terms. All the films mentioned above achieved a degree of commercial success on release in UK cinemas (*The Selfish Giant* grossing £318,875, *Under the Skin* £1.2 million, *The Double* £785,985), with only *For Those in Peril* failing to match critical acclaim with a paying audience (a disappointing gross profit of £22,804). Does the fact that fewer people saw Paul Wright's film on a cinema screen diminish its achievement? Of course not. What it demonstrates is that no matter how targeted the release some titles have limited appeal, perhaps owing to subject matter, a formal approach or that they were made and released on limited means.

Analysing British cinema can be like comparing apples with pears. Standing tall among the titles mentioned so far in terms of critical and commercial achievements is Steve McQueen's *12 Years a Slave*. This multi-award-winning adaptation of Solomon Northup's memoir grossed over £20 million in the UK alone and became the British cinema success story of the year. What is perhaps most interesting about McQueen's journey from *Hunger* to *Shame* and then *12 Years a Slave* is that the director is a Turner Prize-winning artist whose early forays into cinema were cine-literate as well as experimental. Although his accomplishment is unparalleled, McQueen is emblematic of the current crop of British film-makers working across multimedia platforms whose films could be classified under the umbrella term Artists' Cinema. This category also includes Andrew Kötting, Ben Rivers, Iain Forsyth and Jane Pollard.

Like other national film industries, British cinema is one of peaks and troughs, with both established and emerging voices susceptible to economic and cultural factors. However, the vibrancy and diversity of current British film-making, along with a vital support network, enables it to reach the screen and, on occasion, be enthusiastically received by audiences. In an industry that is fast changing – with on demand and digital downloading – there is a genuine collective desire to empower British film-makers. The radically overhauled BFI Film Fund has played its part in this, as have schemes such as Microwave and organisations including the consistently innovative Film4 and the BBC. Independent producers, distributors, festivals and cinema programmers are also 'on message' in regard to giving British cinema the chance to flourish.

New British Cinema analyses the current state of our contemporary national cinema, filtering many contributing factors through the voices of the directors who are actively involved in making it. An intensive editorial process has resulted in extended interviews with film-makers both on the margins and at the heart of what is happening in British cinema today. There are established figures here whose work and methodology will be familiar and others who have only recently emerged, such as Hong Khaou. Each of them has an interesting story to tell and an important role to play in the continuing evolution of cinema in Britain. Although we made every effort to include all the key directors, some politely declined, preferring to let their work speak for itself.

Jason Wood and Ian Haydn Smith

About Curzon

Ask people why they come to Curzon venues and you'll get a varied response: atmosphere, comfort, location and, for those who like a drink, the bar. But there's one constant above all others: the film programme. We're incredibly lucky to have a loyal audience who trust us implicitly and come week in, week out to watch films. Curzon is known as a place to discover other worlds and cultures, or see a different perspective. It's also a place where the drinks and conversation flow in equal measure, where cinema is a truly memorable experience for a broad range of people. Those curious about the world and hungry for everything life offers might not be film aficionados – they might not even know exactly what's on at Curzon, but they do know what they'll get. We believe there's always something to take away with you, always a surprise, always a conversation point, and always a reason to come back.

Why are we fortunate enough to be trusted? One reason is that we've been doing what we do for a very long time. We've championed the new and been a home for film-makers from foreign lands with something to say. Unexpected sensations, surefire hits and the odd spectacular flop have all featured along the way. But perhaps it's the same restless, questioning spirit that inspired Harold Wingate, our founder, to import unknown films during the post-war period that still drives the business today. As a company that buys, distributes and shows films, we're different from other cinema chains.

However, cinema is changing, and so are audiences. We launched our 'at home' service in 2007 and all sorts of people were up in arms about it. Films at home on the same day as they're released in the cinema? But that's against everything cinema stands for, surely? Nonetheless, Curzon Home Cinema now reaches over three million homes and is growing fast.

The Curzon (as it was then known, long before other venues came along) opened in Mayfair in 1934. It was taken over by the Wingate family in 1940. In contrast to the picture palaces typical of that era, the Curzon had an almost austere interior, in keeping perhaps with the seriousness with which it approached film. During the war it was exceptionally busy – somewhere warm at a time of unheated homes and, like other entertainment venues, a place for London's itinerant population of young men and women in uniform to meet for dates. The running of the cinema was very much a family affair, with Mrs Wingate – fluent in French and taking courses to improve her kitchen Italian – translating and subtitling the films imported by her husband.

Happily, film buying and distribution at Curzon is now a well-oiled machine, and we've picked up more than one or two awards for it. Most recently, *The Great Beauty*, which ran for eighteen weeks, received a BAFTA and an Oscar. At the same time we released *Blue Is the Warmest Colour*, which won the top prize at the Cannes Film Festival. (In the last seven years, we've distributed five Palme d'Or winners.) When Artificial Eye became part of the Curzon stable in 2006 it felt like a perfect fit. Our film buying remains respectful to Artificial Eye's incredible heritage – keeping powerful human stories and quality film-making at its heart – as we look to widen the company's vision in distribution and exhibition.

As for exhibition, we're welcoming new audiences – and bringing Curzon to communities currently underserved by high-quality cinema – as we open beautifully designed venues across the country. Live broadcasts of the world's finest opera, ballet and theatre have changed what cinema means to many, reaching new audiences and opening up the arts to more people. Curzon Home Cinema also allows us to share our love for independent film with millions via its online platform and partnerships with the likes of Freesat, BT, Samsung Smart TVs and Amazon Fire TV.

About Curzon

Curzon has had its fair share of notoriety over the years. In 1950, Max Ophüls's *La Ronde* helped usher in the X certificate, but it didn't stop people turning up to see it at the Curzon during its initial seventy-six-week run. Over half a million people eventually came to the cinema to see it. Luis Buñuel's *Belle de jour* (1967) also sailed close to the wind. But it was Marco Ferreri's *La Grande Bouffe* (1973), with its combination of gluttony and sex, that brought a private prosecution against the Curzon under the nineteenth-century Vagrancy Act (we were acquitted).

Curzon is a brand that has stood the test of time, albeit with the constant changes required to survive in an ever-evolving industry. However, what gets us out of bed in the morning remains the same. As filmgoers are presented with more and more choices, we do what we've always done: offer films that we believe are worth sharing, that spark conversation and stay with you long after the lights come up.

Lenny Abrahamson (photo: Peter Rowen)

Lenny Abrahamson

A graduate of Trinity College, Dublin, Lenny Abrahamson's work initially explored Irish life, from both working and middle-class perspectives. *Adam & Paul* (2004) charts the exploits of two drug addicts over the course of one day in Dublin, as they attempt to steal, score and get high. It showcased Abrahamson's innate skill in balancing comedy with high drama, which would be mined further in *Garage* (2007). Starring Pat Shortt, better known to local audiences as a comedian, Abrahamson's second feature is a beautifully realised character study of a good-natured man with learning difficulties. Josie lives and works in a garage in a small rural town. Popular with everyone around him, he sparks up a friendship with a young lad who works alongside him part-time. However, what Josie believes is an innocent act leads to him being ostracised by the town and left alone in the world. A prizewinner at the Cannes Film Festival, *Garage* cemented Abrahamson's position as Ireland's most accomplished film-maker.

After directing the TV series *Prosperity* (2007), Abrahamson returned to cinema with *What Richard Did* (2012), adapted from Kevin Power's novel *Bad Day in Blackrock*. The film focuses on Ireland's middle class and a handsome, popular schoolboy whose affections for his best mate's girlfriend have tragic consequences. Filmed on a broad canvas and portraying an Ireland rarely seen on screen, Abrahamson perfectly captures the excitement and ennui of teenage life. As with the director's previous work, *What Richard Did* presents a subtle examination of the impact of mental illness, both on the afflicted and those around them.

Frank (2014) also touches on mental illness, within the framework of a fictionalised biopic of Chris Sievey, aka Frank Sidebottom. Loosely inspired by Jon Ronson's experiences as the keyboard player with the Oh Blimey Big Band, the film charts the progress of an offbeat group as they journey from obscurity on the fringes of the British music scene to infamy at the South by Southwest music festival. Abrahamson skilfully shifts from the earlier comedic scenes to much darker territory during the film's closing moments, aided in no small part by Michael Fassbender's and Domhnall Gleeson's excellent performances.

Abrahamson's next project is an adaptation of Emma Donoghue's *Room*.

This interview was conducted over a period of two years, between the completion of *What Richard Did* and the release of *Frank*.

Looking at the number of people you've continued to work with over the years, collaboration is quite an important aspect of your work.

I really like the collaborative process of film-making. Sometimes I have to trick myself into starting work. One of the ways of doing that is to start on something that I can't extract myself from, usually with me relying on other people who have expectations of me. In that way, if my outlook on a project gets pretty bleak I have to keep going. My sense of responsibility always trumps my innate nihilism about the films I'm making. I always value what I've done at the end, and I certainly value the work of everyone involved with me, but when I'm working on a project I can go through periods of self-doubt. One of the reasons I've avoided writing fiction, or writing screenplays on my own, is that it's too easy to walk away from them. However, that's just the negative side of things. On the positive side, I relish the collaborative environment and the spirit of sharing ideas – the particular stimulus of bouncing different ideas around.

I think that's why accidents and mistakes can be so stimulating. Your films are never quite as you imagine them to be. They're always going to be a bit different because of something happening on that day, or the moods of the people, or the way that the light works, or you might arrive at a location and it's changed in a particular way. In those moments, when material is thrown at me, it unlocks an immediate creative response. Those accidents, that kind of unpredictability in a collaborative situation, really suits me. Even if someone has a bad idea, I find the process of addressing it a more reliable and robust process than the part when I'm sat on my own.

You worked with the writer Mark O'Halloran on three projects.

I would love to work on another film with Mark. To be honest, I'm not sure why we haven't. We've never had an argument or fallen out. There have been projects that haven't worked out. One of the reasons there was such a long gap between *Adam & Paul* and *Garage* was because we had a go at something and it didn't work out. Various things have happened that affected him, but now he's writing like crazy, so I can see us working again at some point. In the best scenario, we've both gone off and done our own things and they have been successful, so we can come back together and, kind of . . .

. . . reaffirm your vows.

[Laughs] Yes. Exactly. And perhaps forgive each other our in- fidelities!

What was the process like between you two on Adam & Paul? *The film has a more freewheeling feel than* Garage *and yet there's still a precision to the narrative structure.*

I am fascinated by how those two seemingly opposite elements can exist. It's connected to that idea of chance and mistake. Even though I hope each of the films I make is well balanced and has that sense of precision, I hope that the things being thrown at me – the freewheeling element – gives the film a sense of energy.

Whatever happens, the structure has to shift to accommodate it, but it must still exist and make sense within the context of the narrative. I think all of my films are a mix of the found and the made. Whether it's lengthy discussions with Mark over what we're going to include or, like many of the scenes in *What Richard Did*, it comes out of watching the kids and how they respond to each other, it all has to fit together to make a coherent whole, which fits in with the film's ideas.

Adam & Paul was great because we hadn't worked on a film before. It came about with no pressure. It's scary on one level, but there's also a sense of abandon. And when you're working on your third or fourth film you realise that, by comparison, it wasn't scary at all.

The tonal range of the film was agreed on at the very start of the writing process. Mark had given me sample scenes for a possible idea, with an overall outline, which eventually changed. But the musicality of those scenes, between those two characters, was there right from the beginning. It was a joyful thing. Even though the film is dark in places, the real heart of it is a celebration of a style – an old-fashioned comedic tradition, mixed with a more modern Beckettian twist. What I think I brought to the project is something that's fascinated me since I watched Laurel and Hardy as a kid, and that's the absolute beauty of two lost individuals sitting together and letting the world occur – a certain existential situation. To turn the camera on two addicts and have them be just that – that was there from the beginning.

There is this seamlessness in the way that your narratives shift between comedy and high drama.

It's a comedy of tenderness. I don't do black comedy. When you look at people on their own in an environment, if you filter out the noise, what lies at the heart is a sense of uncertainty and need. That behaviour exists on the thin line between the humanely funny and the desperately sad.

4

I think that part of what allows me to move between different tones in a film, particularly with *Adam & Paul* and *Frank*, are the various digressions that unfold throughout those narratives. They allow me to explore those facets of character. Novels do it to an extreme degree. Proust managed to combine the highest philosophical meditations with the comedy of the party scenes.

Another constant in your work is the strong focus on complex characterisation – the nuances in each personality, which surface the more time we spend with them. It's there no matter how much your style of film-making changes, which it has significantly across the four features.

I'm a fan of story but not plot. Tell me what happens to this person, but don't give me a mechanism that creates this false, imposed tension. The tone of *Adam & Paul* is in the frame before anything happens. It's almost a way of allowing the time that passes to set the tone. I've heard conductors talk about the way they respond to the orchestra in front of them – a response to the musicians they see in that moment. It can change the music with each performance. I understand that.

These things have to be thrashed out with the actors – in rehearsals and in the casting – whether it's a hint that makes them attack the opening phrase of a line that can change everything. When it really works it should appear as one vision. Like conducting, directing is a series of mechanical decisions and instructions, but it should appear as one single flowing action. Look at Kaurismäki's films. Tonally, he is one of the most recognisable directors at work today. You can never mistake his work. I had seen his films before I made *Adam & Paul* and they were a powerful influence on me.

There's also something beyond character. It's the presence of the person in that space at that moment that I find so interesting. When you're talking generally about character, that's something you could transpose from a film to a book. It's character as presence that really fascinates me – what that person feels like in a room. I haven't really talked about this before, so it's quite interesting to think it through.

You know when you're in a car, looking out at the landscape? I would get that same feeling – of watching the world at one remove – when I was young and in a room surrounded by adults. They tend to sit still a lot. So as I watched them I saw one person tapping their finger. Another was watching television in a particular way. Someone would say something that wasn't heard by the third person. Then things would all settle back down again. It was like a sculpture, or a machine or a . . .

. . . composition.

Yes. Those energies in a room fascinated me before I was sophisticated enough to say, 'He's a depressive and she hates her, which is why she isn't listening.' Before I was able to decode that into the language of desire and tension – the psychological stuff – I felt there was something beautiful in how people operate in those spaces and how time flows through them.

I feel I've still only scratched the surface of this. The films I make are really just the receptacle, the container, which holds these precious things. And so narrative comes later. You certainly need to know why you're there. So in a film like *Garage*, you have Josie pottering along, but he is pottering along with some direction – a destination within the construct of the narrative. However, it's in the journey that all the interesting things happen.

With your interest in exploring this space, was there a decision – as you progressed from Adam & Paul *through* Garage *to* What Richard Did *– to explore different facets of Irish society and in particular class?*

That was actually a happy accident. By the time of *What Richard Did*, I was aware that I had covered the urban poor, the rural and the prosperous. I heard someone refer to the films as the 'Celtic

Tiger trilogy'. That's not something that ever occurred to me. I think the change of location was bloody-mindedness on my part. In France, people started to talk about the 'Loachian' aspects of my work. I have a huge respect for Ken Loach's films but I'm a million miles away from what he's doing. I consciously made *Richard* because I didn't want to be slotted into a specific role as a film-maker.

What distinguishes *What Richard Did* from most other films made in Ireland over the last few years is that it takes place among the middle class. It's a leafy, attractive world of nice houses and good-looking people whose lives are not so dominated by the usual concerns that might affect many of us – of just getting by. Irish cinema has, like a lot of cinema in our part of the world, concentrated on people who are on the margins and living harsher, more challenged lives. We're used to seeing the gritty streets of inner-city Dublin – I've filmed them myself – or, in the case of *Garage*, an isolated and fairly dysfunctional rural community. So it does make a change to see Dublin looking pretty, with people going to summer houses and walking on lovely beaches. Ireland's a beautiful place and, outside of the more saccharine Hollywood representations, we haven't tended to show this aspect of it.

Alongside the comedy of tenderness is the subtlety of the palette you employ. What Richard Did *accentuates the beauty of Ireland that you feel is rarely captured on film.*

I worked with the cinematographer David Grennan, who is young and relatively new. This is his second feature as cinematographer, but he's worked a great deal as a camera operator. We watched a lot of films together and talked about approaches to lighting in scenes. These discussions are partially aesthetic, so you're talking about how black the blacks should be and whether the image in a particular scene should feel crisp or whether you want it to be softer. They're also practical – how I want to shoot and how much freedom there is to move the camera. This impacts on his work. If I want to be able to shoot in all directions, that's something Dave is going to have to facilitate, whereas if I was shooting in a controlled, pre-planned way, then he could light a location more specifically. We had these discussions all the way through, so by the time we shot the film it was a very easy working relationship and we were able to find an approach to a scene very quickly.

Jack Reynor is remarkable as Richard. How easy was the casting process?

It was a long process. Louise Kiely, the casting director, went to so many schools, sports clubs and drama groups – anywhere she could find kids who would understand the drama of the film. That took several months. At the same time, we were also looking for experienced actors. It wasn't really until we found Jack that I knew we were going to make something interesting. It's an obvious thing to say, but if you don't find the right Richard for a film called *What Richard Did*, then you're in trouble. He's such a great actor and he knows that world intimately. He went to the same school that the school in the film is modelled on. He has the same charisma that Richard has, which is crucial. Likewise, Róisín Murphy is amazing as Lara.

What makes the characters so credible are the stories they tell. Their conversational style feels natural.

The script was mostly written, with about 20 per cent improvised. The stories the actors tell are almost all real. So Jack's story about drowning his pet gerbil when he tried to give it a bath actually took place, when he was five years old. That scene wasn't planned. He told it as we were setting up and we just recorded it there and then.

I spent almost a year working with the cast and these stories cropped up all the time. My co-writer Malcolm Campbell and I would note them down and then remind an actor of things they had talked about, so that they could incorporate them into a scene. That kind of fluidity was really exciting. Even during the shoot, while travelling from one location to another, you would overhear something the guys were saying. Once or twice we took those and put them into a scene we shot later that day. So they were really fresh and there was a lovely immediacy to it, and the textures of their delivery were the same as when they first told it.

These conversations also shift audiences' expectations about what they're watching.

I enjoy the challenge of thinking about structures within a film that aren't just off-the-shelf creations. In *Adam & Paul*, you allow the audience to become comfortable, thinking they're watching a certain kind of comedy. Then you turn that on its head and make it a much less comfortable film. I think there are things to learn from structure, which is an expressive element. So those choices are made not just to keep an audience interested and to surprise them. They also inform the film at a deeper level. They allow you to explore some interesting ideas. In *Garage*, you think you know who Josie is at the beginning of the film; you're invited to participate in the town's image of him – that's he's a village idiot – but he defies that categorisation by the end of the film. It makes you think how easily you consign people to stereotypes and how dangerous it is to do that. So the structure of the film can challenge you on those assumptions.

In *What Richard Did*, while there's always a tension in the film because of the title – you know something's going to happen – it's not possible when you watch the first twenty minutes to work out where you're going to find yourself emotionally at the end of the film. As a film-maker, I do like to allow myself to discover things about a character and the story as I make the film. If you know everything in advance yourself, what is there to explore? It's important for me to have that. That then makes the editing process exciting, because there you can refine the film.

The editing shifts with the change in tone, from a looser style in the early stages then becoming tighter as the film progresses.

That's true. The film has an observational style at the beginning, watching this group of youngsters, as you would if you were at the same bar they were in. Then, halfway through the first beach section, when Richard's character gets up to walk through the garden to the dunes, the film creates more of a sense of an interior. It's also the point where the music comes in for the first time. It's not as observational and the subjective elements become more apparent as the film continues, until, by the end of the film – or at least close to the end of the film – it is a strong evocation of the state of being of the central character, before leaving the audience with an image that is external and asks lots of questions. These shifts in perspective and tonal changes are what I'm most interested in with regard to film, both as a director and audience member.

The film, like your previous work, refuses to assign blame or point fingers. Yet there is a morality at work here.

I don't believe it's the director's job to tell an audience what to think. It's not my job to judge. My job is to present things as truthfully as I can and to create that intimate encounter between the audience and the characters. If you can do that, what is amazing is that the audience has a natural tendency towards empathy. It's almost impossible to stop that feeling. If an audience spends enough time with a character, provided they're not a monster or a psychopath, they can become very connected to them. It allows me to have characters doing awful things, yet still manage not to alienate the audience; that character can still be cared for.

I think of myself as a humanistic film-maker. I try to present people – to the extent that my skill allows – to the completeness of their humanity. That humanity can't be switched off because people do terrible things.

The music in What Richard Did *is beautifully restrained.*

Stephen Rennicks has composed the music for all my films, including *Frank*. We've been friends for over three decades. *What Richard Did* allows for a more expressive score than *Garage*, which featured very little. We agreed that the film wouldn't be the music of the characters. It's not a teen movie – it's a film about teenage people told from an adult perspective, and as such should appeal to all ages. In a way, the film is imbued with a nostalgia that comes from an older person thinking about younger people. So there's a longing in the music.

Frank *is the perfect example of a film where knowing nothing about it is a great way to see it.*

Yes, it's the best way to see it. It is such a strange film that you just have to go with it from the beginning – just let it do its work. If you have too many expectations when you go in, you'll probably be off the mark. So that's a good way to see it.

Did you ever see Frank Sidebottom play live?

I never saw him. The closest I got was seeing him on *Top of the Pops* as a kid and then on some kids' TV programme. If you were living in Dublin then, back in the 1980s, you only got BBC1 and BBC2 – we were a little outpost of British TV – and so I saw him there. He definitely made an impression on me as a kid. I never became a big fan. I think he was just that bit too 'other'. But the image of him stayed with me.

How did you become involved with the project?

I was sent a script by my agent. She said, 'You've got to read this. It's by two brilliant writers and this is a really strange project, but bear with it because I think there's something in it.' It's the first thing that I've worked on that's come from outside – where something landed on my desk. I read the script, which was very different from the one we shot. I was immediately taken with the central section, where they get lost in the wilderness to make their album, which was loosely inspired by the stories surrounding the recording of Captain Beefheart's *Trout Mask Replica*, and any other number of stories about people going completely mental and getting cabin fever in the wilds. There was something very freewheeling, anarchic and playful in the writing of that section, which was the right side of quirky – it was strange and lovely, and tender and childlike. It was also moving. These scenes were where Jon Ronson and Peter Straughan really let themselves go and just enjoyed the world and the characters – the least narratively driven part of the film. There was something about those scenes that I responded to, so I met with them and we got on well, and started working together on the script. We worked on the overall structure, particularly the sections that bookend the scenes in the wilderness.

How much had Jon Ronson's own story, of being a member of the Frank Sidebottom Oh Blimey Big Band, been excised before your involvement?

It had already been established that it was completely fictional. Once Jon and Peter began talking about the project, they moved quite quickly away from the real story and towards an 'inspired by' character, one that captured [the real Frank Sidebottom] Chris Sievey's punk anarchic spirit. Only the physical shape of Frank Sidebottom remained. I think Chris himself was keen that they did that. It also made sense to me. I never wanted to make a biopic. It could have been interesting but it wouldn't have appealed to me in the same way. So I entered the fray with the story fully fictionalised and we just went from there.

The film touches on mental illness in a way that is not too dissimilar to your previous films, What Richard Did *and* Garage.

That's true. It's so often the case that you see these patterns after you've done the work. *Frank* deals with this material in its own particular way. It remains true to its comedic heart, even though it goes somewhere that is emotionally quite affecting. I would hope that the brush with this topic doesn't in any way over-balance the film for anyone watching it. I don't think it does.

It doesn't.

If anything, I think it adds a certain depth to it. It must be a preoccupation of mine, or something that I'm very moved by – by people who struggle with their own internal difficulties. Also, anything that is broken or flawed helps us understand the way we work. You look at things that aren't working in order to understand how things really work.

The film is also a study of the creative impulse.

We have an instrumental idea of creativity. It's valued because what it produces is success. At least in the mainstream that's how we rate it. We talk about someone 'never really making it' as a waste or a pity but never engage with the work itself. If that work loses its value then the whole thing becomes an empty pur-suit of approval.

It's so interesting to see how social media works now. Some people are championed and others are vilified. If someone puts a foot wrong then they are eviscerated on Twitter, which emanates a great sense of its own moral authority. I think that we're so conditioned to measure value in terms of success. The way we present ourselves in that space is so false. It lacks any sense of humility or the basic human recognition of fallibility. And you look at a character like Frank, who is so fallible and messy and could never function as his own marketer in the way that Jon [Domhnall Gleeson] does and in the way that so many people in the creative world are encouraged to work, as their own PRs, as if that's empowering. It's like, 'Okay, you don't need a record contract any more, you don't need a big film company behind you. You can make your work and you can promote it.' While in one sense that is freeing, in another it turns you into your own cheerleader, which I think is a really unpleasant split in a person. That's what Jon is. Actually, he's just the cheerleader – he doesn't have the talent. And Frank is just the talent without any of the other. They're two parts of what is expected of one person in many cases today. Frank is the authentic, flawed, creative part and Jon is the egotistical, self-promoting, put-your-best-foot-forward, be-positive, social-media-avatar part.

So this is a film that celebrates the process and not the end result?

Yes. As my editor says, you can't cheat the process. When you start editing a film, which is a big, unwieldy task, you initially feel that you're getting quite close and this isn't going to be one of those long edits. At least, you think that. And then you realise you have always got to go through it, living this process and questioning it. Things are always better for that. And that has value. The film really affirms that. They may never play to hundreds of thousands of people. But what they're doing is great.

The music here is so starkly different to its role in previous films you've made. Not just because it's about a band, but for the way it works so integrally with every element of the film.

I loved it, although it was very daunting. For one thing, when you're putting music in your film as opposed to on your film, you've got to know what a lot of it is before you start shooting. That said, we didn't record in advance. Everyone played live and was filmed live, which was a challenge but adds to the authenticity of the film. But you need to know what the tracks will be, and they're big colours to nail to the mast from the outset.

I've played in a few bands, and although I'm not a great musician I do have a strong musical impulse and this was the first time I was really able to actively and constructively use it. So while Stephen was writing the music, I was working with him, listening to it and responding, and I ended up writing quite a lot of the lyrics. I also worked with some great musicians, testing out ideas in the studio of how this band might operate. We tested out really interesting principles. Not just discussing what style they were going to play. That felt like the wrong question. It was more like, 'What if they're astronauts and are exploring the furthest reaches of musical possibilities?' So we began looking at the tiniest objects they could use to make a piece of music. Or, let's have them write something and see what can be extracted so that you still know it's the same piece. This experiment, or process, which is as much about the philosophy of how you might make a song as it is about the music, is then distilled to create some songs, like the last one that Frank sings. But it also creates more playful music – half music, half spoken.

We went for a total looseness. The really tricky thing was maintaining that while going through the very mechanical process of making a film. We had to create pieces of music that we knew the band could actually play. They didn't have the luxury of being in a studio rehearsing for three months. The pieces aren't technically difficult, but they are loose enough to still be changed on the day. That's also why we didn't pre-record. If we did that, everything would have had to be simpler. Instead we allowed the performers to respond to what was happening there and then. It was a hard process to anticipate. Having a real drummer and a gifted actor who could play the bass really well was also important. Domhnall even wrote the really bad stuff he performs, which was great.

I have to pay tribute to Stephen. We thought he would write the score and then we would get a band in for the songs. We got demos from some pretty amazing people, but everything Stephen did was always closer to what it should be. And we just work together well. I really enjoyed it.

With your film and Terrence Malick shooting at least one of his upcoming projects there, the South by Southwest festival seems like the place to go for making a film. What was it like filming there?

We didn't. It's so great that people think we shot there, and even when we attended the festival proper – to screen the film – the audience still thought we shot there. We actually shot the US scenes in Albuquerque, New Mexico. Texas lost their tax break, and not quite having the budget of a Terrence Malick film, we had to shoot somewhere that suited us financially. It also helped that the desert landscape around Albuquerque is gorgeous. We just studied South by Southwest and reconstructed parts of it. Going there then, with the film, was really funny because I found myself registering it in exactly the same way that the band does in the film. And the whole place was just jammed with hipsters. I think we all thought we did a pretty good job replicating it for the film.

The bright desert scenes offer a contrast to the narrative. By the time the band arrives in the US the story has become significantly darker.

The counterpointing visual shift was just luck. And I guess there was a little luck involved in the ending too. If you have actors like Michael, Maggie and Domhnall, and things work out, you can create something special. The tension we had in the film, which was building up, really found a release at the very end. The script only hints at what we achieved in the end thanks to the actors and the music. It floored me and, I think it's because of Michael that it turned out that strong.

Michael Fassbender is brilliant as Frank. But Domhnall is the person who really holds the whole thing together. Both in his relationship with Frank and with Maggie Gyllenhaal's character.

He's pretty despicable in the film. That appealed to Domhnall because he's played a lot of lovely guys. And he is a lovely guy.

Michael rightly gets amazing plaudits for this film, and I think it is a great performance. But I think it overshadows how great Domhnall is. It is so hard to play that part. On the one hand, he has to be the straight man, because that's how the comedy works in the film – he's the butt of the jokes. But that character also has a big journey to go on. So he has to balance the fact that we have to be rooting for him, because at some point he seems right, but at the same time we then have to realise how selfish and destructive he actually is. If you get Frank's character right, the rightness is massively visible. But if you get Jon right, he sort of disappears.

Domhnall's work with Maggie is great too – the way they spark off each other. Maggie is terrifying. She brought a much more serious darkness to Clara than I would have gone for initially, and it took me a while to realise just how right she was. Rather than have a comic foil, she transformed Clara into a very rich character. And the sex scene is hilarious. I'm really proud that I've made a film that could include a jacuzzi scene alongside that incredible powerful ending.

Hossein Amini (*centre*) on the set of *The Two Faces of January* with Viggo Mortensen (photo: StudioCanal)

Hossein Amini

An acclaimed screenwriter, Hossein Amini has worked with Peter Kosminsky (*The Dying of the Light*, 1994), Michael Winterbottom (*Jude*, 1996), Iain Softley (*The Wings of the Dove*, 1997), Shekhar Kapur (*The Four Feathers*, 2002), John Madden (*Killshot*, 2008), Mikael Håfström (*Shanghai*, 2010) and, most recently, Susanna White (*Our Kind of Traitor*, 2015). His screenplay for *Drive* (2011), directed by Nicolas Winding Refn, stripped James Sallis's novel to its bare bones, creating one of the finest American crime dramas of the last decade.

The Two Faces of January (2014) is a boldly imagined adaptation of Patricia Highsmith's novel. As richly rewarding as Amini's screenplay for *The Wings of the Dove*, the film is also notable for its strong visual style, particularly in the use of location as a metaphor for the characters' desperation and despair.

What is it about Patricia Highsmith's work that attracts you?

She creates a two-way mirror between the characters and their psychology and the reader. She has this ability to put you in the criminal's shoes. Her writing can reflect a lot of the weaknesses or a darker side in me as a reader. For example, there are times in *The Two Faces of January* when Chester is tender with his wife, Colette, then in the very next moment he says something mean and biting. It struck me that I've done that, and it's a characteristic I don't like about myself.

She's certainly more interested in character than she is in plot. I've never read her books because of the plots, and all the really good adaptations have been fairly free with them but have mined the characters she has created for all they're worth. Unlike the Ripley novels, which have at their centre a psychopath, *Two Faces* takes a very weak, conflicted, jealous and drunk older man and makes him both the hero and anti-hero. You feel compelled by him throughout the whole journey. It's Highsmith's ability to be so non-black-and-white with her characters that makes them so alluring.

Like the main characters in your adaptations of The Wings of the Dove *and* Drive, *Chester falls between the cracks of a criminal and someone who has taken a few wrong turns in life.*

Characters like Chester bring those criminals closer to us. It's that very thin line between leading our everyday lives and suddenly, through fate or circumstance, we can be dropped into a dark and dangerous situation. In the way that you could step out into a street and be hit by a car, everyday life is actually out of our control. We reassure ourselves that we're okay, but we don't know what lies in wait. It's that element of those stories – they embody the lack of control we have over our lives. I also love mythology and the roles played by fate and destiny. You have that in a lot of Highsmith novels, but particularly in this story.

I gather you researched Highsmith's life and read her own collection of writings on the art of the novel before embarking on this screenplay.

Yes. I wanted to see how she approached suspense. The other book I read, which was more influential in terms of writing the screenplay, was the Hitchcock–Truffaut interview. Highsmith's novels are thrillers without thrills. It can be quite tricky getting the suspense right. It tends to be much more about the psychology and putting the audience in the criminal's shoes. Hitchcock does that so well, whereby the criminal is terrified of being caught and, by extension, the audience is terrified of their being caught.

At what point does an adaptation cease to be another author's story and become yours?

In terms of adapting, I'm attracted to the books that feel difficult to adapt, because that leaves me enough space as a screenwriter to find a way into the story, incorporating my own personal reactions to it but also my life experiences, so that they almost become half original and half adaptation. *The Wings of the Dove*, *Drive* and *Two Faces* definitely have that element. *The Wings of the Dove* was written so that it's reporting what happened, *Drive* features a fantastic protagonist but I created more of a story around him, and *Two Faces* allowed me to impose certain plot elements. All my favourite books give you these amazing characters who allow you to invent scenes that aren't in the original story. The authors have created such a strong base with them it's easy to know how they would react in the situations you create for them. A book that feels structured like a screenplay is less interesting to me because there's less space for me to bring myself to it. I'm looking for that space between the book and an adaptation.

Did you write differently knowing that you were directing the script?

Absolutely. For instance, there was a scene that didn't make the final cut, in which the main characters are driving through Athens at night. If I had written that just as a screenwriter, I would have had exterior shots of the car. But knowing how impossible it was going to be to get that kind of budget, I wrote the entire scene from inside the car. I think there is a degree of self-censorship involved. I don't know if that's a good thing. It forces you to think much more clearly about the practicalities of shooting a scene, whereas in the past, when I've been writing for other people, it's possible to cheat. I could write a line like, 'We feel all the pain inside him,' and the director has to interpret what I mean by that. I think the writing is a little less lazy, because as a director you're the one who has to solve those problems.

It's funny how things changed as I progressed with the project. There's one scene where Chester and Rydal are on a boat together. It was the longest dialogue scene in the script. My brother reads all my scripts, and he said, 'You really don't need all this dialogue.' Gradually, I kept cutting away until, after the rehearsals with the actors, I realised that what they said was repeating things from an earlier scene, so I finally decided to cut all the dialogue. It's now one of the scenes I am most proud of, because it's just about the two actors staring at each other and saying nothing.

We write dialogue to tell the story and help tell ourselves the story. But then, once you become familiar with the story, you realise you don't need all that dialogue. With every film I've worked on, dialogue is slashed in an editing suite. If a scene can survive without lines, then the fewer lines it has the better.

Did your approach to screenwriting change in terms of the rhythm and pacing – the musicality of what you were writing – knowing that you would be directing?

I've never been a fan of the basic three-act structure, because screenwriting is much more 'musical' – it's about fast, slow . . . slow, slow, fast. What I really learned during the editing of this film is that you could start off with a drama, have it turn into a thriller, but then it's really hard to go back to it being a drama. With writing it's easy to shift tempo, but with a film there's a tyranny of rhythm. In the editing room you realise how important momentum is in a film. It influenced my writing of the Le Carré script [*Our Kind of Traitor*]. I cut fifteen pages out of it, because I learned so much editing this film. I've been in a cutting room before, but I think there's something different when you're directing too and your head's on the block. It's very different to when you're giving suggestions. So that musicality is the most important thing for a film.

Did you write the script with specific actors in mind?

Not at first. What I tend to do is write with nobody in mind, and then when the actors are cast I tend to rewrite quite a lot for them. I'm at the same agency as Viggo [Mortensen] and my agent slipped a copy of the script to his agent. He reads a lot, but I didn't know he had a copy of it. Suddenly, I received a message saying he was interested. I went to Madrid to meet him and he was very gracious, saying he would be happy for me to direct. Kirsten [Dunst] also read it without me knowing and expressed an interest. When I gave the script to Oscar [Isaac] he hadn't been cast to play Llewyn Davis [the main character of the Coen brothers' 2013 film]. He said he liked it but felt it was going to be quite hard for me to cast him because I had no clout as a first-time director and he wasn't that well known. However, he suddenly – and fortunately for me – became a star.

It's another great performance by Oscar Isaac.

He has a wonderful quality. There's a scene where they're all sitting in this Greek taverna and an argument is unfolding. What's great with his performance in this scene is that he can switch from making a pass at Colette to remembering that Chester is there and, when he turns to him, he gives him the sweetest smile. Oscar has this ability to make the tiniest shifts in character incredibly quickly, without revealing any element of process. It makes him such a great and natural actor, and I think he's going to be a huge star.

Why did you decide to change the location of the final stages of the story from France to Turkey?

I love the idea behind these three Americans being in a place of comfort and familiarity, which is Athens, and then travelling further and further east in a state of increasing discomfort. So the idea of coming back to Paris felt more modern and familiar to them than Athens and Crete. It felt like they were going in one direction and then back again, not just geographically but also in terms of comfort and a state of mind.

I wanted to make the world around them more and more alien as they went along. America was once their safety net, and so I take them as far away as I can from that. And Istanbul is a film noir city. That element worked perfectly within the narrative. The idea of shooting in a place with those minarets, the hustle and bustle of the bazaar, and neon lights littering the streets was great. We didn't quite have the budget to show huge vistas of Istanbul, but it works well. It was a fairly modern city in the 1960s, but it had these pockets of exoticism, particularly in terms of sound. The idea of Chester being isolated in the city because of these strange sounds, which torment him, really made me feel that Istanbul was so right.

The visual style of the film also appears to shift as we progress from Greece to Istanbul.

I wanted to change the visual style of the film through three stages. In Athens I was looking for a clichéd, almost touristy look – a picture-postcard version of the city. I sifted through countless Kodachrome pictures from the 1960s and worked with Marcel [Zyskind, the cinematographer] to recreate these. In these moments everything seems right. But then in Crete, when they're on the run, I wanted a minimalist look – dustier and harsher in terms of lighting, moving away from the pastel colours of the early scenes. Then, in Istanbul, I went film noir crazy. I wanted the visual side of the story to reflect the psychology of the characters, but also for the landscapes to change and become harsher, as if the gods are somehow punishing them. I had this notion that we're in the lands of the gods and I wanted to get across the idea that they're always being watched.

The actors' physicality plays a huge factor within this tensely knit triangle.

In some ways it reflected what was happening on the set. You have Oscar as the up-and-coming young star and Viggo is the established star and father figure. There's always a little competition between two great actors. It's also one of the reasons I wanted to cast Oscar, because there are very few young actors who can go toe to toe with Viggo. I think it worked.

Amma Asante (photo: Hazel Thompson,
True Image Media Ltd)

Amma Asante

Amma Asante first made a name for herself as one of the cast members in the popular children's drama *Grange Hill*, before making appearances in *The Bill*, *Desmond's* and *Birds of a Feather*. She was the head writer on *Brothers & Sisters* before moving into directing. *A Way of Life* (2004) was one of the first films to look at teenage and young adult life in Britain in the new millennium. This hard-hitting drama set in South Wales examines racism, economic inequality and the ramifications of an entire community deprived of a voice in contemporary society. At the BAFTAs that year Asante received the Carl Foreman Award for Special Achievement by a British Writer, Director or Producer in their First Feature Film.

Belle (2013) is an imaginative, visually lustrous account of the life of Dido Elizabeth Belle, the illegitimate mixed-race daughter of Maria Belle, an enslaved African woman, and Captain John Lindsay. At a young age, she was entrusted to the care of William Murray, the first Earl of Mansfield, who became Lord Chief Justice. The story focuses on Belle and Mansfield at a time when the subject of slavery and its abolition lay at the heart of British politics. Asante's film is a fascinating study of attitudes to race, class and gender during this era.

Was acting a way into film for you?

It was the way in, although I didn't realise that at the time. I was a very shy child and my father decided to send me to stage school at the age of ten. He thought it could be a way of bringing me out of myself and also nurturing my creativity. He realised that I was a creative kid and this would be a good route for me. He was quite progressive in this way. If you're the child of an African father for whom formal education is important, there's normally a pressure to be a lawyer or a doctor. My father was very good at looking at what the three of us – I have a brother and sister – were interested in, or showed a talent for, and then encouraging us in that direction. So I ended up in stage school not really knowing what it was and what it was going to mean to the rest of my life.

After acting in a number of TV series, was writing Brothers & Sisters *a stepping stone towards directing for you?*

At the time, no. Directing just didn't seem to be an option for me, for someone like me. I didn't even know it was something that I would enjoy. By the end of my teens, I realised that acting just wasn't for me. Mainly because I realised that I wasn't good at it. However, I was fascinated with television's ability to connect with its audience – I was enamoured with storytelling.

Around this time my mum insisted that I went to secretarial college. That gave me the ability to type. At first, I was just intent on getting my typing speed up so that I could temp. I really thought I was going to leave the industry. However, I realised I had this story in me. And because the script format was the one I was most familiar with, I just started to type out my story in the form of a screenplay.

Has your experience as an actor informed you as a director?

What really made a difference was working on *Grange Hill*, more than anything else. We had two scripts a week and were turning over two episodes a month. Doing that for three years meant everything. I was constantly surrounded by actors and crew, and the language of film and storytelling. So I guess *Grange Hill* and learning to type were key. I know that sounds crazy but being able to type allowed me to get my ideas out really quickly.

Directing was thrust on me when I was forced by one of my financiers at the BFI to direct my first feature. I wasn't keen because I didn't want to ruin it. I thought the script was the best thing I had written at that point and I wanted a great director to take it on. The Film Council felt that I was the one person who knew this material inside out and was the best placed to direct it. In the end they were right.

Why did you choose to set the film in Wales?

I met the producer Peter Edwards – the head of drama at what was then HTV Wales – at a BAFTA event and we started talking about the difference between parts of Wales and London, where I was living at the time. I was fascinated by the fact that Wales has some of the oldest black communities in Europe and was convinced that Wales had something to show the rest of the UK in terms of diversity. Peter, who would become the producer on the film, immediately disabused me of that notion, and it was after this that he contacted me with an idea about a drama set in Wales.

Peter originally ring-fenced money for me to do a TV piece, which eventually evolved into a feature. That's how Wales became the location for the drama. But it was also fortuitous. I wanted to explore race, class and status, and this was perfect for it.

You seemed keen on exploring various facets of racism – from outright bigotry and prejudice as a by-product of ignorance to an aggression that grows out of frustration, often economic.

Absolutely. Frustration is key because I wanted to explore the idea of racism as a symptom of something else. I don't believe that we're born racist.

That same frustration is also present in Belle, *albeit witnessed through a very different section of society.*

With both films, I wanted to look at the idea of society defining you and whether you allow society to do that or not. *A Way of Life* looks at what happens when you let society define you – when you let society tell you who you are. Whereas *Belle* shows the flipside of that coin. It looks at what happens when you say, 'No. I define myself. I will not let society tell me who I am.' In both cases, the two lead characters go through various stages of frustration, but one comes out the other side whereas the other doesn't.

You could have created characters who were completely dislikeable or victims. Instead, they are complex and challenge our sympathies.

Yes. I think that when you're creating characters you're working in grey areas. That's where the interesting drama lies. An audience is going to identify what feels true or authentic to them. The story has to resonate with them. Dido Belle has her faults. She's pompous, she's status-driven early on. She looks down on John Davinier. And Leigh-Anne clearly has her faults in *A Way of Life*. Huge faults. When I create characters I have to love them for better or worse. I have to understand them and walk in their shoes. But I have to be absolutely honest about who they are. And in that process it generally means me being honest about who I am and where I'm coming from with this.

You chose to present A Way of Life *from the point of view of a racist. Was this a stumbling block during the project's development?*

Being female and a woman of colour probably made it easier for this film to get made – to convince financiers to let me tell the story from this particular perspective. The more traditional viewpoint would have been Leigh-Anne's neighbour, who is killed. Or to see it from his daughter's perspective, where she witnesses the murder. But I wanted to explore what racism is from the inside out. That allowed me to explore the cause and, as the film shows, it's all about class and exclusion. It makes clear that when you don't let members of society contribute to the world they live in, however small or great that world may be, you're creating problems for that society.

The bigger problem, which the financiers were concerned about, was how to get audiences to stay in their seats. How do we encourage them to go on this journey with Leigh-Anne, when she's so reprehensible in so many ways? That was a challenge, and there were a lot of elements in the script that I had to work on. It comes back to this idea of my associating with that character, ensuring that her vulnerabilities are as visible as the negative aspects of her personality.

How difficult was the casting for A Way of Life?

It was really tough and took a long time. It lasted around a year. I didn't find Stephanie James, who plays Leigh-Anne brilliantly, until quite late in the process. I found Nathan Jones, who plays Gavin, almost immediately. I shot a pilot the year before for the BFI, which was part of the process of them trying to convince me that I could actually direct the film. Nathan was on board for that. But as far as the remaining cast is concerned, I ended up seeing over a thousand kids.

Gary Howe, my Welsh casting director, knew where to go in order to find the right kids, so we spent a lot of time in the Valleys in South Wales. We set up Saturday morning classes and had open auditions. Gary would also bring in people he'd seen in drama schools. In the end, all the kids were non-drama school because I wanted something authentic.

Nathan was my lynchpin. He was used throughout the casting process. After the open auditions, I formed teams and started to shoot them, with Nathan acting against them. We matched everybody against him. Stephanie was in one of those Saturday morning classes, around six months before we began filming. She was funny at the beginning because she didn't want to say the swear words or act out any violence – even kicking a chair. But there was something about her.

There was a long gap between A Way of Life *and* Belle. *You were caught up in development with projects that never materialised. Was it difficult to keep going?*

Like a lot of film-makers, I fell foul of the financial crisis in 2008.

I had three projects on the go. After winning the BAFTA, I took everyone's advice and didn't just put all my energies into one film. There were three that were quite far along and they all collapsed. But I don't believe in this idea of 'development hell'. These all fed into future projects, and without the experience they gave me I wouldn't have had the experience that allowed me to create *Belle*.

How did Belle *come about?*

The producer Damian Jones had been trying to get a movie off the ground around the story of Belle. He had secured money from HBO for what was going to be a TV drama, but it didn't come to fruition. Misan Sagay was on board as the writer and was exploring the history. The role of the painting in the story came and went with various drafts. The same went for Belle. Sometimes she was in it from the beginning and then in other versions she didn't appear until very late. As a result of that, Misan received a WGA [Writers Guild of America] contract.

Shortly after that, Damian came back to the UK and the BFI were interested in a film based around the picture, but felt that a new vision had to come on board for it. The BFI have developed every project bar one, and so they were very aware of my writing. I was working on a 1940s drama at the time, which became one of the ones that fell through, and to which I've now returned and will shoot in late 2015. That story centres on the experiences of a young woman in 1940s Berlin, who is an outsider but wants to belong. So the BFI suggested to Damian that he meet with me and talk about the project.

When I saw the postcard of this painting I immediately saw a combination of politics, class and history. It was a gift of an image, and I had yet to explore the full history but I felt there were themes that I wanted to explore and ones that an audience would connect with.

I tend to do several months of research on each project, so looking into this period and what history there was about Belle took some time. Aside from being an extraordinary character herself, she was associated with Lord Mansfield, who fascinated me completely. He reminded me of my father. Here was a progressive man who bucked against the system in terms of what he thought and yet was also stuck within this system of order. So there were these two elements within him that were always in conflict. From there, it was about incorporating the love story between Belle and John, and the paternal love story between Belle and Lord Mansfield.

The film raises interesting questions relating to history as a factual text. Can we really discuss the past in such concrete and definite terms, or must we accept that everything is interpretation and so it's better to try to capture the spirit of the past?

I had two motives in mind when writing. Firstly, I knew that I was aiming for an emotional truth. Beyond that, I wanted to be clear that I was presenting my interpretation of who Dido might have been and how the relationship with her great-uncle might have developed. Alongside this, we decided to commission an accompanying book, laying out the actual facts of her life, should anyone wish to read it.

It was important for me to tell people that this woman existed. However, to ensure that it was very clear to audiences that this was an interpretation and not a factual retelling of her life, I decided that we wouldn't use the real painting of Dido and Elizabeth during the film, but would show it at the very end.

Both films grapple with balancing heightened emotions and the issues that lie at the heart of the stories.

That's something there at the beginning of the process and stays all the way to the end. You have to be sure that balance is right. I am sentimental and I have to be careful. In the case of David Gray and Rachel Portman, who composed the music for the films, it's ensuring that I don't go too far – finding the right balance. And you never really know until a film reaches an audience.

Richard Ayoade (photo: Dean Rogers)

Richard Ayoade

A former president of Cambridge University Footlights (1997–8), Richard Ayoade graduated to television with *Garth Marenghi's Darkplace* (2004), based on a series of stage shows. He followed this with roles in *The Mighty Boosh* and *The IT Crowd*. Ayoade also appeared in the feature film *The Watch* (2012) and is a regular guest on a number of TV shows. He has also directed music videos for Arctic Monkeys (for whom he also directed a concert film), Super Furry Animals, Vampire Weekend, Kasabian and the Yeah Yeah Yeahs.

His adaptation of Joe Dunthorne's novel *Submarine* (2010) is a cine-literate coming-of-age tale that details the life and loves of Oliver Tate, a precocious fifteen-year-old attempting to cope with his parents' rocky marriage while his hormones go into overdrive. Balancing the ideals of youth with the realities of everyday life, Ayoade's feature debut attracted critical acclaim and played at the Toronto, London, Sundance and Berlin film festivals.

The Double, adapted by Ayoade and Avi Korine from Dostoevsky's novella, is a visually stylish, darkly comic exploration of one man's inability to escape the shackles of low self-esteem. Featuring Jesse Eisenberg as Simon James and his doppelgänger, James Simon, Ayoade's film is a stark contrast to his debut, but once again exhibits the sure hand of a director with a strong vision.

Did you always want to direct?

Not really. I always wanted to write, and I had fallen into performing at university. I was writing with John Oliver, and the way it seemed to work there was that people performed their own material – performing came out of the writing. Directing was just a way of furthering the writing – realising how much the directing impacted on how the writing came across – so the first thing I directed was a show called *Garth Marenghi's Darkplace*.

Do you perceive your role as director as being indivisible from that of a writer?

I once directed something I didn't write. It was an episode of *Community*. But even then I knew the terrain we were covering, and it was being written as we filmed, so I was able to go into the writers' room and speak with them. I never received a completed script, so I wasn't faced with having to work out how to shoot it as a whole. I find that idea quite intimidating, although I have high regard and respect for directors who can do that – someone like Mike Nichols, in particular, who can take that material and interpret it so well.

Much of your work is based on collaborations. Did that attract you to an adaptation – working with material that already existed?

I didn't consciously want to adapt something. Events unfolded that way. Around the same time, two things happened. One was the arrival of the script of *The Double*, a first draft written by Avi Korine, which was given to me by Robin Fox and Amina Dasmal [the film's producers]. I read that and was interested in working on it. I hadn't had such a strong feeling before of reading something and thinking I could really do something with it. I also read Joe Dunthorne's book (at the instigation of Warp Films) and thought that it would be worth having a go at writing an adaptation of that.

I had co-written two shows for television and both had only gone to one series, so I'd reached a point where I wasn't sure what to do, I guess. I'd also made music videos, but they were collapsing as a concept – you can't really survive by being a music-video director any more.

I liked Joe's book. The genre really appealed to me. I have always wondered why there was really no English equivalent of *My So-Called Life*, *Dawson's Creek* or the films of John Hughes. People have made films about childhood in England, but not consistently.

What was Joe's input?

I think Joe had initially been asked if he wanted to write the script, but I believe he felt he was done with the story and didn't really want to go back into that world, as opposed to starting on another novel.

For my part, I wanted to ask Joe as many questions as I possibly could in order to work out what he thought and felt about the adaptation. He is very different in terms of giving notes compared to what I'm used to, which is usually regarding big, broad, structural things. His notes were more specifically about a line where he's not convinced that a character would say something, which was really good because you rarely get those notes. I guess his role was as a kind of script editor.

The film has a strong visual identity. Did you decide on the look of the film while writing?

It's hard to define. There are often certain absences in a novel that you don't necessarily think about when you're reading it, but when it comes to adaptation you realise you need to address these things. The novel doesn't give a description of Oliver, and his own descriptions aren't like Dickens, where you can visualise the scene. You think about these things the moment you start writing, even in terms of cuts – you see this, then this, then that etc. But then there's a reality that kicks in when you begin scouting for locations and you literally see things that make you judge what's right or not for the film. It's at that point that you begin to feel intuitively as to what best reflects a specific character or scene.

How has your work on music videos, playing with abstract imagery, fed into your work?

What music videos allow is the opportunity to do something

without dialogue, and to tell the audience something through imagery and editing. It stops you relying on dialogue, because often when you sit and write something you end up just having people talking. It forces you to think in terms of images and pacing. But at the same time you're powered by the music, so you can get away with a lot of things, like repetition, which you can't with a feature film. So many music videos do everything they're going to do in the first forty seconds, and then they just recycle it.

Both films feature protagonists who aren't entirely sympathetic. Nor are they particularly articulate.

Well, that's partly the source material. However, it's interesting to me to have someone in a crisis. I think people in a crisis aren't actually able to express themselves. If you could, if you are able to talk about it, you would probably be closer to understanding the situation you're in. As for a sense of sympathy, I think so long as someone is human you can feel for them in some way. Take Travis Bickle in *Taxi Driver* (1976). He does atrocious things but you feel for him. In that conversation he has with Albert Brooks, where he says he doesn't know what life is about, you can see his vulnerability in the way he's attempting to reach out. But he also challenges the audience's sympathy. All dramatic characters, all great characters, are flawed in some way, otherwise there wouldn't really be a story.

In the way that Taxi Driver *has moments of humour, both your films are funny but they're not comedies.*

I like films that are both funny and sad, like *The Graduate* (1967). Would you call that a comedy?

At times it feels like a tragedy with funny moments.

Yes, but even the worst bits are funny. When Elaine's father confronts Benjamin, it's really tragic and awful. Mrs Robinson has said that Ben raped her, and yet it's a funny scene. How can that be funny? But it is. I like the tension in the fact that awful things can be funny. I think it's truthful in some way.

How difficult was the shooting of Submarine *and* The Double?

It wasn't easy. In terms of working with the actors and crew it was great, but at times I felt like the whole thing was beyond my capacity. I have a feeling of how I wanted the films to turn out, but it can always feel far away from what I am capable of achieving. It's very hard. But you keep going until you get there. I remember Scorsese saying that film-making is like an awful compulsion. You never feel you've got it totally 'right'.

Both films are so starkly different in terms of style. Was it a conscious decision to challenge yourself this way?

The style was dictated by the story. In *Submarine*, I looked back to how I felt when I wasn't in school, when I was free to do what I wanted. The light in that part of the day took on a certain quality. It was a crepuscular, magic-hour light, which is also in tune with how Oliver sees himself – in that romantic kind of way. That romantic glow is central to the biopic of his life as he imagines it.

There's something nightmarish about *The Double* unfolding entirely at night. It felt like there should be a hint of a wider universe. When a city only has artificial light, there's no sense of anything beyond it. The light is there as a function and nothing else. It closes down that world.

In the way the world is presented in The Double, *including the fact that we never see the sky, Simon isn't a prisoner; he's not trapped in this world in any way whatsoever. It's a stark contrast to a film like Terry Gilliam's* Brazil, *to which* The Double *has been compared.*

That's true. He's not a prisoner and he's not the product of a wider system. The Colonel isn't an authoritarian figure. He's someone that Simon wants to know, who might recognise something special in him if he can only get close enough. The Colonel is a benevolent figure, in a way. What Simon is ultimately trapped by is his self-pity, which he can't get over.

It also helps that you have such an evocative location.

We filmed in an abandoned industrial park in Crowthorne [Berkshire]. There were a few places we saw that had certain elements. The post office sorting space in Holborn was pretty good, which gave us some ideas for the layout of the office. But this place had all the buildings we wanted, which allowed us to create a complete world. We had that moment when we saw that this world could actually exist. Up until that moment it can be worrying.

Submarine was also tricky because we specifically wanted a white house on its own on a hill, and there just aren't that many places like that. The place we used was an old vicarage. The production designer changed it a good deal, but so much of it was already there. When you find something like that house, or the location in Crowthorne, that's when the film starts to feel real.

Both films are also interesting because of their indeterminate time period – neither feels particularly enslaved to one specific era.

I think for a long time that applied to all film. There weren't many silent films that were contemporary. And that idea of time-lessness was accentuated by films being shot on sets, existing in their own kind of dream world. Realism came about in the 1940s, with directors like Rossellini, and became more prevalent as cameras developed and were more portable.

I think it's important to create a world that suits a story visually and not have to accept that it is locked into a specific moment. With *Submarine* you have a character who views himself and his life in such a romantic way that it feels completely out of time.

There are many reasons as to why *The Double* feels like this. One is that this kind of deference to authority doesn't exist in the same way it once did, particularly in the concept of the work structure in the nineteenth century and how different it is to now. We had to create an environment where the character couldn't just escape – where you wouldn't think that he should just move away or get another job. We needed to create something dream-like, and as a result those places tend to be out of time too.

The way you employ sound adds to this otherworldliness in both films. It's particularly strong in terms of The Double.

We were much more concerned with sound in *The Double*. We spoke to the sound designer before we began shooting, even creating some of the noise that would be in the background to play on the set, so that people would speak at the right level for what we were going to put in. It was going to be loud and uncomfortable for people to speak. That was an important element. We were trying to collect sounds as we went along, which could be manipulated later.

With *Submarine* all of the ambient sound was recorded on location, whereas almost all of the sounds in *The Double* were processed after shooting was completed. They were manipulated in some way, perhaps slowed down or created from animal noises. There's a disjuncture between the image and the sound in *The Double* that isn't present in *Submarine*, with the exception of a few very subjective sequences.

How early do you involve the composer Andrew Hewitt in the process?

As early as possible. He was working on the music for *The Double* a year before we started shooting. It was the same with *Submarine*. We had conversations before filming began, so we had some of his music by the time we actually started filming, and all of it was with us before we finished the edit, so that we were able to edit the film to the music tracks. It's great to have his music so early – it really helps.

Clio Barnard (photo: Nick Wall)

Clio Barnard

Clio Barnard's work deals with the relationship between documentary and fiction, particularly the subjectivity of recollection. In 2006, Film and Video Umbrella commissioned Barnard to make *Dark Glass* as part of the 'Single Shot' touring programme. A psychological microdrama that moves from the sanctuary of a domestic garden to the half-remembered shadows of a house, the piece looks back into a semi-veiled interior world of fraught, ambiguous memories.

The tactic of constructing fictional images around verbatim audio (and vice versa) was brilliantly utilised in *The Arbor* (2010), Barnard's remarkable debut feature. Andrea Dunbar wrote unflinchingly about her upbringing on Bradford's Buttershaw estate, and was hailed by fellow playwright Shelagh Delaney as 'a genius straight from the slums'. Dunbar's first play, *The Arbor* (1980), originally written as part of a school assignment, described the experiences of a pregnant teenager with an abusive, drunken father.

Dunbar died tragically in 1990 at the age of twenty-nine, leaving her ten-year-old daughter Lorraine with bitter childhood memories. In the film, Barnard, who also grew up in the Bradford region, visits the Buttershaw estate to see how it has changed in the two decades since Dunbar's death. She also catches up with Lorraine in the present day. Now aged twenty-nine, Lorraine is ostracised by her mother's family and is in prison, undergoing rehab. The film follows Lorraine's personal journey as she is reintroduced to her mother's plays and letters, then reflects on her own life and begins to understand the struggles her mother faced.

Over a period of two years Barnard recorded audio interviews with Lorraine, members of the Dunbar family and residents from the Buttershaw estate. These interviews were edited to create an audio 'screenplay', which forms the basis of the film as actors lip-synch to the voices of the interviewees. This footage was intercut with extensive archive clips, as well as extracts from Andrea's stage play, which was filmed as a live outdoor performance on the Buttershaw estate to an audience of its residents.

Very loosely adapted from the Oscar Wilde short story, and again set on the outskirts of Bradford, *The Selfish Giant* (2013) concerns two rebellious young lads – Arbor and Swifty – and their involvement with a local scrap dealer. At first their earnings seem to roll in, but as jealousy and resentment begin to drive the boys apart Arbor resorts to a desperate act of greed, the tragic consequences of which will tear apart the lives of everyone involved. A bold and gripping work that exposes life on the margins of society, the film also counts among its many assets compelling performances from its two non-professional leads.

Your work has repeatedly demonstrated a concern with the relationship between fictional film language and documentary. How did you wish to engage with previous representations of the Buttershaw estate on stage and screen? And what was it about the techniques of verbatim theatre that struck you as being appropriate for The Arbor?

Andrea's fiction was based on what she observed around her. She reminded the audience they were watching a play by her use of direct address when the Girl in *The Arbor* introduces each scene. I see the use of actors lip-synching as performing the same function, reminding the audience they are watching the retelling of a true story.

My work is concerned with the relationship between fiction film language and documentary. I often dislocate sound and image by constructing fictional images around verbatim audio. In this sense, my working methods have some similarity to the methods of verbatim theatre, which, by its very nature (being performed by actors in a theatre) acknowledges that it is constructed. Housing estates and the people who live there are usually represented on film in the tradition of Social Realism,

a working method that aims to deny construct, aiming for naturalistic performances, an invisible crew and camera, adopting
the aesthetic of Direct Cinema as a shorthand for authenticity. I
wanted to confront expectations about how a particular group
of people are represented by subverting the form.

I used the technique in which actors lip-synch to the voices of
interviewees to draw attention to the fact that documentary narratives are as constructed as fictional ones. I want the audience
to think about the fact that the film has been shaped and edited
by the film-makers. Through these formal techniques I hoped the
film would achieve a fine balance – so that, perhaps paradoxically, the distancing techniques might create closeness, allowing a
push–pull, so an audience might be aware of the shaping of the
story, but would simultaneously be able to engage emotionally.

Above all, my hope is that the film will provoke compassionate thought and reflection.

*You recorded audio interviews with Lorraine Dunbar and other
members of the Dunbar family over a two-year period to create an
audio screenplay. To what extent did you allow this audio screenplay to form the basis of the film? And was it during this process
that you decided to make Lorraine one of the central voices of
the film, thus opening up the project into a consideration of inter-
generational neglect as well as a dissection of Andrea's legacy?*

The audio screenplay is the basis of the film, and it was always
the intention to approach it this way round. I knew Lorraine
was important because of her words at the end of *A State Affair*
[Robin Soans's play of 2000], which linked back to Andrea's
play *Rita, Sue and Bob Too*.

At the point the film was commissioned, I knew I wanted to
speak to Lorraine because of these words, but I didn't know what
had happened to her in the ten years since [*A State Affair*]. Neither
did I know how autobiographical Andrea's play *The Arbor* was
until I met Andrea's sister, Pamela. Realising the character of

Yousaf in the play was Lorraine's father really was key. Her play, combined with the interviews with her family, means that the film can look across three generations of a family and three decades of a particular place. I hope that this allows some understanding of the destructive effects of poverty, racism and addiction to emerge.

The lip-synching technique you employ, in which your actors have to not only learn words but also master pauses and speech rhythms, must have been challenging. What casting process did you employ, and how did you help the selected actors cope with the rigours of the production?

I worked with a brilliant casting director called Amy Hubbard, who brought in lots of actors who were up for the challenge. We asked them to try out the technique during the casting process. I have huge respect for the actors. It was very, very demanding on them. Manjinder Virk described it as like learning a piece of music, and like circular breathing. It meant that they had to be very present – never thinking ahead or they would trip up. The actors were incredible and I'm indebted to them, not only for their remarkable technical skill but also for their ability to give true performances.

The approach you take with the material and your concern over the boundaries between fact and fiction make for an incredibly immersive experience for the spectator. Did you wish to encourage an interpretative approach from the audience to what is on screen?

I wasn't totally certain what the effect of the lip-synching would be, so it has been fascinating to learn about that from people who have seen it. People say that paradoxically the distancing technique draws them closer. I think it may be because all the people on screen look you in the eye. Perhaps you actively listen as a result.

I understand that The Arbor *was not originally intended for cine-*

ma release. *How did the positive critical reaction and the numerous prizes it has steadily accrued contribute to the film being allowed to find a wider audience than you perhaps originally intended?*

Artangel commissioned *The Arbor* as a feature-length film for TV. The UK Film Council became involved during development, and that was when it became intended for cinema release. Tracy O'Riordan, who is a brilliant producer, made certain that UK distributors saw the film as soon as it was finished. We were lucky that Verve picked it up. They have been great at getting the film out there, working alongside Rabbit PR – lovely, committed publicity people who made sure the critics saw the film. The response has been amazing and unexpected. I don't think you ever know how people are going to respond. I'm grateful to all the critics who were very open to and excited about the challenges of the film, and to audiences for going to see the film and for their feedback.

Alongside recent works by Steve McQueen, Andrew Kötting, Joe Lawlor and Christine Molloy, and Gillian Wearing, The Arbor *highlights the continuing strength of artists' film in British cinema. Does this feel like an incredibly fertile period in which to be working?*

I'm a great admirer of all these film-makers. It is great that there has recently been this strong strand of risk-taking British film. It's wonderful that these films are getting made and fantastic that they have found an audience. It's exciting to think that *The Arbor* is part of that.

One reviewer described your approach on The Selfish Giant *as 'narrative scavenging' in relation to your taking only the essentials from Oscar Wilde's source material.*

Taking a Victorian fairy tale as the inspiration for a story about contemporary marginalised teenagers was a deliberately incongruous provocation. In a Victorian fairy story we might idealise children, but it seemed to me some contemporary teenagers were far from idealised, and were instead demonised and most certainly criminalised. The original story is about children who are excluded. The children I met when I was making *The Arbor* were also excluded, both from school and from society on a more general level. It made me angry that the children I had got to know and care about were undervalued – that people didn't understand the day-to-day pressures and struggles both they and their families faced.

In the original fairy tale by Oscar Wilde, the children are excluded from a giant's garden. It's the story of real values that are lost if those in positions of power are selfish and greedy. I think the essence of the original story is still there in my adaptation. The first draft was written from the giant's perspective and was closer to the original, but I realised I was more interested in the children – I wanted to tell the story from their point of view instead. At that point I considered changing the title. However, I felt that although the relationship to the original was now tangential, enough of it remained for me to keep the title.

As with The Arbor, *you filmed on location in Bradford. Landscape is key to your work and is essential again here. I sense that with the film you wanted to have a contrast between the urban and the rural. Was this element fundamental for you, or was it more a function of the narrative?*

Landscape is really important in the film. I was interested in liminal places and liminal people – places that are in a state of flux. I wanted to explore the threshold between urban and rural, not industrial or agricultural, but forgotten and undervalued places – just as teenagers are in a state of flux between being children and adults. As well as referencing the past with the horse-drawn vehicles, I also see the film as a vision of the future. The disused power station is a redundant place, the remnants of an unsustainable, diminishing resource that made a few people very rich but which became increasingly inaccessible to those with little. It's also Arbor and Swifty's territory, a place where they can get away from the pressure of home and school – a place where they can come of age. I find the pylons, the cooling towers and substations very beautiful – they are giants in the landscape. They are also the viaducts of tomorrow – the remnants from today of an industrial past.

The film rightly drew much praise and attention for its casting of Conner Chapman and Shaun Thomas. Was it difficult to find two young lads who could work so well and so naturally together? And did you cast from within the environs of the local community?

The Selfish Giant grew out of *The Arbor*, so the casting director and I knew exactly where to start looking. We found Conner Chapman on the first day. It was something about his voice that initially drew me to him. Then I understood, although he was quite shy, that he's a brilliant storyteller.

We also needed a child who could ride and had a real connection with horses for Swifty, so we went to an area of Bradford called Holme Wood, where there is a settled traveller community and a big horse culture. That's where we found Shaun Thomas. At first Shaun found it hard to get his head around the idea that, within the fiction, he had to take orders from a twelve-year-old who is smaller than him. Shaun was fifteen at the time and a good boxer, which meant he really had to adjust to play Swifty. Both boys have an incredibly strong instinct for story, so it was great working with them. I loved it.

DoP Mike Eley has one of the most diverse CVs I have ever seen. His work runs the gamut from award-winning documentaries, such as Touching the Void *and* Marley, *to* Nanny McPhee. *What caught your eye about his work?*

I wanted naturalism – realism but with an edge of something that alluded to the fable, a subtle edge of something more transcendent. What Mike achieved was beyond what I had hoped for, particularly the shots in the power station, of the cooling towers and the sheep in the mist. His photography is beautiful in a completely unselfconscious and uncontrived way, attuned to the landscape, performance and story. He has such strong instincts, following the actors and finding the right shots, while giving them lots of room. And he was great at working with natural light in the most incredible way. He has a calm nature and made the children feel completely at ease. And he is incredibly experienced, so he knew how to handle the more complicated scenes, like the road races.

The film draws much-needed attention to the plight of people like Arbor and Swifty, who are pretty much thrown on life's scrapheap from the start. Given that the film was so highly regarded and well received, is there a hope that lawmakers might actually pay attention to the people you depict? For instance, Nick Broomfield's Juvenile Liaison, *which was set in Lancashire, led to wide-ranging changes regarding the youth justice system. Could a film today have such a sweeping impact?*

I haven't seen Nick Broomfield's documentary, but direct effect in terms of a change of policy or legislation is more likely to come as a result of a documentary rather than a narrative film. It's unlikely that a film like *The Selfish Giant* would lead to direct changes in policy. I think its themes are too broad for that. There would need to be a huge shift in ideology to be able to say it had had a direct effect. And I think it would be naive to think that David Cameron might go to the cinema, see the film and say: 'Tell you what, let's reverse our policies, from renationalising transport networks and natural resources, so that everyone can benefit from them. Let's not have profit as the priority, and look to making the most from what we have so that more can share in it.' If I were optimistic, I would say we are in a state of flux and that Arbor and Swifty are showing us the way forward. We need a societal coming of age where we understand what we stand to lose if we continue with this ideology of greed.

Did you allow yourself to draw on any specific film references?

I watched realist fables – about children and for children – with my own (then young) kids. We watched *The Bicycle Thieves*, *The Apple*, *Kes* and *The Kid with a Bike*.

What did you think of the film's reception, which was uniformly positive? You enjoyed acclaim with The Arbor, *but* The Selfish Giant *reached a whole new level and was also seen and enjoyed by a much larger audience.*

I had no idea how audiences were going to respond, whether audiences would feel anything for these two boys, or find the layers that I hoped were there in this simple story. So the premiere in Cannes was wonderful, as it has been since, with the film opening around the world and the positive reviews pouring in. It's a wonderful feeling to be understood – to be heard.

Does the film's reception make securing funding for future projects easier? Is it currently healthy in terms of finance and support here in the UK? Or do you have to go through a similar process each time, given the social and political nature of your work, and the fact that they don't fall into the starry, British heritage cinema bracket?

I couldn't have asked for more support than I've had from both Film4 and the BFI. Lizzie Franke, Katherine Butler and Tessa Ross were behind *The Selfish Giant* right from the outset and remained committed to the end. My experience of film executives has been a good one – they want films with social and political content, just as audiences clearly do.

Yann Demange on the set of '71
(photos: StudioCanal)

Yann Demange

Born in Paris and raised in London, Yann Demange started out filming live concerts and cutting music promos before studying film at the London College of Printing. His graduation film, *Joe* (2001), was accepted as part of the British Council's international festival programme. Following an MA in directing at the National Film and Television School, he began directing for television. After directing episodes of *Secret Diary of a Call Girl* (2007), *Coming Up* (2007), *Dead Set* (2008) and *Criminal Justice* (2009), Demange collaborated with writer Ronan Bennett on the acclaimed drama series *Top Boy* (2011). An exploration of gang culture in contemporary London, the series eschewed clichéd representations of gang life in favour of detailed characterisation. The drama also explored the notion of masculinity amongst a younger generation of boys and young men, a theme Demange would explore further with his feature debut.

Nominated for BAFTAs in Outstanding British Film and Outstanding Debut by a British Writer, Director or Producer, *'71* (2014) is a powerful thriller set at the height of the Troubles in Northern Ireland. Mainly unfolding over one twenty-four-hour period, the film details the plight of a young British soldier (Jack O'Connell), who has only just begun his first tour of duty when he is separated from his unit and forced to run for his life through the streets of Belfast. Demange's muscular direction, which saw him awarded the Critics' Circle Breakthrough British Director Prize, is a stunning exercise in suspense and a detailed portrait of a young man, ignorant of the politics of the world he has entered, desperate to reach the safety of his barracks.

What attracted you to the script of '71?

There are so many anonymous films out there – films you watch in the cinema, and by the time you get home you've forgotten about them. I've always wanted to make films, but stumbled into television by accident. I'd had ideas for feature films and I'd written a screenplay, but I was always really critical of anything I had done. I'd ask myself, 'Was it worth making?' After two years of working on that screenplay I decided not to do it.

You might not get a chance to make a second film, and we're saturated with so many new films, so I had to ask myself if there was a good enough reason for the film to exist. I knew that my first feature had to be worth it, and it took me a long time to find the right project to work on.

I had a meeting with Tessa Ross at Film4, who has played a part in almost all my favourite British films of the past decade. And she said to me that she wanted to work with me on my first feature, which was great news. But then I kept saying no to everything. She – along with Sam Lavender at Film4 and Lizzie Franke at the BFI – kept sending me scripts, as did Dan MacRae at StudioCanal . . . probing me for what might take my interest. I did have a few things in development but they didn't work out. They were all really patient with me.

'71 was sent to me by the producer Angus Lamont, who initially had the idea for the film, and Robin Gutch. Film4 were already on board financing the screenplay and they were keen that I read it. They thought I would respond to the writing; to be honest, I was a little apprehensive when I was told the story took place in Northern Ireland during the Troubles. After *Bloody Sunday* (2002) and *Hunger* (2008) I thought, 'I ain't touching Northern Island.' But then I read the screenplay. It was the most muscular and visceral piece of writing I'd ever come across, yet it had so much humanity at its core. I never normally read a screenplay in one sitting, because I'm so ADD, but I just smashed my way through it.

I loved it but had strong opinions about what direction I would want to steer it in. So I met with the producers and the writer and we all hit it off. They responded to the ideas and it was a great collaboration. We worked through about four drafts together. Well, passes really. Essentially, 70 per cent of it didn't change a great deal. I remember when I read the scene of the young loyalist boy bossing around the guys at a barricade. I loved it – it was the best scene I'd ever read and we never changed a word of it.

So the four drafts that followed after you came on board were mostly cosmetic changes?

I wouldn't call it cosmetic. I introduced the idea that he has a younger brother. It felt to me that we needed a reason to root for him. He is so silent through most of the film, it somehow makes us closer to him to know he is responsible for someone else. The brother also represents this idea of kids caught up in conflict. We had a scene that ended up being cut, where I specifically identify him as Gary's brother, but it doesn't matter if the audience think he might be his son. It's a positive ambiguity. What's important is that by having kids litter the film we see the impact of it on Gary. He sees them through a different gaze – that of his own experiences. And it reminds him of the responsibility towards the kid he has back home.

There were some issues with credibility too, here and there, which is always the case with thrillers. After the pub explosion, for instance, we needed to figure out why Gary was still on the run. The ending also needed some work, and I was keen to push the entire narrative towards a more ambiguous area, where we were dealing in shades of grey. It was a great process because there was no resistance to any of the changes we made. We were just bouncing ideas off each other, the producers, the writer and myself. I need that, I rely on my collaborators. For instance, I've worked with my DoP [Tat Radcliffe] and editor [Chris Wyatt] for nine years now, and I need them to react to what I'm doing.

They'll ask me if I really need something, and my reaction is normally, 'Fuck! No, you're right. I don't.' They probe and challenge everything in a healthy way, they're rigorous. We all need to be, I guess.

Most importantly, we wanted to humanise everyone. I'm not a polemicist. It wasn't the subject that ultimately attracted me – it was the human story. That transcends the specificity of the Troubles and had a universality, it could almost be contemporary in that it could take place in Iraq, Afghanistan, Syria, the war in Algeria, many conflicts that have taken place and are taking place. It felt really pertinent. It immediately made me think of *The Battle of Algiers* (1966) and Alan Clarke's *Elephant* (1989). Alan Clarke has been a huge influence on me. It was tragic that he died so young. That refusal in *Elephant* to give any motive or explain anything – just to watch it unfold – it's phenomenally powerful. Tat and I watched that film before we started filming, and we talked about many different cinematic references and exchanged films and images. I love that process.

Its power lies in the refusal to offer up answers, but to constantly question.

That's right. The best I can ever do is present a situation that allows people to grapple with it. I'm in no position to give answers or relay messages – at most I can pose questions. And try to humanise everyone, attempt to genuinely engage with the different points of view. At the same time, it's finding a way of presenting it in a way that engages the audience's hopes and fears, that elicits an emotional response. Alongside Alan Clarke and *The Battle of Algiers*, I'm a huge fan of Walter Hill and John Carpenter. It's essentially a chase film, with layers, of course, but it also had to deliver as an exciting chase movie on some levels. And there's nothing wrong with genre cinema. I can't tell you how many times I've watched *The Warriors* (1979). So I embraced the genre elements, but we had a responsibility to make sure it always felt grounded and that we didn't slip into 'movie moments'.

The film also touches on the notion of masculinity in crisis, a theme that surfaced in the Top Boy *series you directed for Channel 4. It's an interesting area considering how young these characters are, rather than a more conventional mid-life crisis narrative that often plays out in dramas exploring aspects of masculinity.*

I'm fascinated by people attempting to define who they're going to be in life, especially when they're anchorless. I imposed that idea on *Top Boy*, asking, 'Who is going to be the top boy? Is it the joiner or the kid who decides he's going to be his own man?' My focus was much more on the kids than the drug dealer narrative, which we've seen so many times. There's something fascinating in the narratives of these young boys who often have no fathers, no male role models, and yet they are trying to define their own sense of masculinity and who they're going to be in life.

That's what's so important about the implication that Gary came out of an orphanage and the decisions he makes with his life. He's looking for a home – a place, a sense of tribe and family, somewhere he can belong.

Was Gary based on a real character or a combination of characters you and Gregory [Burke] had encountered in your research?

He was Gregory's creation. What's amazing about Gregory is that he completely understands these worlds. He's utterly forensic in his research and facts without ever losing sight of the characters at the heart of the story, what makes them tick, who they are. There's a long tradition of writers coming from the theatre and writing for the screen in the UK. Often they fetishise the dialogue over finding the image that can capture the essence of the moment without words. He doesn't. The first time I met him he just said, 'I fucking hate the theatre.' And I thought, 'He's my man.' One of our first conversations was about Michael Mann's

Thief (1981), and he kept quoting lines from it. He just loves movies. Beyond that, he grew up in an environment where the people he knew were joining the army. He can write about men in a way that I think is really rare. It's honest – warts 'n' all. I've read some things that offer up an approximation of what they believe an alpha male to be, and it's all wrong. He gets the balance right – it's experiential, not imagined. Shane Meadows is the same. He understands the worlds and people he depicts completely. He understands the nature of boys hanging out together. He's listened to these people and he gets it.

Did Gary's character change much when Jack O'Connell came on board?

The character kept evolving. He was initially seventeen years old. I didn't want the age to rise and, ironically, in our first meeting I said we need to find the next Jack O'Connell. There was a poster of *This Is England* (2006) on the wall at Warp Films' offices, where we had our meetings [O'Connell played Pukey Nicholls]. At the time, Jack was working on the *300* sequel [*300: Rise of an Empire*, 2014] and he looked ripped. I really wanted him but I thought, 'It's too late. He looks too old.' Then I met him some time later. He'd lost weight and I thought he could easily look nineteen or twenty. We spoke to Greg about the change in age. He's not precious at all, unless he thinks you're making a mistake. And so he set about making a number of changes. It also worked better with the younger brother, giving the relationship a more paternal angle.

I think Gary may be a patchwork of the people Greg and Angus knew growing up. Jack was an extension of that – he grew up either wanting to be a footballer or to join the army. He was from Derby, so we changed Gary's birthplace to there (from Leeds). Jack then became the expert on the character and we would discuss how he would react as the story progressed.

It's also important for me to keep the writer involved. We

would always refer any decisions back to Greg, and he kept writing throughout the production.

The rest of the casting works so well, particularly Sam Reid and Sean Harris, whose characters are polar opposites, with Gary trapped in between them.

It really came together when I actually met the actors. Sean Harris gave me a strong idea of who his character could be, and that then made me think about who I would have to find to cast opposite him. It's important in an ensemble piece like this to cast the relationships right. The script featured rough approximations of each character, but there was room to explore how best to place these men up on the screen. That is not to say Greg didn't write strong characters. It's more that we remained open to meeting actors that excite and could in turn influence or shape the character in the script.

Gary is a very passive protagonist. It's the people he encounters who move the narrative forward, so it was essential to get them right. Most are only on screen for a very short time, but you need to feel that they're completely rounded, utterly believable characters. They're archetypes in a way, but we had to be sure that we weren't just presenting lazy stereotypes. They needed to feel like people with a free will that existed beyond the frame.

The film may not engage with the debates surrounding the Troubles, but it is scathing about the power structure of the military, whether it's a state army or one organised to oppose it. Both structures are split by fissures, with satellite groups more extreme in their outlook and actions.

As soon as humans organise, we're fucked. The moment we group together, the potential for corruption increases. We're all fallible, so the only way we could attempt to deal with this situation was to accept that it doesn't matter which side you're looking at, there's always going to be some kind of rot in it.

How much of a challenge was it not filming in Belfast, instead having the production unfold across four locations in England?

From a practical point of view it was a nightmare. Shooting in four places is tough on the budget we had. It was expensive for a first film, but cheap for what we were aiming to achieve. This was important for me because this film had to stand out. Not against other British films, but against all films in general.

The spaces had to have the right scale. And there was nothing in Belfast today that allowed us to film there. It also had to break out of the terraced-house street stereotype. That was such a staple of the TV when I grew up and I wanted to find a way to challenge that. That's when I found out about the Divis Flats. It's this stunning building made in a Brutalist style. During the Troubles the army wouldn't actually enter the building from the ground floor. It was too dangerous. They took the top floor in one of the tower blocks and airlifted men in and out. It was the visual representation of what I wanted and allowed the action to become more claustrophobic.

Greg loved the idea. So we went to Belfast, only to discover it had been torn down. But by then it had become the primary location with almost thirty pages set in the one location, so we started to hunt for something similar. I still wanted to shoot in Ireland. It is their story and it made sense to. I felt a responsibility to shoot it there. But we couldn't make the locations work. Funnily enough, after travelling everywhere to find a replica of the Divis Flats, from Scotland to the south of England and a tour of the North, we actually found it in Sheffield – Park Hill estate. You wouldn't believe it, but you can literally see it from Warp's offices. It had been in front of us all the time.

The building was uninhabited, which was great. But it had no electricity and most of the windows were broken or boarded up. That said, once all that was fixed, we had the run of the place for three weeks.

The riot at the start of the film was another problem. We had another search for a location, and that's when you have to hold your nerve as a director. You have the pressure of the machine – of the [completion] bond, of the finance, of the line producer – wherein you have to try to make things fit when you know that it won't do the film justice. It's knowing when to put your foot down and say it won't work that way. And, most importantly, having producers that support you in those moments. I have to say Angus Lamont and Robin Gutch were incredibly supportive. They were risk-takers. They backed me and their support gave me strength. So we ended up going to Blackburn to film the riot, which added pressure to the production and an extra expense, but it was the perfect fit.

As for the chase, that unfolded over three cities: Sheffield, Blackburn and Liverpool.

It's stunning. The complexity of it reminded me of the sequence Kathryn Bigelow shot for Point Break *(1991), although in this film we're with the pursued, not the pursuer.*

Exactly. That was a major influence. I love that chase scene – it's possibly the best foot-chase scene ever.

The logistics were a nightmare for us. It's probably the toughest thing I've ever done technically. Actually, the riot is probably the hardest thing I've ever done. [*A long pause.*] You know what? This whole film was the hardest thing I've ever done!

Working out where everyone was geographically was tough, from the soldiers arriving, to where people were on the street. But when it came to the chase, I knew it had to deliver – it had to have this sense of power. And it also had to be an experiential thing; we have to feel what the protagonist is going through. Gary has no idea what is going on around him. He's just running for his life. So we don't need exposition or context. We need to be as lost as him. Therefore, the camera should behave as he does. It needs to be married to him during these scenes. We are trapped in the moment, whether it's with him running or the violence we witness. It has to happen first-hand and we can't be ahead of him. That's what governed it.

There are some great chase scenes out there. The opening of *Narc* (2002) is a good example, and there's a good one in *Inception* (2010) too. But *Point Break* is the one. Bigelow burns through so many locations for that chase. It's incredible. That's what I wanted, and I think we achieved it. But stitching together so many locations from three different cities was tough.

How was the challenge of shifting from 16mm for the daytime shots to digital at night?

It was a challenge for Tat. We worked really hard on the look for this film. We knew we wanted to shoot anamorphic. And all the archive footage we were looking at for research was shot on 16mm. Moreover, when we looked at the colour palette for the green uniforms, the red of the brickwork and the skin tones, digital just didn't do it the way we wanted. It was too sharp. We tested 16mm and it looked just right. We could have played with the digital in post but it wouldn't have been the same. There were some heated debates, but I screened some tests and everyone agreed that a combination would work in the end. It's crazy how people now get so nervous the minute you mention shooting on film. 16mm is an amazing format – I'd hate for it to disappear.

I'm particularly proud of the lighting at night. Tat and the gaffer sourced the actual bulbs that would have been used at the time in Belfast. There was no fill light. That's the beauty of digital – we captured the images exactly how they would have looked back then. So we were able to get the best of film and digital for this story in the end.

The shift also works on a metaphorical level. The straightforward chase in daytime between the 'good' and 'bad' guys becomes increasingly complex and morally ambiguous as night descends.

Absolutely. As the sun goes down we move further away from

straightforward realism and the film takes on a slightly mythical quality as this guy wanders through the night. We wanted to present scenes impressionistically – with the hellish flames burning across the town. This guy is travelling into his own heart of darkness.

Jane Pollard and Iain Forsyth on the set of *20,000 Days on Earth*,
with Nick Cave and Susie Bick (photo: Amelia Troubridge)

Iain Forsyth and Jane Pollard

Iain Forsyth and Jane Pollard met and began working collaboratively at Goldsmiths College. They initially became known in the 1990s for their recreations of highly charged cultural moments, which pioneered the use of re-enactment within contemporary visual art through a series of major live art commissions at London's ICA. This body of work culminated in their critically acclaimed *A Rock 'n' Roll Suicide* (1998), a painstakingly faithful live recreation of David Bowie's final performance as Ziggy Stardust, twenty-five years after the original event.

They have since continued to employ the mechanics of live performance and repetition, while shifting focus to work predominantly in video and sound installation. In 2003, they produced *File under Sacred Music*, a remake of an infamous bootleg of The Cramps playing at Napa State Mental Institute, California, in 1978. The artists meticulously restaged this performance with an audience from local mental health arts organisations, in order to reshoot each pan, tilt, zoom and jitter of the original.

Performance and music culture plays a significant role in their work, and this has led to some notable collaborations. Their video *Walking After Acconci* features the acting debut of young rapper and actor Plan B (aka Ben Drew). *Silent Sound*, their live performance and ambisonic installation, was scored by Jason Pierce (from the band Spiritualized), and when re-presented at Art Basel Miami Beach in 2007 was described as 'one of the fair's biggest word-of-mouth hits' by the *New York Times*. They have established an ongoing working relationship with Nick Cave, with their various projects together including producing the 3D audiobook of his 2009 novel *The Death of Bunny Munro*, and directing a series of fourteen short films, collectively titled *Do you love me like I love you*.

In 2009, the British Film Institute commissioned a major project, *Radio Mania*, their first stereoscopic work – a multiscreen 3D video installation with ambisonic 3D sound and a cast including Kevin Eldon, Caroline Catz and Fenella Fielding. Crossing the illusion of cinema with the presence of theatre, the work conjures up a psychological, conceptual and physical state between reality and hallucination.

2011 marked Forsyth and Pollard's first show as a duo, *Publicsfear*, presented at South London Gallery, and *Soon*, their first major commission for the City of Toronto, as well as *Romeo Echo Delta*, a radio broadcast reworking of *The War of the Worlds* for the BBC. In 2012 they were shortlisted for the inaugural Samsung Art+ Prize.

20,000 Days on Earth is their first feature film. It premiered at the 2014 Sundance Film Festival. A synthesis of fact and fiction that follows an imaginary day in the life of iconic musician Nick Cave and the recording of his *Push the Sky Away* album, it is the most innovative portrait of the creative process since *Zidane*.

The duo were travelling at the time of the interview, which was conducted in writing; they chose to submit their answers in unison.

Could you expand on the origins of 20,000 Days on Earth?

This film was only possible because of our existing relationship with Nick. Had that trust not already been firmly established, it couldn't have happened. The origins of the film were accidental. Nick called us and said that he'd begun working on a new record and asked if we'd like to film the writing sessions that he was about to go into with Warren [Ellis]. It's unusual enough for Nick to be happy to have cameras with him in the studio, so to be allowed in at such an early stage was unheard of. Without any thought to the final outcome, we jumped at it.

We continued to film as the record began to take shape, and eventually found ourselves in the residential studio in France where the Bad Seeds had assembled to record the album. Once we began looking at the footage we were blown away by what we'd been able to capture. It was at this point that it became obvious to us that this stuff shouldn't just get churned up in the promotional machine, ending up as snippets on YouTube.

Nick was completely behind the idea that we should make a long-form film, but was initially very dubious of the form it should take. Realising we all shared a healthy cynicism of the conventional rock-documentary form, we threw ourselves into trying to figure out how the idea should evolve. It was at this point that we borrowed the notebooks Nick had used to write the album, and among the scribbled lyrics and song fragments we found a number of phrases that resonated with us. One was an abandoned song called '20,000 Days on Earth'. There was something off-kilter and epic about that phrase, something that spoke to us about how we all measure the time that we have, and the things we choose to do with our time alive. That began to shape the film we wanted to make. The idea evolved further when we found the phrase in Nick's notebooks that ended up opening the film – *'at the end of the 20th century I ceased to be a human being, I wake, I write, I eat, I write . . .'*

Performance and music culture has always played a major role in your work, from your use of re-enactment in visual art to music promos and the recreation of iconic cultural moments. Was it a natural progression to move into a more feature-length project, and how conscious were you of balancing your interests with a need to create some sort of narrative that more 'traditional' audiences could grasp?

We've worked together as artists since meeting at art school more than twenty years ago. Since the beginning, music has always figured large in our work. Not really as a subject, but we've always been drawn to the way that music is able to connect with an audience – the deep relationship we're able to feel

with music and the way we use it to shape ourselves and communicate with others. The seeds of this were really sown during
our time at Goldsmiths. Being there in the wake of the YBA
years, it was a time when many students viewed it as a kind of
finishing school for art superstars. There was all this big, shiny
and ultimately vacuous work being made, and everyone just
expected that at the end of the course Charles Saatchi would
breeze in and pick out the blessed few. That attitude made no
sense to us.

We were also massively influenced at that time by DIY music
culture, friends running tiny clubs, writing fanzines and putting
out 7-inch singles, all that stuff orbiting the world of music
made sense of collaboration, and it was really in that spirit
that we began working together – we felt we could achieve
more together than individually. Maybe that's why the transition to film-making has actually been really comfortable for us.
Art-making is so often about the ego of the individual maker,
but we've never had that; even working 'alone' we were always
part of a team.

20,000 Days on Earth is, at its heart, a film essay about the
creative spirit. So we felt a very conscious need to create an
accessible, familiar narrative for an audience. The conceit of a
day in the life of Nick Cave felt like a device that would give us
an anchor, something we could always return to. When people
hear you are an artist making a feature film, there's usually an
assumption that what you're doing will be inaccessible, difficult
and somehow wilfully obtuse. But accessibility has always been
important to us; we've always made work that operates first and
foremost on an emotional level.

Were there any specific reference points with the film?

A huge reference for us, although not really for Nick, was
Lindsay Anderson's *O Lucky Man!* (1973). It's a film we return
to often, that gives us a creative shot in the arm whenever we

need it. The scale, ambition and absurdity of it is vast. It contains multitudes. With Nick, so many of our shared references were about understanding what we *didn't* want to do. We all hated the thought of making a fly-on-the-wall style documentary. We had no interest in the widely accepted conceit that this type of film-making is somehow able to get 'behind the mask' and reveal truth. Nick's been performing in public for more than thirty-five years now, and our assertion was that there is no mask. Nick is every bit the creature he's created and the truth is right there on the surface. Seeing him drive the kids to school or making a cup of tea doesn't truly reveal anything.

There were very few films that we really referenced, but there were two that, although flawed, both shared a sense of ambition that really appealed to us. Godard's *One Plus One* (1968) and *Led Zeppelin: The Song Remains the Same* (1976) [directed by Peter Clifton and Joe Massot] both seemed to be reaching for something. It's that grasping for greatness, while always being open to failure, that we feel so acutely in *O Lucky Man!*

The synthesis between drama and reality is another aspect that I sense fascinates you, and which is given full exposure in 20,000 Days on Earth. *What are some of the origins of this fascination?*

Truthfully, this goes way back for us – to some of our art experiments with re-enactment. For us, re-enactment wasn't about revealing something about the past but rather attempting to understand something about the present. What can the act of superimposing a past performance or event onto the present tell us about the culture that engages with that? How does it affect the psychology of those experiencing something new in the here and now that is totally built on the past?

There was a search for some kind of truth, some kind of new understanding of authenticity, of reality, in the midst of a culture that seemed increasingly obsessed with artificial or constructed strategies. Over the past ten years or so there's been a landslide in culture that has engulfed these odd tensions between the real and the copy. And as this comprehension has become absorbed into the mainstream it's become a less interesting area for us, as artists, to explore.

Even though our interests have evolved in different directions now, without this work we wouldn't have made *20,000 Days on Earth* in the way we did. We approached it with some firm principles in place. Firstly, we needed to make the situations that we put Nick in feel real for him. This isn't about a delusional suspension of belief that there aren't cameras and it isn't a film set, but it is about making them a secondary concern. The primary concern is the cohesive sustained reality of what is happening in the room. This means longs takes; it means we can't use actors; it means we can only run a scene once, and – most importantly – it means accepting that some things will fail.

I also wondered if there was a conscious attempt to not entirely ostracise Nick Cave's large and quite possessive fan base? For all its brilliant technique, your film also contains just enough archive footage, music and glimpses into working methodology to appease more traditional Nick Cave fans.

The fan base was never a consideration. Not that we deliberately wanted to ostracise them, but we knew we weren't making the film for them. For it to be interesting to us, for us to commit so much of our time, and demand so much of Nick's time, we had to make something that would speak more universally.

Fans of anything are always a very difficult group to please, and we're sure many of Nick's fans will have their own particular reasons for being interested in Nick that they feel should have played more of a role in the film. There are probably aspects of his life or work they'd like to have seen more focus on, people they feel should have featured more prominently, and so on. It's completely natural. That's really part of the job of being a fan. It was never something at the forefront of our thinking.

Although the lunch with Nick Cave and Warren Ellis is fictionalised, it does effectively capture the extent of their friendship and collaborative synergy. Was it always clear that Ellis is a major figure in Cave's life?

Absolutely. Nick's relationship with Warren is very special. Nick talks in the film about needing these 'remarkable creatures' to collaborate with – and there's no creature more remarkable than Warren! We knew he would play a pivotal role in the film. We wanted to cast him almost like a court jester, the Shakespearean fool – a character who we'd meet around the middle of the film and who would cut through everything. As well as teasing out the remarkable friendship and camaraderie between Nick and Warren, we also felt he was the only person who could give the audience a little break from Nick, a different voice for a short time before we move into the second half of the film.

The film is remarkable for many aesthetic and conceptual reasons, but I think it is important not to overlook the contribution of DoP Erik Wilson. He has done outstanding work with Richard Ayoade and on Paddy Considine's Tyrannosaur. *What was it about Erik's visual sensibility that attracted you, and what kind of mood and tone did the three of you talk about creating?*

We love Erik. His work is remarkable and he's a very special person. We met a few cinematographers, some incredibly talented people, but ultimately Erik was the one who seemed genuinely excited by the unique considerations thrown up by this project. Working essentially with non-actors means you really only get one shot at everything – you can't just reset and go again. We also have some pretty strong ideas on how to arrange and manage a set in order to get the best out of someone like Nick, which does ultimately put additional demands on the crew. Everyone needs to be completely on their game, and invisible. So it's a lot to ask, but Erik totally understood it.

As well as being in tune technically, we had a strong creative connection with Erik. We wanted to create a series of worlds that Nick would exist in that were visually cluttered and cinematically rich, without becoming clichéd or pretentious. Erik's idea to use anamorphic lenses played a major part in defining the look of the film. The shared ambition was always to create a very slightly enhanced version of reality, not super-stylised, but heightened – recognisable to the audience, but still somehow off-kilter.

Have you been surprised by the incredibly positive reaction to the film?

It's been very inspiring. To not be overwhelmed by such a universally positive reaction you'd have to be dead inside. You always hope your work will be well received, but audiences do seem to really get this film, and that wasn't something we'd anticipated. We worked incredibly hard on developing universal themes and speaking to ideas that would resonate with an audience beyond Nick Cave fans. But a real audience is the only real test and, so far, we've been blown away. We're in Australia at the moment, where the film is opening the Sydney Film Festival, and it's incredibly gratifying to see how well the film is playing in front of an Australian audience.

What plans lie ahead? Do you wish to continue working across various disciplines, or do you now have a burning desire to begin work on another feature-related project?

We'd love to work on another feature project, and we've been discussing some ideas, but we're always most excited by things that scare us. We like to be continually challenged. So we've begun developing a multi-part project for TV. It's based on a real historical figure, but as always we're not going to let the truth stand in the way of a good story.

Alex Garland with Alicia Vikander on the set of *Ex Machina*
(photo: Susie Allnut / © Universal)

Alex Garland

As a novelist Alex Garland has written *The Beach* (1996), *The Tesseract* (1999), and, with his father, the illustrator Nicholas Garland, *The Coma* (2004). He has written the screenplays of *28 Days Later* (2002), *Sunshine* (2007), *Never Let Me Go* (2010) and *Dredd* (2012), and has written and directed *Ex Machina* (2015).

Ex Machina *functions as a very effective thriller but it obviously also operates on a number of deeper levels. Could you outline some of the more complex human and psychological issues you wanted to explore?*

I was interested in various questions about both human consciousness and artificial intelligence, and what each indicates about the other. Much of this becomes about how people relate to each other, irrespective of issues around AI, such as how we establish or fail to establish what's going on in someone else's mind. Other questions flow directly from this, for example about gender, and where it resides.

I read a comment from you where you stated that as well as not feeling paranoid or fearful of AI and computer technology you wanted to make a film about this subject where your sympathies were with the robot. This reminds me of Jonathan Glazer's wanting to make a film from the perspective of an alien in Under the Skin *(2013). Can you explain in more detail how your empathy with the robot manifested itself in how you approached the material and in how you constructed Ava?*

I empathised with the robot – fell in love with her, almost – right at the start of the writing process. I saw her as a sentient being, unreasonably imprisoned, and Ava was always the hero of the story. Past that point, much of the film-making task was in disguising from the audience that Ava is actually the protagonist.

I loved *Under the Skin*, which in many ways has an opposite position to *Ex Machina* with respect to the protagonist, in that the alien remains alien to us until the very end, and in *Ex Machina* it's the other way round.

The film suggests a future where humans are inferior to machines and computer technology and yet, as with the object of your sympathy, doesn't present it, as other films and works of fiction have, as some terrible dystopia. Do you feel there is an inevitability to the eventual dominant role AI will play in our lives?

It's not inevitable that AIs will supersede us, but it is certainly possible. That might seem alarming, but for me it becomes less alarming if you see strong AI as continuation or extension of us, rather than something entirely different. The relationship I imagine is something like parent–child, where we hope of our children that they outlive us, and have an existence at least as good as ours, and hopefully better.

The recent screening I attended was for the benefit of scientists and science journalists. What was the research process for the project and how deeply did you need to immerse yourself, although technology is a theme of your work, in the world of science and technology? There is a line of thought that science fiction is at its best when rooted in science.

I don't think I need science fiction to be rooted in science, but I do generally like it to be rooted in ideas. So, for example, I like *Alien* (1979) and *Starship Troopers* (1997) very much, neither of which strike me as scientific. In the case of *Ex Machina*, I felt that there was a need for accuracy about some of the issues surrounding the subject matter, so I immersed myself as deeply as I could. Mostly that took the form of reading, but when I felt the script was in reasonable shape, I showed it to three people – Murray Shanahan, Gia Milinovich, and Adam Rutherford. Between them, they were able to examine the science, gender questions, and philosophy, and test them.

In terms of the other works referred to above did you allow yourself to be influenced by any key films or texts? The Turing test aspect obviously invokes Philip K. Dick and the subsequent film adaptation, Blade Runner (1982). *I imagine you'll quickly tire of this question but . . .*

I personally think this film is more influenced by *2001* (1968) and *Stalker* (1979) than *Blade Runner*. That said, I did use *Blade Runner* in other ways, essentially as a misdirection. I felt fairly sure that most viewers of *Ex Machina* would be familiar with *Blade Runner*, and would consequently start to suspect that the 'real' robot in the film is Domhnall Gleeson's character, Caleb, and that they have second-guessed the narrative. The film deliberately nudges them towards this idea a few times, to draw attention away from the motivation of the actual robot in the film.

There is a strong feminist element to Ex Machina. *The AIs Nathan constructs are all female and conform to a certain aesthetic regarding beauty. Like Bluebeard's young wives they are all also quickly discarded. There is a liberating aspect to Ava's physical and spiritual escape from Nathan's grip. Was this something you also wanted to stress?*

Yes. In intention, it's a key part of the narrative.

I also found the film very interesting on the subject of employer–employee relations and the abuse of power. I think that Domhnall Gleeson perfectly articulates this in his performance. The production notes contain a quote from Gleeson where he describes Caleb as containing elements of your personality. Do you feel this to be true?

It mainly makes me feel I should have read the production notes . . .

For all his flaws and faults, Nathan is perhaps the most honest character. He is completely upfront about what he wants and, ultimately, what he will do to get it. And yet, his wealth, power and reclusiveness see him teeter on the precipice between genius and insanity. There is something Kane-like and General Kurtz-like about him. Did other similar figures inform your creation of the character?

Nathan is extremely honest in some key regards, and sometimes the honesty is despite himself. Kurtz was definitely a character that Oscar Isaac and I discussed – in particular the idea of having spent too much time up-river, with behaviour that is increasingly unmodified by contact with people/things. I was also interested in Oppenheimer, who is frequently referenced in the script, regarding the weight of responsibility versus intellectual ambition, when working on a foundational scientific breakthrough that may contain the means of mankind's destruction.

It's interesting, and striking, that unlike with Kyoko, there is no attempt to hide the fact that Ava has been artificially created. Could you talk me through the design process for Ava and some of the directions you wished to avoid? Also, how did the synthetic nature of Ava affect Alicia Vikander's performance in more practical terms? I imagine she had to work wearing a restrictive suit to enable the later addition of CGI.

The initial design process was more about what Ava didn't look like rather than what she did. I worked with an artist called Jock, testing various designs, and we quickly learned about which visual cues we needed to avoid. Gold metal triggered thoughts of C-3PO, a metallic breastplate triggered Maria from *Metropolis*, white plastic triggered Chris Cunningham's famous Björk video, and so on. This was a problem because we didn't want our first view of Ava to feel as if it was referencing other films. Eventually, we came to the idea of a geometric mesh that covered her skin, which allowed a view to her internal machine form, and also describe a female exterior form under certain lighting conditions – and that seemed to crack it.

Alicia wore a grey full-body suit, like a black-and-white Spiderman costume, which in some areas of her body (chest, thighs) became the practical effect. She said she didn't find it restrictive, happily, and gave her an approach into the character.

I was interested by your creation of Nathan's compound. It must have been a challenge to set something in the near future and to reveal the living environment of one of the world's richest men. What was your approach in this regard and where did you film it? The glass and concrete play a key role in the film and in how the different characters visualise the world and each other.

The compound did create a challenge, partly because Nathan's character had limitless resources, but the film production didn't (the budget was $15 million). We knew we could extend the sense of his property's scale by 'adding' to a found location on a soundstage build, but we still needed to find a location as a starting point, and the location needed to be architecturally bold and representative of Nathan's wealth and personality. On top of that, it also needed to be in a dramatic landscape, with a sense of uncontrolled nature outside the door, to juxtapose with the fiercely controlled man-made environment inside the doors. Otherwise we would be locked into VFX shots every time there was a view through a window, etc. These competing issues led to a search – initially online, and eventually on location hunts. In the end, we were just incredibly lucky to find a location in Norway, in an exceptionally dramatic landscape, that ticked all the boxes.

I also wanted to ask about the Geoff Barrow and Ben Salisbury score. It's very impressive. Were you a fan of Drokk and how did you come to work with them?

I'm a very big fan of Beak, which is one of Geoff's bands. In terms of working together, initially we collaborated on the *Dredd* score (which eventually was subsumed into their Drokk project). Although *Dredd* didn't work out with them, I loved their approach to composing and immediately contacted them when *Ex Machina* went into production. They are ideal collaborators on every level. Left-field, experimental, brave, open-minded. On top of this, they aren't trained in film grammar, so their approach to scoring scenes is innately original – which is an amazing asset.

Finally, you are keen to stress filmmaking as a collaborative process. How have your previous experiences working with Danny Boyle and Andrew Macdonald informed this perspective and how, as director, did you seek to create an atmosphere of collaboration between all the different departments of the crew?

I learned a great deal from working with Danny and Andrew, and I still work with Andrew. Danny was an extraordinary director to encounter. Aside from my being able to witness his great skill on set, he is not intimidated by writers, and he would bring me into prep, rehearsals, the cutting room, and so on. Both men were entirely generous in sharing their immense knowledge about film-making, and they created a perfect environment to learn the ropes.

My own approach to directing is in some respects to deliberately undermine the perceived importance of the role. I see the cast and crew as a collection of film-makers, of which the director is just one part, and sometimes not the most important part. This is a firm separation from any expectations that stem from traditional auteur theory – which I see as a kind of monotheism that doesn't stand up to much inspection. To be slightly more specific, you can make a reasonable case for auteur theory, but only with a very limited number of film-makers, and not all of them are directors. In that respect, I create a collaborative atmosphere by making it clear that it is the collaborative aspect of film-making that I find most interesting and rewarding.

Jonathan Glazer (photo: StudioCanal)

Jonathan Glazer

Jonathan Glazer first found fame after his revolutionary pop videos for Radiohead's 'Street Spirit' and Jamiroquai's multi-MTV-award-winning 'Virtual Insanity'. His work on commercials such as the groundbreaking Guinness 'Surfer' (1999) further marked him out as a supremely gifted visual stylist.

With his feature debut *Sexy Beast* (2000), Glazer earned a BAFTA nomination and created a work that entered the lexicon of modern British crime movies. The tale of a retired criminal living the good life in Spain but reluctantly coaxed back to the UK for one last job, the film displays a gift for visual set pieces and a talent for working with leading actors, an often underlooked facet of the director's work.

This facet was again at the fore when Glazer worked with Nicole Kidman, Danny Huston and Lauren Bacall on *Birth* (2004). An unsettling story of a young boy's attempts to persuade an emotionally scarred woman that he is her deceased husband reborn, the film has an eerie otherworldliness that presaged Glazer's next direction.

Marked by a lengthy pre-production process and Glazer's perfectionist streak, *Under the Skin* finally emerged some ten years after Glazer began working on it. An adaptation of the Michel Faber novel, the film jettisons all but the title and the central concept of an alien woman arriving on earth in search of prey. It's a bold and brilliant vision that effectively captures the sense of what it must feel like to look at the world from an alien's perspective. Scarlett Johansson shines in the central role. Mica Levi's electronic score is similarly effective.

It ended up taking ten years to make Under the Skin. *Can you talk about the process of bringing it to the screen?*

It certainly took a long time to find a way of doing it that we liked. Over the years, the screenplay became a lot less similar to Michel Faber's source novel. The pillars of the screenplay are similar but the way the story is told is very different. We wanted to make it a story very much told from the alien's perspective.

There was a kind of phase one, where we had a script written by Walter Campbell. We then had a script co-written with Walter that we were prepared to go out into the world with. However, there was then a second phase where we realised that we would be unable to make the film as it was written because of how much it would cost. We then took the decision to strip the script – to distil it to an almost documentary aesthetic, focusing solely on a particular character.

What attracted you to making a film about Earth from an alien viewpoint?

We're slightly limited by the fact that we are inhibited by the human imagination. It's a lovely idea but difficult to achieve. What we tried to do is find a way that represents or evokes this concept of an inscrutable identity – and in our case a slightly malevolent one. I wanted the alien to be like a force and an all-consuming appetite. What I then tried to do was emphasise the difference between this alien entity and us, so I incorporated scenes that attempt to dramatise that. I wanted to depict a slow, osmotic change in the character, towards a more human sensibility. We employed an extreme emphasis on colours and sounds to do that.

You play around a little with the idea of predatory behaviour. The alien is initially the predator, but then you show that humans have predatory instincts too.

I was interested by the idea that for someone – or something – to love, something else has to die. On top of that is the dispassionate nature of things. The alien is very much the conduit for this subject. There is also a sense of the hunter becoming the hunted at the end. It's at the point that the alien becomes more human – when she is vulnerable to the men she has exploited before. There's a certain irony in that, I suppose.

One of the turning points of the film is the scene involving Scarlett Johansson and Adam Pearson. The alien seems to become alerted to the notions of compassion and kindness.

It's a big scene and certainly key in terms of the journey. It is a turning point, but other key moments have also unfolded prior to this scene. I see it as a more gradual drift, and by the time the alien meets the character played by Adam it is ready for some kind of deeper connection. Maybe what she sees is someone like her, an outsider. She doesn't judge his appearance, as others do, because she isn't at all interested in what he looks like. It's also important that the character played by Adam grows more comfortable by the very fact that he doesn't feel rejected.

People tend to categorise you as a primarily visual director, perhaps because of your work in advertising, but this overlooks your work with actors such as Ray Winstone and Ben Kingsley on Sexy Beast, *and Nicole Kidman on* Birth.

Thank you very much! I think it's important when you film something to think about everything the audience is going to see, and, of course, the actor is very much at the centre of that. In many ways, the actor is the reason why you are there, and you have to believe in them. I also recognise that if I don't believe in the actor then I can't expect anybody else to either. It is perhaps the most vital aspect of the film.

This is a very brave performance from Johansson.

Scarlett was in our orbit for a while for the role. I met her quite early on and then stayed in contact as the script went through various changes. As soon as I had finally arrived at the film I wanted to make, it had to be Scarlett. There was a point where

I did consider the part uncastable, because it was so difficult to believe that someone we had seen in other films or on magazine covers could play this role. We did, for a brief period, think about casting an unknown, but then we just decided to go for it and make Scarlett the star.

It also helps extend the idea of alienation. I would imagine that, for Scarlett Johansson, driving around Glasgow in shabby clothes in a transit van is not an everyday experience.

It's interesting because now I am asked quite regularly if she was recognised. You don't expect Scarlett Johansson to be driving around and asking those questions, so we got away with it pretty much all of the time.

There is a vérité *aesthetic – you film for real in real-life situations with hidden cameras.*

There is an interesting dichotomy between the creative excitement of doing this and the reality of filming it. There was a concern that we may not capture the 'happy accidents' that we need to drive the narrative forward. Or what would happen if Scarlett was constantly recognised and the spell was broken? However, our confidence grew the more we filmed. The first shot we tried was in a busy Glasgow shopping centre on Saturday lunchtime, and once this worked we knew the set-up would be okay. For the nightclub scenes, which were filmed on a Friday and Saturday night in a real Glasgow nightclub, we had to have signs up outside – as we did in the shopping centre – to cover us legally. We also avoided lingering on any specific faces. For the driving scenes we had to get the people that were filmed to sign a release. Most people did, but a few didn't. Regrettably, one of the best moments involved a couple breaking up, which Scarlett interacted with. Not surprisingly, the couple didn't want to sign a release form.

The opening sequence with the eye locking into place is terrific.

We spent a year in a warehouse and shot pretty much the entire construction of a human being. Once we began to strip the film down we realised that we needed only one element and, as the film is very much about looking, we decided to concentrate on the eye formation. The eye is also an intensely human thing, so it felt like the right step-off point.

The Mica Levi score is very impressive, especially as a first score.

Mica was actually suggested by our music supervisor Peter Raeburn and his colleague Jay James. Peter has worked with me throughout my career, and they played me various pieces of music. One of them was from Mica's *Chopped and Screwed*. I was immediately struck by it.

Joanna Hogg (photo: Ellis Parrinder)

Joanna Hogg

Joanna Hogg started her career as a photographer before becoming interested in the moving image. She attended film school in the UK and, after several short films, became a prolific director of television drama. Hogg used this as a testing ground for developing her aesthetic as a film-maker, and, in particular, working with actors to obtain performances of authenticity and depth.

Unrelated (2007), Hogg's feature debut, won critical acclaim and numerous awards, including the FIPRESCI International Critics' Award at the London Film Festival, the *Guardian* First Film Award and the *Evening Standard* Most Promising Newcomer Award. An examination of bourgeois values in an affluent middle-class family holidaying in Tuscany, the film was remarkable for its naturalistic performances and frills-free aesthetic. A film of silences and recriminations, it announced the arrival of a major new British film-making talent.

Archipelago (2010) follows the travails of an upper-class family on holiday in Tresco (the Scilly Isles) and, once again, looks at what happens to the carefully calibrated equilibrium when simmering resentments surface. In many ways a deft comedy of manners, the film is refreshing in its honest portrait of upper-class values and concerns. It also established Hogg's close working association with fast-rising young British actor Tom Hiddleston.

Exhibition (2013) is an intimate, austere and engrossing study of a marriage and a revealing investigation into memory, architecture and the artistic process. When artists D and H decide to sell the home they have loved and lived in for two decades, they begin the difficult process of saying goodbye. The upheaval causes anxieties to surface, and D struggles to control the personal and creative aspects of her life with H. Dreams, memories and fears have all imprinted themselves on their home, a container for their lives and an axis of their marriage. How will their relationship – and their art – exist without its confines?

This interview began with the release of *Archipelago* and ended after the release of *Exhibition*.

You've described Archipelago *as being less autobiographical than* Unrelated *but more personal. Can you elaborate a little on this comment?*

I would say *Archipelago* is not autobiographical, in that it's not based on an account of my own life. *Unrelated* was more directly inspired by a specific moment in time that I had experienced. Though I would still argue it wasn't autobiography, which suggests a moment-by-moment story of a person's life.

Archipelago sprung more from my imagination. However, I was concerned that by using my imagination in this way, the characters and story would be somehow untrue to my own thoughts and feelings. Actually, this was not the case and in some ways it helped me to get even closer to the 'truth'. I am learning to use my imagination more, but it continues to be a challenge. The ideas are still based on my own emotional experience. But this avoidance of expressing a literal truth is very freeing, and opens up so many more worlds and possibilities.

A different facet of myself inspired each character in *Archipelago*. For example, Cynthia is based on a part of myself that is controlling and intolerant. Edward is based on a more indecisive, oversensitive aspect of myself, and so on. I am fascinated how such contradictory traits can exist in one person, and if *Archipelago* had been four hours long then those traits would have become visible in each of the characters at different times. It is a challenge to convey such complexity in cinema.

You have a background in photography and you've also spoken of your interest in painting. How has this helped shape your distinct film-making style?

It is difficult to understand precisely what has shaped my style. It's such an instinctive thing and has evolved over so many years. No doubt my background in photography has played a part and influenced my eye. To a degree, I think I put my 'eye' on hold in the ten years I worked in television. There was no place for my imagination there, certainly not in the genre of television I was working in. I had to pick up from where I left off, which was a very fertile creative period between the ages of nineteen to twenty-eight. Only when I started painting again in 2001 did this artistic side of myself spring to life. I view those lost TV years as colourless ones, from a creative point of view.

I don't remember deciding to create a style of long takes and static camera shots. This happened naturally. It could possibly have been my reaction to the conventions and limitations of TV drama. Now I believe this approach has become a convention in itself and I'm wary of using it for its own sake. Hopefully, my style will continue to evolve, though I find it hard to separate style and content.

What did Tresco come to contribute to Archipelago, *in terms of atmosphere and tone, and its actual physical characteristics?*

Tom Lubbock, in his brilliant 'Great Works' series for the *Independent*, wrote of Constable that he 'turned the natural world into a grand theatre of emotional expression'. Landscape gives form to my imagination. It is a springboard into the story. Actually, the landscape is the story. I want it to mirror the characters' feelings and emotions. I cannot separate the landscape of Tresco from the story. One wouldn't have happened without the other.

I already knew Tresco from my childhood. It was a place I grew up in, through years of going there for Easter holidays. Its associations were happy ones, and I surprised myself that *Archipelago* shows a darker, more melancholy side of the island. The island fascinates me because it has a dreamlike quality due to a kind of condensation of the landscape. There are quasi-surreal juxtapositions which I haven't seen anywhere else. On the

one hand, in the northern part of the island you have wild moorland, such as you would find in the highlands of Scotland, and on
the other, a lush tropical landscape that's more characteristic of
Cornwall. So it almost represents a miniature United Kingdom.

In Archipelago, *as in* Unrelated, *you use no incidental music, but
when we spoke before, you explained how for you a film can be
musical without having an actual score. For example, birdsong
features heavily in your new film.*

I absolutely love music but in cinema it is an incredibly powerful
tool that needs to be handled very carefully. You can show an
image of a flowerpot, but coupled with a Wagner opera it can
spring to life and be very emotional. So it's an easy trick to use,
and most films, for my taste, use it far too often.

I also love natural sounds. I am very aware of them in everyday life and enjoy recording them. I have a particular fondness
for birdsong, though, like certain music, I can find it excruciat-
ingly sad. In *Archipelago* I wanted to explore the idea of birdsong and communication. I liked the idea of counterpointing the
awkward silences between the Leighton family with the constant
chattering of birds.

The only musical idea I had was for Cynthia to sing a song to
her brother – that in a song she could communicate everything she
is unable to say directly to him. I told Lydia [Leonard], who plays
Cynthia, about my plans for the song a few days before recording
it. The idea needed to land with her at the right time emotionally.
I wrote the lyrics but we needed a melody, so I rang my friend Viv
Albertine, who sang the song to Lydia over the phone. I thought
Viv would respond to the ideas and emotions, which she did.

*How did you approach the casting? You strike a successful bal-
ance between actors and non-professionals such as Amy Lloyd
and Christopher Baker. What dynamic are you looking to explore here?*

The idea to cast Tom Hiddleston again, and also to write a part for Christopher Baker, arrived around the same time. Yet I had no idea how the two characters would converge or even if they would be in the same story. I enjoy observing people and imagining how I might place them in a film. It is a kind of 'game' I play with non-actors and can result in the beginnings of a story.

I like the way the actor and the non-actor communicate with each other. I want the actor to stop acting, and I find the non-actor helps this to happen. Actors' tricks don't work so well with a non-professional. The actor is forced to use their instincts and be in the moment. Of course, if you're not careful, it can work the other way round and you find the non-actor wants to start acting!

The decision to work with Tom again was an easy one. He is totally tuned into the world I am trying to portray. Christopher Baker is my painting teacher and already has an understanding of my creative process, so we are halfway there before we start.

For the character of Rose, I knew I wanted to find a professional cook. I interviewed many cooks before finally meeting Amy Lloyd. It turned out that *Archipelago* was Amy's first film role and her first professional job as a cook. This part was a real leap of faith for her. She knew nothing about the story when she agreed to play Rose, and was brave enough to remain in the dark pretty much throughout the shoot.

I'd also be interested to learn how you develop the interplay among your cast.

I begin with a melting pot of actors that I have met individually, but there has been little or no communication between them. The cast arrived on the island a week before the shoot, with the exception of Amy Lloyd, whose arrival coincided with her character's arrival at the family's rented house.

Amy and Christopher knew nothing about the story except the setting, so they never knew what turns the story was going to take. The actors, on the other hand, knew the story, but part of the process is that I change things as we go along. Shooting in sequence allows this to happen. It gives me so much more creative freedom and means new ideas can always be part of the process.

The actors playing the characters living in the rented house actually lived there for the duration of the shoot. The rest of the cast and the crew stayed in other houses on the island. This approach definitely adds a level of reality to the story, yet I know it is challenging for the actors, who have to make this same space their own when we're not filming. The locals told eerie ghost stories about the house during the shoot, and I expected rebellion at any moment. Fortunately, this didn't happen, and that's a credit to the actors' endurance.

Edward strikes me as a man completely shackled to his family, and the notion of family, yet desperate to attain a sense of personal freedom. Was this a concept that interested you?

Edward, and how he is in relation to his family, is at the centre of what is interesting to me about this story. This theme is the heartbeat of the film, and one I suspect I will continue to explore in future films.

I had an inspiring conversation with Tom when I was first thinking about the character of Edward. We were talking about how a sense of oneself can so easily vanish in the family fold – the struggle to keep hold of one's self when your family refuses to acknowledge you as an individual and as an adult.

The theme of the family obviously holds a recurring interest for you. What is it about this theme that continues to fascinate you, and how does the notion of family relate to the title?

The family and my interest in it is buried so deep within me that I am unable to extract it and hold it up to the light. There are so many levels to my fascination with it. It is a love–hate relationship that is as old as I am. I can only structure my response as a series of questions, because I am still trying to understand it myself. Actually, I don't believe it is helpful for me to try and articulate it too much. I will leave that up to other people who see the film. I am curious to hear how they interpret it.

The title relates to the family as a group of islands, linked together beneath the surface. What often links a family together goes unspoken and unacknowledged. Families are a way of protecting individuals from what they don't want to hear, with clever techniques for avoiding the real issues. The Leighton family are just like this. They are also masters of competitive self-sacrifice.

It struck me that for all the tension and awkwardness in Archipelago, *there is also a rich sense of humour at play.*

I was aware during the making of *Archipelago*, and then during the editing of the film, that the tension in some of the scenes was very funny. I think the humour comes out of those situations that are so uncomfortable and awkward that laughter is the only response. It wasn't a conscious decision to make *Archipelago* funnier. But it has a darker tone than *Unrelated*, and I relish depicting awkward and embarrassing social situations. These situations naturally become so uncomfortable you just have to laugh.

I love that audiences have been laughing during screenings of *Archipelago*. I find it is a very satisfying response to the film. Helle le Fevre, my editor, and I laugh a lot when we're working together and I think some of that rubs off in the timing of the scenes. The humour is often about where you cut out of a moment, the timing of a specific line of dialogue or the timing of a look, which can make people laugh. These ideas are, of course, not new to anyone making comedies.

As a first feature Unrelated *enjoyed great critical success. What lessons have you learned between your first feature and your second, and how do you think critics and audiences will react to* Archipelago?

Something that has changed since *Unrelated* is the way I develop a story. With *Unrelated*, I went through a conventional screenplay process but ended up with a simplified version of it when it came to the shooting. I didn't go through the same laborious writing process with *Archipelago* because I knew I could do without that blueprint.

It was an easier process with *Archipelago*, perhaps because it was second time around, but also because I had some of the same crew, who understood my methods. I felt more free creatively and also more confident, in ways that allowed me to experiment more. I took my ideas much further, and as a result I think *Archipelago* is more coherent. There may not be the sunshine of Tuscany to seduce you with, but there is a depth to *Archipelago* that I hope is more satisfying. Also, because it explores the complexities of family relationships, I think more people will be able to identify with the story.

What were some of the thought processes behind Exhibition?

I'll play around with ideas for months before I settle on my story. Then something takes hold and ideas begin to pull together. With each film I am engaging my imagination more. This time, I tapped into my dreams and pushed myself further in terms of a less linear narrative and creating different levels of reality.

Actually, it was this process of creation that I wanted to depict in the film. It's quite rare in films to see people working, and I wanted to see an artist during the act of creation. To show inspiration in motion and how sexually charged this can be, but to offset this with the challenges of being in a relationship and the different roles required to keep everything in balance, especially from a woman's point of view.

Above all, I wanted to depict this marriage from the inside out, and it felt like riskier territory for me as it was naturally going to connect with my own personal life. So I needed to find a way of visualising the story, which would create some distance between myself and my characters. The house, which I had encountered through my friendship with the architect James Melvin, seemed to be the perfect container for that story.

When we've spoken previously, you always described Unrelated *and* Archipelago *as forming part of a trilogy. How does* Exhibition *complete that trilogy, and how do you see the films fitting together as a whole?*

I hate saying goodbye to my films. Hanging on to elements from the previous film is one way to make this transition easier. After *Archipelago* I thought I would go back and see what the relationship between Anna and Alex from *Unrelated* might be like back home in London. I had finished *Archipelago* wishing I had explored Edward's sexuality, so then this gets pushed into the next film. A lot of time passes between the films and my ideas are changing and adapting and responding to new situations. I never look back at my work, so I don't know how they look in relationship to one another.

Again, in the context of all three films, you described Unrelated *as being partly autobiographical,* Archipelago *as less autobiographical but more personal. Where does* Exhibition *stand in all this?*

Did I? Actually, I'd say now that none of them are autobiographical but all of them are personal – in very different ways. In the end, I'm unable to say what is personal and what is not. It's not relevant to the films and, anyway, I forget. Even if it starts off as intensely personal, it ends up just being the film. I have to divorce myself from it, in order to keep my sanity and move on to the next project.

Can you talk about the casting process? You have always adopted a very original approach and this continues with Liam Gillick and Viv Albertine, both of whom are terrific in their roles.

Casting is where I get my kicks. The high is taking a risk, or you could say trusting my instinct, yet not knowing exactly how it will work out. It's exciting to bring someone new to the screen. I saw many people for the roles of H and D, including actors, artists, married couples, even dancers. I wanted this story to rely less on dialogue and more on body language, so I was looking at how my characters would move around the space. It was a long process but eventually I found what I was looking for. Viv had been there all along. I have known her for thirty years, but had never thought of casting her until ten days before the shoot. It was different with Liam. I knew his work as an artist but didn't know him personally. I spoke to him on the telephone and was struck by his beautiful voice.

If I'm casting non-actors, it's because of who they are and not because I want them to skilfully transform themselves into someone else. I may have written D in a certain way, but then I look at Viv and realise I'm going to have to take on board the differences between what I've written and what is now in front of me. I have to do some letting go here, and this isn't always easy, but the pay-off is it's going to be a flesh and blood 'performance' that doesn't feel like a performance. And it'll be one that hasn't been seen before. This is what I find less interesting about casting well-known actors – they have been seen in a myriad of ways before and I won't be surprised. Non-actors generally ask fewer questions. They can be more willing to be led and take each moment as it comes. I think the best actors can do this too – if they're willing to let go. This is the hardest thing. However, I'm increasingly reluctant to distinguish between actors and non-actors, and really it is simply a question of finding the right person for the role and less about whether they're trained or not.

Tom Hiddleston is something of a talismanic figure for you, and takes a smaller but key role here. I imagine it's getting harder to afford him. How has your relationship with him developed, and do you take a special pride in seeing how he has conquered the acting world while retaining a genuine passion for his profession?

Tom will always be interested in work that challenges him. He doesn't differentiate between mainstream or independent when it comes to portraying a character. I remember when we shot *Archipelago* he would sometimes refer to Loki – from *Thor* (2011) – as someone who was also struggling to define himself within his family.

Exhibition *is a poignant and affecting work, especially on the subject of how communication falters and breaks down between people. This is a subject to which you return often in the film, both through the use of the intercom system and the general silences and spaces in the dialogue. Is this one of the primary thrusts of the film?*

I've noticed different audience reactions to H and D. Some people see them as a loving couple. Others believe the film is about the breakdown of a marriage. They think H and D are unpleasant to each other and won't stay together [after the film]. I think if you've lived with someone for a long time, niceties go out of the window. Communication can be terse and abrupt, but that doesn't mean the relationship is not working. We're simply not used to seeing this kind of 'reality' on screen.

I was also interested in depicting H, the husband, as the rational and intellectual one and D as the instinctive and emotional one, but then at times contradicting this. That's life. In relationships we act out many different roles and moods.

Location is always incredibly important to your work. What was the role of the house in this instance?

My personal relationship to the space is key. It's one of the springboards for my imagination. My feelings surrounding a place become the foundations of the story. Once I decided on this house, then so many of the visual and aural ideas followed on from there. The sponge-like nature of the house, the way it soaks in sounds from the outside so they appear to be coming from the inside. The reflections – how you can be looking out of the window and see the dining chairs floating in the garden. It was a simple matter of observing what was already there.

It became like a magic box into which I could place my dreams, memories and nightmares. I recognised from the places I have lived in that homes have mood changes just like us. But maybe these mood changes can be our own projections. This house is at different times frightening, loving and possessive – it demands to be looked after. It's needy like a child.

You've always been very exacting in terms of your aesthetic. Can you talk about your approach here? You play around more with both the sound design – which is very impressive – and with the editing. What were some of the meanings and emotions you wanted the spectator to experience?

Bresson's dictum 'The ear is more creative than the eye' is always ringing in my ears, and I believe this wholeheartedly. As I mentioned, one of the many aspects that struck me about this house was the way sounds from the street penetrated the space inside. Sometimes it was as if a noise, like a car door shutting or a voice in the street, would appear to be coming from inside. This inside–outside aspect informed the soundscape. I wanted D to imagine entire stories in her head through sound, and to create the idea of a frightening world outside.

In the edit, I challenged Helle and myself to make less sense and have the film work on a more unconscious level, so the connections would be more freely associative and less linear. I want to go further and further into dreams and the connections between different levels of reality, and by doing this make it possible for the audience to get inside a character's head.

Having now completed your third feature, how do you feel you have navigated the British film-making system? You work regularly with [producer] Gayle Griffiths, and seem to have quite an autonomous position.

I have deliberately created this position for myself. After more than ten years working in television drama, within a structure created by others, I felt it was time to work by my own rules. This mindset formed the basis of my first feature, *Unrelated*. It's why I may not venture into big-budget territory; it's difficult to maintain this position when financiers have a lot of money at stake.

Since I like to keep each part of the film-making process alive and mobile, it can make planning difficult and be frustrating for those trying to pin me down. I have a very patient producer in Gayle Griffiths. She is super-organised, but I believe there is a part of her personality that enjoys spontaneity and chaos. Likewise, I sometimes enjoy being organised. So we work very well together.

How do you view the current climate for contemporary British cinema? A number of recent articles have mentioned a deep vein of talent, including people such as yourself, Andrea Arnold, Clio Barnard, Amma Asante and Peter Strickland, to name but a few. It's good to see so many female film-makers in this list. Is this a fertile time for talent?

We're all individuals and I don't think it reveals anything new about us to be defined as a group. I am interested in the work of all those film-makers you mention, and some of them are friends – but I still resist this idea of any movement. There are some interesting films being made in the UK, but I'm wary of saying this, as it only helps draw an even deeper line between us and film-makers from other countries, and I don't really be-lieve in this idea of national identity. I don't experience feel-ings of nationalistic pride. My creativity comes from feeling like an outsider. I don't make a distinction between myself and a film-maker, say, from Indonesia. What links us together [as film-makers] is more about a desire to make sense of the world through our films – this is much more interesting.

D. R. Hood (photo: John Hoare)

D. R. Hood

The director of a number of acclaimed short films, D. R. Hood's feature debut is an impressive drama centred on the terse relationship between two brothers, as seen through the eyes of the eldest brother's wife. Set within a small farming community in the Fens, *Wreckers* (2011) opens with Nick, having completed his military service, arriving at the ramshackle and half-decorated home of David and Dawn. No sooner has he settled in than the friction among the three increases, with Nick's presence reviving memories from David's past. Excluded from this world, Dawn finds herself isolated and questioning her marriage. A nuanced exploration of relationships, Hood's film is visually ravishing, employs sound and music to unsettling effect, and features excellent performances by Benedict Cumberbatch, Shaun Evans and Claire Foy.

Because the film is very different to what we normally see in British cinema, and certainly in terms of the social strata of British society, did you encounter many problems in terms of funding?

It was impossible. It was funded independently, with a great deal of input from two post-production houses. We went to the major funding bodies at every single stage of the film, with no luck – from development to post-production.

The comments I received were actually quite instructive. In development, I was told it was a shame that the film is almost a thriller but not quite a thriller. And yet when Steve Jenkins bought the film for the BBC, one of the first things he said was that it's great the film is a thriller yet not quite a thriller.

So films are problematic if they don't fit within a certain category of recognisable parameters?

Yes. During post-production, concerns were raised over who the audience would be. I don't know who the audience would have been without Benedict [Cumberbatch] and his immense fan base. One can't speculate. If we'd cast someone else, it would obviously have been different.

Wreckers is, among other things, an unusual study of class.

The characters are middle class, but they're lower middle class because it's a farming family. The idea is that both brothers got out, albeit in very different ways. Nick remained within the class but also escaped from it to a degree by going into the army, whereas David 'improved' his class status. Something that isn't discussed at all in the UK is how, within families, people can move between classes, both up and down. That fascinated me because we are still very class conscious. In some villages, there is a cross-section of this system that operates in a feudalist way.

I didn't specifically set out to make a film about class, but rather one about a village, because I come from one. Within the village, people get out in various ways and that can affect their position within the class system. I'm pleased with the way that the two brothers have gone in different directions but you still buy into the idea that they're brothers.

The casting had a huge impact on how the characters would be perceived. Dawn was originally meant to be a little less 'posh' than she is in the film, but I didn't want to change Claire [Foy]'s accent. Benedict, who wasn't as famous when we cast him as he is now, certainly isn't from the background described in the script, but he brought elements to the role that worked brilliantly – this extraordinary ambiguity in the character – and I think he and Shaun [Evans] really do convince as brothers.

How did the story originate?

It began a long time ago when I read a book of Fenland tales, which were very graphic and brutal. I wrote a couple of shorts, and I had also written a script for a short that involved Gary, the garage owner in *Wreckers*. But that didn't get made because it was too high-end. A few years later, I wrote a ten-page outline about a soldier coming back to his village, who now feels something of an outsider. He stays with his brother, who at that time was Gary, and Gary's wife Dawn. It was told from Nick's point of view. Then a year later I added a character called David, who appears at a party and is pretty sadistic in that scene. Suddenly, I realised that Dawn was married to David not Gary, and that she was the point-of-view character. From there the script really came together.

It was always based heavily on atmosphere and images and about someone coming into the village and creating havoc. One of the Fenland tales details the devil arriving in a village and he walks over rooftops in the snow, leaving his footprints behind in the morning.

Why did you choose the Fens for the story?

It's very similar to the landscape I grew up in. But where I grew up is now a commuter belt. So the intact rural life and the Fenland stories benefitted my story. The villages are still intact there, with agricultural industry – they're not just commuter villages.

It's a very open landscape and yet the film feels incredibly claustrophobic.

That came partly out of the process of filming. We had to cut costs quite a lot, so we shot the drama first and then the landscape shots. The script was written more generally within the landscape. There were a few scenes we had to cut. But the claustrophobia works in terms of Dawn's experience.

Do you see the role of nature, particularly the creeping effect on the walls of the house, as a major theme in the film?

Not so much nature as fertility. Later in the script development I began reading Viking myths, and you could say that Dawn is Freya, Nick is Loki and David is Odin, who sees everything with only one eye. There's also the cherry tree carol that played into the story. So the flower and bird images painted on the walls of the house tap into that idea.

So you have fertility on one side, but also this sense of a simmering violence beneath the veneer of quiet country life. Nick seems to be the open wound in exhibiting this – someone who has experienced violence first hand, in open combat.

Yes. I feel that we know we're capable of violence but it's often carried out by soldiers in foreign lands. That's a topic I'm going to explore further in another project. We're exporting our wars. At the same time, I know that violence can come from within, from within families. Look at Michael Haneke's *The White Ribbon* (2009), which I saw after we completed this film. The effect of this kind of violence leads directly to conflict on a huge scale. I think there's something about the life the brothers have lived that comes home to roost.

The violence in the film seems to erupt from the inability to communicate, to express frustration or anger in any way other than through pure brute force. Both Nick and Gary are like this.

Gary is definitely someone who isn't able to speak at all. It's not class-based. I think there's a reticence and a pride among the English that covers all facets of society. David is angry and doesn't know where to place his anger at all – not that he's a bad man.

The past comes across with such a sense of menace. It's a

secret world that Dawn isn't privy to.

I didn't necessarily think of it in exactly that way. The backstory is incredibly important to me – and I am obsessed with the past. Perhaps too obsessed by it. Most families do have secrets generally and these things fester. And sooner or later it affects people's lives. What David is holding back is ultimately going to affect the relationship.

I always thought of the situation as: Dawn clearly wants to know about her husband – who he really is. But what I liked doing here is that in most films someone finds out the secret and then does something about it. But here, Dawn goes right to the very edge and then decides she doesn't want to know, and she and David find a way to live with that.

It becomes an exploration of the breaking point in relationships – how far can you go before there's no turning back, when the trust is gone and the relationship implodes?

That's right. And in the first draft of the screenplay they did fall off the edge. It was much more like a conventional thriller. However, the performances didn't support that scenario and, ultimately, I don't think we really had faith in that ending. Frankly, those scenes didn't work. So it becomes more a portrait of a marriage.

What was wonderful when we first showed the film to the crew, the London Film Festival and potential distributors, is that we saw people becoming very tense as they watched it, which was nice, because we cut it so that it became an examination of relationships and the tension arises from that.

Part of the thriller element – the mystery of the past that draws us in – is the way you capture snippets of dialogue. Sometimes it feels that we're privy to a private conversation, but often only part of it. More often than not, these scenes revolve around two of the characters.

That was constructed to be like that, to give a sense of unease. It's mostly Dawn on the outside, but not always. We improvised those scenes in rehearsal – two characters with one always outside, and mainly Dawn as the outsider – and then we shot it like that, to give you that strange feeling.

I'm glad you realise the fragments of information and feeling are intentional. We weren't sure whether we had achieved that, and so it's good when people point that out. Originally, it was more of a Russian doll structure, with Dawn looking back. But that seemed a bit too tricksy.

The ambiguity of the film is present in the way it was shot. It is both very real, yet possessed of an ethereal, dreamlike quality.

I thought of Peckinpah's *Straw Dogs* (1971). I've only seen it once – perhaps once is enough! – but I think it's an amazing film. And *The Wicker Man* (1973). Annemarie [Lean-Vercoe, the cinematographer] made me watch a number of Korean horror films, like *A Tale of Two Sisters* (2003), because they're so creepy. And David Lynch. I remember watching *Twin Peaks* – normally from halfway up the stairs because it was so scary – and you always knew the episodes he had directed. They're so simple, yet terrifying. We also watched Tarkovsky. We specifically took something from *Stalker* (1979), which is to de-saturate the green in the grade.

When we were preparing to film we looked at a lot of photographs and picture books, Edward Hopper among others, but in terms of the shooting style, we spoke a great deal about close-ups and landscape. And we had a lot of discussions about point of view. We also played with thirty frames a second. There are a few sequences in the film, such as when they're coming down the towpath, that are just that little bit slower and the effect is wonderfully subliminal.

This contrast between the dreamy and the real was worked

out in the edit. We discovered how powerful it could be to juxtapose the dreamy scenes with moments of violence. It was through experimenting with structure, and it worked out so well.

Sally El Hosaini (photo: Francesca D'Ascari)

Sally El Hosaini

Prior to making her feature debut, Sally El Hosaini worked for over two years as a script editor and specialist researcher on the 2008 HBO–BBC drama miniseries *House of Saddam*. In the same year she was awarded a BAFTA for her short film *The Fifth Bowl*. Her second short, *Henna Night*, was selected for the 2009 London Lesbian and Gay Film Festival, and played in competition at the Rotterdam and Raindance film festivals. That same year, she was voted by *Screen International* as one of the 'UK Stars of Tomorrow', and also participated in the Sundance Directors and Screenwriters Labs to develop the script of *My Brother the Devil*.

Hosaini's feature debut is a remarkably assured film that explores the lives of two Muslim brothers in East London. Rashid is a leading member of a local gang, but his growing ambivalence towards the route his life has taken finds him discouraging his younger brother from travelling the same path. A chance encounter with Sayyid, a French photographer, makes Rashid question everything he believes in and, ultimately, places his brother in danger. Hosaini's film challenges lazy stereotypes of Muslim culture, instead offering a richly textured drama whose narrative complexity weighs against the simplicity of most British urban dramas, the tropes of which it both employs and undermines to impressive effect.

Your film was a long time in development.

It took six years to make *My Brother the Devil*. I've since heard that isn't too long for a first film, but it certainly felt long. Like many first-time writer–directors, I kept hearing that it was a great idea, or great script, but execution dependent. Of course it's going to be execution dependent when it's your first feature! It's hard to get people to take a risk and believe in you. I was repeatedly told that my ideas for the film were too ambitious. The main issue was that it wasn't quite an 'urban' film, as it had too much poetry and sensitivity, and yet it was not some 'art house' film either, as it was genre and had commercial ambitions. So I think the main issue was the cross-genre nature of it. For me, that was the entire point. Why would I want to make a film I've seen before? And the excitement lay in subverting an audience's expectation of films about that world and those characters.

Even successes along the way, like getting into the Sundance Lab, didn't help me raise money or get a producer on board in the UK. I was rejected and turned down by all the main funding bodies and I couldn't find a producer for years. I pretty much produced it myself for most of the development process. Eventually, I did manage to find a private investor, but still no producer. Before I found my producers, I had told myself, 'If I don't shoot by next summer, I'll give up.' It had been over four years of trying to get the film made. When do you stop? It was when I gave myself that deadline and decided not to play by the rules that things started to happen. I went against everything people told me and simultaneously bombarded every producer whose email I could get hold of. I had a very simple proposition – to shoot immediately or I would abandon the whole film. Then I met some producers who were game, believed in it and loved the challenging proposition. They raised the rest of the finance, and before I knew it I was shooting.

I think my message for writer–directors who have a script and are trying to get their films made is that you have to get out of your comfort zone. Put yourself out there and don't give up –

don't depend on public money. There are films made every day with private investment. It's a business – it doesn't mean that your idea isn't good, or your script isn't good, or that your film isn't good. In America, they don't have public money, so it's a completely different attitude. I think British film-makers could benefit from having more of that attitude. Art and commerce are always strange bedfellows, but I want to make films that are actually seen by people. So being savvy about the business side of things is necessary.

How did the idea for the screenplay originate?

When I first started writing the script it was shortly after the 7/7 Tube bombings in London. The way British Arabs – and British Arab youth in particular – were being portrayed in the media, as some kind of terror threat, bothered me. It didn't represent the boys I saw on my estate every day, so I decided to make a film that revealed their lives honestly and conveyed their real struggles. I've always been interested in people on the margins of society: outsiders and outcasts. I'm also drawn to intimate studies of character, so I wanted to make complex heroes out of people that don't already have that kind of iconic representation in cinema. I set the film on a council estate in Hackney because that's where I live. I honestly thought, when I started writing, that I was going to shoot the film on a micro budget on my estate and in my flat. But as the project grew, so did my ambitions.

I knew that I wanted to explore a sibling relationship. I'm both an older and younger sister, so could identify with both brothers in the film. And being Welsh-Egyptian, I know how it feels to have opposed belongings and to live in two worlds that aren't always in harmony. Being on the edge and looking in – never fully belonging in either world – gives me a certain perspective that makes me passionate about telling stories that explore the contradictions of this world. I love capturing the complexity of people and life on film.

The film articulately explores a number of strands. As you were developing the characters of the brothers, did such elements as Rashid's homosexuality gradually appear or was it there from the outset?

It wasn't there when I first started researching for the script, but by the time I'd finished the first draft I had landed on the sexuality strand of the story. I initially knew that I was interested in a betrayal between two brothers, but I hadn't committed to what that betrayal was exactly. It was when I was spending time researching, with the real guys who inspired the film, that I noted what a macho, alpha-male world it was. The homophobia was explicit. It was then that the idea of Rashid being gay took hold. He inhabits a doubly homophobic world, as it's not just the homophobia among his peers and on the streets, but the cultural and religious homophobia of his family too. I realised that Mo would rather have a brother who is a terrorist than gay. This realisation blew my mind! I think it's pretty tragic that in this day and age we live in a culture where a lot of people feel more comfortable seeing two young Arab men holding guns than holding hands.

You've lived in the area where the film is located for some time. How much did you research to explore the vernacular and physical behaviour and banter of the characters? Or is this something the actors also helped bring to the roles?

I did a lot of research and approached the script the way I would approach making a documentary. It was through the establishment of a few key relationships that I was able to gain access to the world of the film. With time, that access turns into friend-ship and trust. I'm very proud that key people who helped me in my research also ended up acting and working on the film. Aymen Hamdouchi, who played Repo, was my script consult-ant. I would read him scenes to check that my dialogue was 'on point'. By the end, even he was surprised as I had pretty much learned a new language.

I often get asked whether the film contains a lot of improv-isation. It was actually completely scripted. This was one of the barriers to getting my film made, because some producers and financiers couldn't see past the vernacular. I even had to supply a ten-page glossary that accompanied the script to explain the urban and Arabic slang.

I was open to the actors changing things if they didn't feel their character would say or do something. A script is a blue-print and I'm not precious about it. Words on a page are not a film. Once on set, I tend not to be tied to the script and use it more as a guide. I like to be in the moment and to follow my gut. When you really use your eyes and ears on set there is so much more around you than you could ever have written, imagined or planned for.

This could have been another genre film, and there's a sense you're playing on the fringes of it while drawing the narrative off into other directions. Was this to give more depth to characters that might appear superficial in other films?

I was very conscious that I wanted my characters to be multi-dimensional people. I didn't want the brothers to be ghettoised like youth often are in urban films. Or symbols for bigger con-cepts, as Arab characters often end up. They are just boys. London boys. They wouldn't last five minutes in the Middle East. They have an ambivalent relationship to Arab or Islamic culture, as it's both familiar and alien to them. Their concerns are the universal concerns of all teenagers. They want to look good, make some money to buy the latest gear, and have sex. Yes, they struggle to survive the gangs, drugs and violence, but they have other needs, desires and dreams.

Can you talk about the way you wanted to represent the female characters in the film, from the boys' girlfriends to the brothers' mother and Mo's friend?

Representing the women was something I struggled with from the outset. I wanted them to be fully rounded characters and so much more than just the mother and girlfriend. But the more women I encountered in the world I wanted to set the film in, the more I realised how narrow their lives actually were – how they revolved around the men in their lives. In the case of Rashid's girlfriend, Vanessa, we largely see her through the boys' eyes. Therefore she symbolises a fantasy for Mo. For teenage boys, it's all about attaining a girl like her. It's shallow, but that's how she is viewed.

With Aisha, Mo's friend, I wanted to show a character who grows up in exactly the same world as the boys, but who has a strong moral compass. I met many girls and boys like her. Just because you live on an estate it doesn't mean you end up getting involved in gang life. These youths exist, and for me she was a nod to that. She symbolised hope, and because of her presence I knew that Mo would be okay without Rashid.

I have met many Arab mothers like Hanan, who literally dedicate their lives to looking after their husbands and sons within the home. I wanted to show the love, laughter and connection she had with her sons. It's not just youth from 'broken homes' that end up being involved in gangs. There is one world inside the home and Hanan has no idea of the other world her kids have to navigate whenever they leave the flat.

The film is brought into stark relief by the fact that the riots broke out in London when you began filming. What was the impact of this?

It was a strange time. The London riots started while we were testing the camera on Mare Street in Hackney. Suddenly there were groups of youths raging down the middle of the road and helicopters in the sky. Hackney had turned into Baghdad. For a second, I wondered how to incorporate the riots into my film, but as tempting as it was, I knew deep down it wasn't my story. I realised how important my film was because there was now, more than ever, a need to understand disenfranchised London youth. It was surreal to be shooting a movie in the midst of mayhem, and the riots did affect the shoot on a practical level, in terms of locations changing and scenes having to be re-written. But the biggest impact I felt was a sense of unified purpose among the cast and crew. The film we were making was important.

I was reminded a number of times of La Haine *(and not because of Saïd Taghmaoui's presence). There's the scene in the art gallery, and where the woman is sat between two pairs of boys at the bus stop. It felt that ideas about racial difference and how people are represented may have been one element in these scenes, but there was also a sense of economic inequality and how someone can feel locked out of a world if they have no money.*

I love *La Haine*! It was one of my favourite movies as a teenager, so it's certainly there in the DNA of the film. It's interesting that you drew those parallels because I had never thought of those scenes that way. My only conscious *La Haine* connection was in building the character of Sayyid. My starting point was: what if Saïd from *La Haine* took a different turn in life, came out, then moved from Paris to London in order to live freely as a gay man. Sayyid is a 'real man' in terms of Rashid's definition of these things, and yet he's gay and fine with it. In many ways he's the most revolutionary character in the film. Saïd Taghmaoui brought an authenticity to the role that made the character very believable. I wrote the role with him specifically in mind, so I was thrilled when he agreed to do it.

The film is definitely about economic inequality. When I met up in central London with some of the real boys who inspired the film, I was quite surprised to learn that they had walked from Zone 2 to meet me because they couldn't afford the bus fare. There is a lot of poverty and economic inequality in London. Most people go about their lives and seem blind to it, but it's there and it's not going away or getting better.

The film is beautifully shot. How did you and cinematographer David Raedeker come to the decision to shoot in Scope, and also to adopt a palette that almost has the feel of a reverie?

It wasn't that I set out to make a beautiful movie. I wanted the camera to stay close to the brothers and to present the world from their perspective – to be an insider looking out, rather than an outside observer. I wanted a visceral camera that translated their emotions and senses. It's their home and to them it's beautiful. Scope turned what normally might feel like a mundane world into an adventure for us. The Scope format enhanced the camera's intimacy as it forces you into these close-ups.

What has been the reaction of the local community to the film?

Gayle Griffiths, one of my producers, has worked to set up a cinema club on the estate we filmed on. *My Brother the Devil* was the first film they screened. They absolutely loved it!

Asif Kapadia (photo: Jimmy Lindsey)

Asif Kapadia

Having won a Cannes Grand Jury Prize and the Grand Prix at the European Short Film Festival with *The Sheep Thief* (1997), his graduation film from the Royal College of Art, anticipation was high for *The Warrior* (2001), London-born Asif Kapadia's feature debut. The expectations were exceeded by an assured, enigmatic and visually astonishing tale that showed a vision and scope far beyond Kapadia's relatively tender years. A critical and commercial success, the film won the Alexander Korda Award for Best British Film and the Carl Foreman Award for the Most Promising Newcomer at the 2002 BAFTAs. Kapadia also won the *Evening Standard* British Film Award for Most Promising Newcomer and the London Film Festival's Sutherland Trophy.

After a troubling shoot in Hollywood with the supernatural thriller *The Return* (2006), Kapadia travelled into the Arctic region to film *Far North* (2007), the second of four proposed dramas inspired by the points of the compass. Based on a short story by Sara Maitland, Kapadia's feature once again explores the notion of myth as a soldier finds himself drawn into a web of desire by two women.

Senna (2010) might seem a change in direction for Kapadia, but the themes that dominate his most personal work are present as he recounts, through the use of archive footage and contemporary testimony, the life of the charismatic Formula One champion Ayrton Senna. It was a critical and box-office hit and won the BAFTA for Best Documentary Film, as well as many other awards.

He is completing a documentary about the life of Amy Winehouse and is about to embark on a new fiction feature, *Ali and Nino*.

[This interview took place over a number of years, following the completion of *The Warrior* and during post-production on the Amy Winehouse documentary.]

Could you talk about the processes involved in making The Sheep Thief, *and how, if at all, it influenced the approach you took to* The Warrior?

When I was making *The Sheep Thief* I had no idea what I was getting myself into, but I knew that it would be my last short film and I wanted to push my crew and myself to the limit. If I screwed it up, at least I had done it while I was a student.

The idea came from a story told to me by a teacher when I was about seven years old. It was an old Bible story of a thief who becomes a saint. I love classical tales. I didn't believe the concept would work if I set the story in Ireland or the Lake District. It needed to take place in a timeless landscape. I had only previously been to India for a week or so, and the idea came to me of shooting the movie there, on location, with non-professional actors, in Hindi and with a minimal crew.

We hooked up with the students from the Indian Film Institute in Pune, raised the finance – around £25,000 – and seven of us went off to Rajasthan with a 16mm camera, to find a location, cast the movie and shoot the film. The process of making the film was the toughest thing any of us had ever been through. We all went a little crazy.

For a first feature The Warrior *is an extremely ambitious undertaking. What kind of elements led to your decision to embark on the project, and how much depended on your sustaining the confidence to pull it off?*

I felt the central idea of *The Warrior* was very strong. I loved the story and was desperate to make it. There was never a doubt in my mind that it would make a great film. Whenever I pitched the tale to people, they seemed to love it too, so I really thought Tim Miller – my co-writer – and I had something good. I was also excited by the idea of shooting something on a bigger scale, with a bigger cast, horses and burning villages. The entire project was a huge leap into the unknown, but it was the challenge that excited me.

I knew it would be hard, but I felt confident. The script was good, my producer was completely supportive, I had my crew from *The Sheep Thief* around me, and I was able to cast the film as I wanted. Film4, who backed the project, were brilliant all the way through. So I felt very confident that together we would make it work.

The film has a very distinct and distinguished visual style. Were your approach and your aesthetic set in place before you began filming, and how much did you allow yourself to respond to the challenging yet picturesque filming conditions?

The style I had been developing with my short films at the RCA continued with *The Warrior*. The script is written so that the story is told through images, with minimal dialogue. I love to use the frame, spend time on the composition and be confident enough to hold a shot. I don't like to cut or move the camera unless there is a motivation to do so. The idea is for me to tell the story with the camera and not to load the non-professional actors with pages of dialogue.

Of course, when you're shooting, anything that can go wrong will, so you have to be prepared to compromise. In the case of *The Warrior*, we began running behind schedule – it was so hot – so we ended up shooting with two cameras on simple scenes and on bigger sequences we had three cameras. That was an education. We had no video assist and the rushes were being sent back to the UK, with a two-week turnaround. I had to learn to explain in great detail what I wanted from the second operator, who was often far away on the other side of the mountain shooting with a long lens. I had to trust my instincts to decide if we had enough to make the scene work or to do the sequence again, which could have involved setting fire to a village twice.

What cultural and technical challenges did shooting in the blazing deserts of Rajasthan and the snow-capped foothills of the Himalayas present?

There were about thirty crewmembers from the UK, France and

Canada. The other two hundred crewmembers were from India, so there was an interesting balance of learning to collaborate. There was also the language issue while shooting off the beaten track in rural locations. The European crew had to learn to work with translators.

The video assists kept blowing up in the heat – we went through about four of them, so we were often shooting blind. Pre-production and casting took place during the monsoon season. When we started shooting, the temperature was about 47 degrees [Celsius] in the desert. We finished shooting in the Himalayas in December, and during certain sequences we were at 10,000 feet and dealing with about six feet of snow.

I had written a big climax to the film in a holy lake with a cast of thousands. In this scene, the Blind Woman was supposed to, in a sense, 'see' the Warrior washing away his sins in the lake. Unfortunately, at 10,000 feet in December it was too cold for anyone to go in the water. The location was on top of a mountain, a four-hour drive up a narrow track. There was no electricity, hot water or any amenities, and we ended up spending the night there, as it was not safe to travel back down the track after dark. So, from a cast of thousands, the scene became a cast of one with only the Blind Woman in it.

Critics were quick to offer comparisons with Kurosawa. Was he in any way an influence?

It's an amazing feeling to see people mentioning *The Warrior* in the same sentence as a cinematic god, but generally the comparison was used as shorthand to explain to the audience the type of film it was.

To be honest, before we wrote the film I hadn't really seen any Kurosawa films on the big screen. They have only recently been re-released in the UK. I love Kurosawa's work but I would say the movies and directors that really inspired me were Tran Anh Hung's *Cyclo* (1995), Zhang Yimou's *The Story of Qiu Ju* (1992),

Bresson's *A Man Escaped* (1956), Hitchcock's *Vertigo* (1958) and *Psycho* (1960), Kenji Mizoguchi's *Ugetsu Monogatari* (1953) and Sergio Leone's *Once Upon a Time in the West* (1968).

When I first saw *Cyclo* at film school it was like a light bulb going on. The director was Vietnamese, he had studied at film school in Paris, and it was a European film by someone who understood Vietnamese culture. It was his second movie and he shot it with a mixture of professional and non-professional actors on location. The movie was a huge motivation for me to shoot *The Sheep Thief* in the same way.

A Japanese folk tale given to you by your co-writer was also a foundation for the film. How closely did you stick to this tale, and what particular elements inspired you?

Tim Miller had travelled in Japan and is a big fan of the culture. He pitched me something he had read in a book of Japanese tales, it was a four-line footnote:

'A young boy training to be a samurai was brought before the Shogun, shown a severed head and asked if it was his father. The boy knew it was not his father but to save his father's life he lied and said it was. To prove it, the boy pulled out his dagger and killed himself. He would rather be dead than live with the shame his father had brought onto the family.'

I thought it was such a powerful scene, which posed so many questions, I decided that this would be the opening of our film. We would then cut to the father and follow his journey, revealing along the way why he was being pursued, and by whom etc.

In the end, the scene comes thirty minutes into the movie. The only thing we changed was that one of the warriors killed the boy, rather than the boy killing himself. This kept alive a strand of tension during the story.

What are the challenges and benefits of working with a mostly non-professional cast?

I spent a lot of time on location looking for actors. I like to use local people, from the area where we're shooting. I like the naturalism and truth I get from non-professional actors – the feeling I get by just looking at their faces and the way they carry themselves. An actor from the UK would just look wrong in the middle of the desert.

The Thief character was a real street kid; he had lived rough on a train station platform from the age of seven. I learned so much from him. The difficulty is that you need to make sure the actors don't get bored, so you don't over-rehearse. I would often shoot the rehearsals, just in case it was the best take. I try not to give the actors marks or expect them to be in the perfect position for the lights. The focus puller has to get the image in focus, the operator deals with the frame, and I have to tell the story with the shots and in the cut. The actors just have to 'be' – the audience need to believe what is happening to them.

Conversely, Irrfan Khan is magnificent in the central role. How did he come to your attention?

I worked with the casting director who did Shekhar Kapur's *Bandit Queen* (1994). It was the one Indian film that had the texture I was looking for. As soon as the casting director Tigmanshu Dhulia read the script he recommended Irrfan. I met him and he had these eyes and a real presence. He was so brilliant. We never considered anyone else.

Given the location and the conditions in which you were shooting, Far North *must have been an arduous undertaking. To what extent was the decision to make the film a desire to return to the more personal form of film-making of* The Warrior, *after the painful experience of* The Return?

I want to make my own films, from my own scripts, based on stories I want to tell, but they take time to put together. I had always intended to make *Far North* straight after *The Warrior*. We had the rights to the short story, the script was in development and I knew where I wanted to shoot it. It just took a long time getting the script together and raising the finance. So I had to make a tough decision to shoot another film. I needed to direct again, as it had been too long since my last film, and I had to earn some money to pay the bills. I just never realised *The Return* would take so long to make. It was a very tough 'political' experience, the post-production in LA seemed to go on for ever. So *Far North* was delayed for much longer than I had hoped. This may be the way I continue to make movies in the future, where I direct a film for someone else in between doing my own more personal style of films.

In a director's statement you describe your initial belief that, given the essentially simple structure, Far North *would be a quick and easy project to complete. It ended up being four years in the making. How did this come to pass?*

I honestly thought that after the complications of *The Warrior*, this would be a simple film; three people in a tent in one key location. I thought we could make it fast and then do something more complicated with the next film. I knew the shoot would be tough but I didn't realise how difficult the film would be to put together. It was partly the issue that the Sara Maitland short story was only five pages long – it gave us the basic structure and characters but it also left a lot of space for us to expand the film into a feature. I think my co-writer Tim Miller and I took a few wrong turns along the way with it.

I had always wanted to shoot the film in a real epic wilderness. We settled on Svalbard and the high Arctic landscape of Norway. This also brought up a few key problems. Norway is a really expensive country. Secondly, there are three months of permanent darkness during the winter months, so we had a small window in which to shoot the film, both with snow and daylight. To be ready to shoot in this tight window, we had to have the script, the cast and the finance in place six months before. A couple of times we missed the window and then had to wait an entire year to try again. There were no hotels or roads close to our locations in Svalbard, so we ended up making the decision to base the entire cast, crew and all of the equipment on a Russian ice-breaker. This ship was where we slept, ate and relaxed. As we slept, the ship would move on to the next location. It was in many ways a brilliant way to make a movie.

I was lucky enough to be able to work again with most of my key team from *The Warrior*: cinematographer Roman Osin, composer Dario Marianelli, editor Ewa J. Lind, and Andy Shelley, the sound recordist and sound designer. My wife, Victoria Harwood, who had worked on *The Sheep Thief*, was art director.

Over the years we've been through so many experiences together, some good, many hellish. I like working with the same team, because when I'm in the middle of nowhere and we're running out of light and it's all going pear-shaped, it's great to look around and see family. We are all in it together, rather than them thinking, 'This idiot doesn't have a clue what he's doing.'

What strategies did you employ to ensure that Roman Osin successfully transferred the stunning beauty and remoteness of Svalbard to the screen?

I spent a lot of time travelling and researching while writing the film. I went to Svalbard and travelled all over northern Norway many times over the years, in all the seasons. Following my recces, I chose not to shoot in the spring, when the sea is frozen solid, the sky is blue, everything else is a blanket of white and temperatures regularly go below minus 40 degrees. I decided to shoot in the autumn. I liked the monochromatic colours of the landscape and the sea sprinkled with intense blue icebergs. We were praying that the snow would arrive before the dark period hit us. In the end we got lucky – we were able to capture the landscape changing, we shot the first snow of winter and the sea starting to freeze over.

*There is an intriguing ambiguity to the relationship between
Saiva and Anja.*

It was never made clear in the short story what the relationship
between the two women actually was. Were they mother and
daughter, sisters, or maybe even lovers? I wanted to try to keep
some of this ambiguity. Tim and I added the flashbacks where we
reveal Saiva's past and how she finds the child and brings her up.

*Michelle Yeoh and Michelle Krusiec will have specific associ-
ations for audiences that are very different to those suggested
by Sean Bean. Was there a certain amount of surprise expressed
when he was cast as Loki, and what qualities do you feel Bean
brings to the part?*

Maybe Sean has a bit of baggage in the UK as he is known for
his work on TV, but he has been in Bond movies, the *Lord of the
Rings* trilogy (2001–3) and a lot of other huge pictures. For me it
was simple – I saw a lot of actors for the role, then my casting director Avy Kaufman suggested I watch *Patriot Games* (1992) and
Ronin (1998) again. I thought he was great in them. I liked the
way he looks – he has a great face, which is key when there isn't a
lot of dialogue. I also liked his presence. He's a man's man, which
is what I needed for the role. Sean understood how tough the film
was going to be and was ready to give everything for the role.

It had snowed the night before Sean's first day on set, so we
had to change our schedule and shoot the end of the film. This
meant Sean's first scene was the one where he runs naked across
the landscape – he did it for real twice, without a grumble. He
was a great professional to work with.

*The prophecy of the Shaman at the moment of Saiva's birth
evokes the love of folk tales and classic fairy stories that perme-
ates your work. From where does this interest spring?*

I have always loved classic folk tales. There is something about them that just interests me, and there must be a reason these stories have been passed on through the generations. And I love the fact they work in all cultures and languages. Partly it is my Indian-Muslim background – I grew up with religion, superstitions and folk tales. They were an everyday part of life.

Did you allow any influences to seep through into the making of Far North? *Thematically, there are faint elements of Don Siegel's* The Beguiled (*1971*).

Actually, now you mention it, *The Beguiled* was mentioned by someone at the script stage, but I haven't seen it for years. There were a few other films that came up at different stages. One of my friends read the script and suggested I watch the excellent 1964 Japanese film *Onibaba*. When I did see the film, it seemed to come from a similar Japanese version of the folk tale. Another writer suggested I watch Bergman's *The Virgin Spring* (1960) for the magical set-up and the powerful violent ending. I remember the feeling I got when I first saw *Audition* (1999) and that shocking climax. I had that film somewhere in the back of my mind, although ours is very different.

It's now been seven years since Far North. *Are you still looking to complete the points on the compass quartet with West and South?*

Senna became the South film, in a way. It's about Brazil and it's about this 'other' place, which wasn't how we set out to make it. Obviously, it's not a fiction film, but there was something fascinating about the place the film was located in and what Senna meant to the people who lived there – that, in my head, was just another point on the compass, even though we don't explicitly engage with that notion in the film. However, the idea is still to do a western and another film that represents South.

It's funny you should ask that question because the project I've just embarked on now, *Ali and Nino*, is almost like the centre of a compass. The film is set around the outbreak of the First World

War and seen from an Asian perspective. Christopher Hampton adapted this novel [by Kurban Said] and the story takes place in the Caucasus region, in what is now Azerbaijan. It's where East meets West, North meets South and where Muslim meets Christian. So it's a real meeting of all those worlds.

Since Far North, *you've returned to making short films. Has this been because of the long gestation period in developing recent projects, or just topics that interested you?*

It's not so much returning to them as it is things coming up. Some were offered to me. For instance, I was approached about a film for the Olympics. *The Odyssey* (2012) was one of four short films made to coincide with the games. The others were by Mike Leigh, Lynne Ramsay and the team behind *StreetDance*. I was very busy but they kept asking me to do it, and the budget was already in place, so I did it.

Making *The Odyssey* got me thinking about the Amy Winehouse film. It was the first film I had made in London for a very long time. So it gave me some motivation, and when 'Amy' came along I really wanted to make a film that was about the city and about the world we're living in, albeit through her.

Have you seen the film I did about Guantánamo?

Standard Operating Procedure (2013)? *Yes. It's shocking.*

Good. It should be. That was an example of a short film made at the last minute. I was approached by a charity and asked if I would do something the next day. There was no prep time. But the subject matter interested me and I said yes. Whenever something like that comes along, the great thing about shorts is that there's freedom in just saying, 'Yeah, let's just do it,' as opposed to the three or four years of talking about it that features involve.

As soon as *Standard Operating Procedure* was released it went viral. It was launched on the *Guardian* website in the morning; by the end of the day a spokesperson at the Pentagon was answering questions on the film and Guantánamo. Then, about two weeks ago [October 2014], a judge in the US ordered that the military had to release the videos of films that had been made which recorded the force-feeding that had gone on in Guantánamo. There was one take, no rehearsals and it was made with no money. We shot it in two hours. And so many people in the US – who had no idea that the base was still open – have seen it. It has made a huge difference.

It would be easy to look at your career and separate the fiction films from your documentary features. However, looking at how you approached Ayrton Senna and thinking about Amy Winehouse's place in contemporary popular culture, they seem to fit in with your fascination surrounding the notion of myths, albeit very modern ones.

Yes. When I started working on *Senna*, I initially thought that I had been hired to just make a biographical documentary. But along the way something changed. I'm not a Formula One fan and I didn't really know much about Brazil, but it became a very personal project to me.

When the film screened in India, the lead actor from *The Warrior*, Irrfan Khan, came to see it. He came up to me later that night and said, 'I can totally see you in the film.' He saw all the scenes in the film that connected with faith, spirituality and God. And also rain, which he remembered playing such a significant role in *The Sheep Thief*. He just felt that although we were telling the story of this man's life, I had drawn out the aspects of that narrative that interested me.

There is something about him and his journey, which is a very male journey – exploring fame, success, masculinity and what all this means for one country. And the pressure of what it is to become that man. The film about Amy, by contrast, has become the inverse of that. It explores what such a situation is like for a young woman who isn't necessarily prepared for all of this fame, success and the pressure that's put upon her. Those two films mirror the earlier features, in that *Far North* was a female perspective and *The Warrior* was male. I wasn't conscious of any of this until I started working on the Amy film and realised how it contrasted with *Senna*, and then how those were linked to my early films.

If there is a link between your early and later work, the more recent films are still structured around real lives, as opposed to complete fictions. Did this make the recent films more challenging for you?

I quite like having those restrictions. You're dealing with real people, so there is a story and a truth that you have to find a way to turn into a film. Documentaries can be so much more difficult because you're dealing with real people and sensitivities. But ultimately, I think you're employing the same rules as any other kind of film-making, as well as the same techniques, just in slightly different ways. Most audiences will likely know the ending, so the film becomes much more about the journey.

Having gained experience on Senna *with creating a narrative film from already existing footage, was the Amy Winehouse film an easier journey for you as a film-maker?*

It's actually been more complicated. You never really know, when you're going into these things, how straightforward they're going to be. Amy's story is much more personal and, of course, more recent. The major thing about directing *Senna* – and this now seems obvious but it didn't feel so at the time – was my instinct that we shouldn't have talking heads. By doing that we were edging more towards a fiction film, but some people were adamant that with a documentary that's just what you do. I thought that there was so much incredible footage, and Senna himself was a charismatic movie-star kind of person, why would I cut to someone now – looking older and talking about this great relationship they had with him – when I could just show it? Also, for anyone who didn't know the story, they would be asking why Senna himself hadn't been interviewed. However, what now seems so clearly the right move was a real battle back when we were making the film.

Senna might not have been the first film to take this approach, but it is interesting to see how many other films are adopting this strategy now. It was also important for me, as director, to take myself out of the film. It would be really easy to have shot a few interviews and put them in with the idea of saying, 'Look, I directed these. There *I* am.' Interestingly, when you don't do that, you get asked what your role actually was, aside from employing a really good editor. But it was the right decision for the story – to make it as emotional, exciting and powerful as possible.

The Amy Winehouse film has been a very different process. There's so much footage of Senna out there already. With the Amy film it was important to get to know the people around her and to have them trust us in order for them to give us personal material that no one had seen before. This would then allow me to connect the dots in a story that I'm not sure anyone has really, truly presented before.

Thinking about their lives, it could be seen that Senna's is about external conflict, whereas Amy Winehouse's is more internalised. At the heart of Senna *is the Manichaean battle between two racing drivers, Ayrton Senna and Alain Prost, while some might regard the conflict in Amy as being within her – the demons that drove her creatively and her personal life. However, having not seen any of the film, this may be far from how you perceive and present Amy's life.*

It's certainly less visual than the issues dealt with in *Senna*. I'm still in the middle of editing the film, so there is an ongoing creative process that's still unfolding. Certainly with *Senna* it was easy to find a way of telling the story through the images. If we didn't have the images to tell certain stories about him then we needed to find a new direction, while keeping faithful to his life. One of the first things I did when I arrived on the project was to narrow the focus of the many rivalries, so that we just had him and Prost. We could have included Nigel Mansell, Nelson Piquet and others, but the film wouldn't have been as focused.

There is a great deal more internal conflict with Amy, but there is quite a great deal that one can show externally, to understand what was happening internally. It's a very different film. *Senna* was a film about a sportsman, so it was an action movie. For Amy, it's about her lyrics. That's when she was at her most eloquent. When I've talked to people about the film, I've described it as a Bollywood musical, except she had already written the songs so the narrative has been created around these.

You're about to return to a completely fictional world with Ali and Nino. *Are you looking forward to moving back to something where you perhaps have a greater control over what's being created on screen?*

I'm almost going back to the universe of *The Warrior*. I've literally just come back from a scout in Azerbaijan, and it's a great story that's going to unfold across a vast, epic landscape. There's a great deal of action, but within it a strong relationship – a love story across two cultures. In a way, it's more grown up, and I'm really excited about working on it.

When you're making films, trying to build a career, you also have other things – a family and a life – that you have to balance with it. While I've been making the documentaries I got married and had children, so I was able to stay around. But a lot of the ideas that I have tend to take me away. I wanted to be here while my children were young, and now they're both going into full-time education, so I'm ready for a new challenge.

It's great to go back to a world where I can create some fantastic images and feel challenged. So I now find myself within a new world, with more languages than I've dealt with before, more complexity within the narrative, and making the film in a place that hasn't seen many films being made. It's been a while, and I'm looking forward to being out there and doing it again.

Hong Khaou (photo: Artificial Eye)

Hong Khaou

Hong Khaou participated in various writers' attachment programmes with the Royal Court, Polka Theatre, Dende Collective and Yellow Earth Theatre. He was part of the BBC–Royal Court New Writing Initiatives, where fifty emerging writers were chosen across the country to take part in in-house writing opportunities for various departments within the BBC and the Royal Court Theatre. He spent seven years at an independent film distribution company, Peccadillo Pictures, managing their Home Entertainment department. He also regularly attended film festivals and film markets as part of the acquisitions team.

Hong Khaou wrote and directed the short films *Summer* (2006) and *Spring* (2011) before his debut feature was produced through Film London's Microwave scheme. *Lilting* (2014) tells the story of a Cambodian-Chinese mother mourning the untimely death of her son. Her world is suddenly disrupted by the presence of a stranger, and we observe their difficulties in trying to connect with one another without a common language. Through a translator they piece together memories of a man they both loved dearly, and realise that while they may not share a language they are connected in their grief.

A touching, intimate film about the common ground that brings us together, *Lilting* features rousing performances from its leads, Ben Whishaw and Pei-pei Cheng, and announces Hong Khaou as a brave new voice in independent British cinema.

You have an interesting backstory in that you previously worked for a UK distributor. What insights did this give you in terms of the UK market, and the perils and pitfalls of directing your own film?

They should have a module in film school on film distribution. It's a section of the industry that can really help a film-maker understand the whole picture. When I worked for the distribution company, I managed home entertainment and attended film festivals as part of their acquisitions team. It gave me an insight into the type of films that are being bought and those that have suffered. There are some very good films that will never get distribution.

I suppose the insight I had was knowing that the subject matter within *Lilting* would appeal to certain distributors. I was aware that if it could become the film I wanted it to be, there would be a life for it, not just in the UK, but also Europe and the USA. When I was in film school, pretty much all the films in my video collection were Artificial Eye releases. I couldn't quite believe it when they said they wanted to release *Lilting*. I had hoped they would acquire it, but that's something you only whisper to close friends.

How easy was the transition from making short films to directing a feature? What challenges and obstacles did you face?

My short films had a crew of about ten to fifteen people. On *Lilting* we had a crew of forty to fifty, which is still small for a feature film. The difference is the enormity of it – everything is bigger, and that can make the whole process less intimate.

In terms of shooting the film and the process by which I went about achieving it, that remained the same. I wasn't able to shoot chronologically. I would have preferred that. It was just impossible with the budget we had and a seventeen-day shoot. Nevertheless, we tried to be as chronological as we could. We were mindful to shoot the scenes in order to help with the emotional journey for the actors. And for myself.

I used to storyboard all my short films. For *Lilting* I didn't do that. We did block the shots during the run-through. That was very liberating. We found some wonderful shots that I wouldn't ever have considered.

How did the three central partners behind Lilting (*Microwave, Protagonist and the BBC) get involved, and what did they contribute to the process?*

The scheme is run by Film London, under the banner of Microwave. A portion of the budget came from the BBC for the TV rights. Film London gave us 50 per cent of the budget, and my producer Dominic Buchanan raised the remaining money privately. Film London looked after us throughout the different stages. I had Clio Barnard as my directing mentor. Dominic, the producer, had Ken Marshall. The mentors were very generous and active in helping us. It was very reassuring to know we could talk to them.

Protagonist Pictures came in later, when we had a rough cut ready to show. Mia Bays, our creative exec, felt it was a good time to bring the sales agents in to view it. This helped to plug a gap in the budget in order to finish off all the deliveries required.

Protagonist really looked after *Lilting*. You could tell they cared for the film. They were very considerate in where to place the film in terms of having the right world premiere. They were so patient in helping us finalise the film.

The film has a universal feel, in that it deals with bereavement, generational issues and problems with communication. Why were these of interest to you, and did you feel it important to make a work that people might respond to for a variety of reasons?

I started writing what I felt was an interesting premise. That premise was language and communication, and having a translator as a prominent narrative device, rather than employing subtitles.

Inevitably, when you write – or when I write and as I mull over my writing – certain themes come to light while others are discarded. The themes of loss and generational issues slowly became clear.

I was also aware the story had to be achievable within the constraints of the small budget. *Lilting* was never going to be a genre film. I felt that if I can be sincere with the story, then I will connect with the viewer. I wrote from an intimate place, about themes that resonate deeply with me. *Lilting* is a very personal film but it's not autobiographical.

You manage to assemble an estimable cast with Ben Whishaw and Pei-pei Cheng. Could you say something about working with these two performers? The film, to an extent, stands on the tentative relationship that develops between them, going from hesitancy and distrust to a blossoming respect and friendship.

The story does hinge on the relationship of Ben and Pei-pei's characters – will they reconcile? These are the small human connections and disturbances I wanted to concentrate on. And both actors are incredible. They're very different in the way that they approach their characters. Pei-pei has very little to say in terms of dialogue but she conveys so much in her expression and her eyes. You then have Ben, who makes every word feel so important. We hang on to his every sentence. There's a real sincerity in their performances.

Ben's character leads us into Pei-pei's world. It's very much a passive place until he arrives. If you're not from that culture it can also be foreign. It is his character that connects everyone's emotions. It was vital to get the right actor for that part. He was so generous, in every sense of the word. He gave himself entirely to the film and to the character. It was so beautiful to see him fighting to retain a sense of the truth all the time.

The film has a unique visual aesthetic. How did you work with Urszula Pontikos to achieve the visual look and tone you required?

The film's aesthetic is very considered. *Lilting* is a conversational, performance-led film and we really had nothing to hide behind. I was concerned people might find the film too contained because of that. I remembered trying to think of ways to give the story a cinematic lift. I wanted grief to permeate the film without feeling weighed down by it. I always knew I didn't want to highlight what was the past or present. It needed a fluid quality – when we are grieving it can be painfully instant, and I wanted to reflect that in the way the camera moves between the different timelines.

This was Ula's second feature – she was also the cinematographer on Andrew Haigh's *Weekend* (2011). She has a wonderful intuitive touch and she connects to emotion beautifully. We talked endlessly about films we like. We also watched a lot of films, as a reference for composition and tone. I wanted the composition and movement of the camera to aid the emotional tone. We had just one rule – the camera can only pan clockwise when we're in present day and anticlockwise in the past.

The final component was the editing. Mark Towns was brilliant. He found this way of pushing the dialogue out of synch, which was never in the script. It reinforced the idea of memory, but memory specifically to do with grieving. It's gives the bedroom scenes this wonderful bittersweet quality. I feel like we're listening in on a very private moment in those scenes. They are some of my favourite scenes.

What about the films that influenced you? The film felt fresh and exciting, but apart from evolving from what can be seen as a new crop of British gay cinema – Weekend, The Comedian (2012) – were there films or film-makers that you referenced?

Thank you for saying that. I love those films you've mentioned. Both are so different and yet there's an 'English' quality that is very reassuring.

There were three films I would say I was conscious of in the writing and prepping for *Lilting*: John Sayles's *Lone Star* [1996], Stanley Kwan's *Rouge* [1987] and Sean Durkin's *Martha Marcy May Marlene* [2011].

I think more than anything it's the film-makers I grew up watching that had an influence on me, and so perhaps on *Lilting*. Eric Rohmer, Tsai Ming-liang, Hou Hsiao-hsien, Krzysztof Kieslowski are just a small handful of key film-making influences.

Lilting has been incredibly well received. What do you personally feel people are responding to?

Having the world premiere at Sundance was very fitting for the film. It's very flattering when I meet people who say they like *Lilting*. I think it does affect people on different levels. Some connect with the emotions, while others find the inter-cultural, inter-generational themes resonate with them. I think those that like *Lilting* find the story and tone sincere, and maybe that can linger with you. At least I hope so.

What are your next plans? What ambitions remain for you as a film-maker?

There are a few things happening. I'm developing an idea with the producer Dominic Buchanan. It's an adaptation of a play. I've just finished a draft of a new script called *Monsoon*. It received the Mahindra GFA [Global Film-making Award] from the

Sundance Institute. It's a present-day film set in Vietnam, about the repercussions of the Vietnam conflict: three characters from different parts of the world, who are products of the Vietnam War but have not experienced it directly.

Andrew Kötting (photo: Gary Parker)

Andrew Kötting

Andrew Kötting was born in Elmstead Woods, England, and went on to become a lumberjack in Scandinavia. Later, he trained at the Slade School of Fine Art in London, specialising in performance and film. He directed several experimental shorts, which were awarded prizes at numerous international film festivals. *Gallivant* (1996), his debut feature film, is a seminal travelogue about his three-month journey around the coast of Britain with his grandmother, Gladys, and his daughter, Eden.

In 2001, he directed the first of his *Landworks* trilogy, *This Filthy Earth*, for Film4, and *Ivul* in 2009 for Artificial Eye. He continues to work on multimedia art projects, including *Mapping Perception*, *In the Wake of a Deadad* and *Louyre – This Our Still Life*, which premiered at the Venice International Film Festival in 2011.

His most recent work, *Swandown*, was made in collaboration with the writer Iain Sinclair, and was shown extensively in cinemas across the UK and as an installation at Dilston Grove in London. The film had its French premiere at the Cannes Film Festival and will be distributed throughout France by ED Distribution.

This year Andrew was commissioned to work with the photographer Anonymous Bosch on a series of pinhole photographs in a cave near the top of the Mountain of Fear in the French Pyrenees.

A one-man industry who works tirelessly across various formats, turning his films into books and installations – and vice versa – Kötting is among the most eclectic, prolific and innovative directors at work in the UK today. Influenced by psychogeography, journeys and jaunting, the director's works draw on personal experience, documentary, audio and visual manipulation, and archive footage, he is an extensive chronicler of British culture – past, present and future. At the time of writing, Kötting has again collaborated with Sinclair on *By Our Selves*, a Kickstarter-funded account of John Clare's journey from Epping Forest to Northamptonshire – accompanied by a straw bear. Kötting thrives on collaboration (he has also released two records with Jem Finer); *By Our Selves* features father-and-son actors Freddie Jones and Toby Jones.

Despite the way in which you present the physical hardship of rural existence in This Filthy Earth, *there is a lyrical beauty to the film. Did you want these sequences to exist in any kind of opposition to the other 'spunk and bones' sequences? And did you allow any other films to affect the way in which you filmed? I was reminded of Malick's* Days of Heaven (1978) *and Alexander Dovzhenko's* Earth (1930).

I haven't seen *Earth* but I was definitely influenced by Terrence Malick and that magic-hour light that can sometimes seem so surreal. Polanski's *Tess* (1979) was an inspiration as well. The harvesting does read as somewhat elegiac, but there is also something ominous, forever present and, of course, the message of the old versus the new.

What kind of atmosphere was it on the shoot, and when and where did the majority of the shooting take place?

We shot in Dentdale in North Yorkshire for everything other than the girls' abode, which was shot in Dent in Cumbria. The atmosphere on set was that of one large and dishevelled spunk-stained family. The cast were always around, even if they were not required for many of the days of shooting. Peter-Hugo Daly, aka Jesus Christ, would wander the Yorkshire Dales in costume, spirit bottle in hand, ready to cure the afflicted.

The film has a certain timelessness to it but still manages to deal very effectively with concerns that affect modern communities, such as the racial abuse suffered by Lek. Were you keen for the film to have contemporary resonance?

Absolutely. We never wanted to write it large, but it was very important.

Demelza Randall is especially good. Are there benefits to working with non-actors?

I was casting intuitively. I had help from casting agents, who were responsible for drawing my attention to Rebecca Palmer and Dudley Sutton, but it was a process of pushing and probing at the interview stage. It was also about look, and how genuine I thought the actors were when I confronted them with the 'real' that I was after. It was important whether they baulked at the idea of full penetrative sex or dead animals. We were hoping to cast at the city farm but this proved problematic, so we had sides of beef delivered instead. Shane Attwooll is from Deptford – like myself – and it was always his look that I had been interested in. I found his picture on Spotlight years before I cast him, and it was this image that informed the Buto character. The fact that he can act despite his Buddy Holly fingers was a real bonus [Attwooll was the lead in the stage version of *The Buddy Holly Story*].

Do you encourage improvisation?

I am always on the lookout for happenstance, whether that be from the landscape, the cast, the crew or the props or whatever. To trust in the cast to improvise is all part of my process.

I understand that you take quite a 'sculptural' approach to film-making, describing it as a 'hunting and gathering process'.

Yes, it is very much a sculptural process – contingent, never set in stone, and always an approximation of what you set out to do. In that way, I'm far less likely to be disappointed or dependent on, for example, take sixty-six. Even though we stuck very closely to the final script on *This Filthy Earth*, I was always on the lookout for the 'other'. This approach can create no end of problems at the editing stage because of all the new possibilities, but that just makes you work harder as a film-maker.

You work in a variety of media, including DV and Super 8. What kind of potentials do these formats present, and how do you see digital film-making as influencing the future of film production?

The impact of the new technologies is profound. I think that a lot of the control is now firmly back in the hands of the film-makers. The power of the labs has been undermined and the industry as a whole is losing its monopoly. It is all very positive, but as far as the different formats within *This Filthy Earth* are concerned, it is as much about texture and feel as it is about being cost-effective. I also use DV throughout in a symbolic way – it's meant to represent the eyes of the landscape as seen through the eyeless character of Joey, the feral vagabond. It is an animistic presence, and in the wake of Joey's sister's death the film goes into a berserk and apocalyptical freefall where madness is almost kept at bay.

There was a long hiatus between This Filthy Earth *and* Ivul.

It's par for the course, I guess, with the kind of work that I make. *Gallivant* came out and did relatively well, and certainly got a lot of people very interested in it after its initial screening at Edinburgh. Even when I was making *This Filthy Earth*, the idea behind *Ivul* certainly existed, but I didn't really know what form I wanted it to take. John Cheetham, Andrew Mitchell and I wrote the first draft together, and the BBC committed to that, but then it went into a vault while they developed their digital channels. Then *This Filthy Earth* came out and I think people thought, 'Do we really want another one of those?' For me, this was quite reassuring and there was a slight sense of relief that I wouldn't have to make it and I could get on with some of the other stuff I wanted to do. Then three years ago ED Distribution, who distribute my work in France, were approached by a young producer, Émilie Blézat, who expressed an interest in producing the film after reading the script. Various meetings took place in Paris and the French Pyrenees – an area I know well – and suddenly the project took on a new life. The catch was that I had to translate the script into French and transpose it to a completely different landscape.

You are among a recent group of British film-makers – including Ben Hopkins and Thomas Clay – who, having found it difficult to get their work financed in the UK, have relocated abroad. How did shooting outside of the UK feed into the sensibility of the film?

I love language. I love to play with language and I have a massive archive – both sonic and visual – that does this. Inevitably, elements from my archive find their way into my work, whether it is in the films or other media pieces. The nuance of French still escapes me, which means that I tended to simplify things. I kept the story and the images simpler and made a point, not something I often do, of telling a story. I think people are also being more forgiving of *Ivul* because it is in French. I have a feeling that people were less forgiving of *This Filthy Earth* because it was located in the Yorkshire Dales and people spoke the mother tongue. Because *Ivul* takes place in France, people seem to be attributing to it a kind of fairy-tale element.

Landscape is tremendously central to your work, which often attempts a dialogue with your environments.

Every film I have made, from *Klipperty Klopp* (1986) onwards, has involved my confronting the landscape in one way or another. I love the idea of getting my hands dirty, and even allowing elements such as rain to come into the lens. For me, the dialogue is corporeal and I like to convey that in the very fabric of the film, often at the expense of the narrative, which is sometimes why the work feels a little bizarre with its strange rhythms.

Ivul is dedicated to your mother, who you credit with keeping the family together. The notion of family is another central element of your work. It was the core of the In the Wake of a Deadad *project, for example.*

I draw on my life for inspiration and feed that back into the work. *In the Wake of a Deadad* was an exorcism in many ways. The father in *Ivul* is the kind of dad I wished I'd had – eccentric and strange and loveable. My mother, like many of her generation, really did hold the family together and had to make tremendous sacrifices to do so. Even as an adolescent I was astonished at what she would do to keep us together as a unit. Marie, the mother in the film, is obviously very different to my mother, and she reaches a moment where she has simply had enough. My mother never reached that moment.

Jacob Auzanneau is remarkable as Alex. It's less a performance, more a performance piece.

He was actually much less intimidated by the physical acts he had to perform – many of which were filmed the winter before we actually started official production on the film – and more fearful of having to act. He was only sixteen when he came down to the Pyrenees to climb trees, and it was just a tiny crew working with him at this time. The following summer, when the money came through and work on the film proper began, the thought of having to scale houses didn't worry him at all, as he's a trained acrobat who has worked with the likes of Cirque du Soleil. It was the acting that worried him. What I tried to communicate to him, and something I carry with me through all the films, is that it is only a film. Of equal importance to everyone involved is the journey of making it. I'm not in thrall to the hierarchy of cinema and make sure I communicate this to my actors. They are free to improvise and act spontaneously, and often it is these unguarded and unscripted moments that find themselves foregrounded in the work.

What influences did you draw on for the film?

The Moon and the Sledgehammer (1971) by Philip Trevelyan is a key work for me, and I used the film as a companion piece when making both *Ivul* and *This Filthy Earth*. I made sure that I showed it to everyone working on the projects, especially the two cameramen, Gary Parker and Nick Gordon Smith. I looked to them to capture that film's sense of spontaneity. On a purely visual level, I am drawn to Matthew Barney's work. You can almost smell and taste his films. Herzog is another film-maker who is always in the back of my mind. Herzog is so primal.

Ivul *is actually part of a planned trilogy.*

That's right. *This Filthy Earth* was the first. That film was set on the ground, *Ivul* is obviously partly set above the ground, and the third part of the trilogy will take place underground. Xavier Tchili, who plays Lek, will arrive underground and meander through the underworld. There are some beautiful cave structures I've been exploring in France, Cornwall and the Faroe Islands. Xavier is a classically trained actor – and, of course, in *Ivul* he doesn't get to speak. I've promised him that when he arrives in the underworld he'll have dialogue. The intention is that he'll meet some of the characters from the other two films. There's no script as yet, just ideas and a landscape.

Having filmed at your house in the Pyrenees over twenty or so years, at what point did you decide to start compiling the material together into what would become This Our Still Life? *I understand that the film began as a series of drawings before evolving into a bookwork and then a film.*

I have always kept a moving image diary of our time at the house. One of my earliest commissions for the Arts Council and the BBC's Late Show drew upon my Super 8 archive from there. I had shot footage for the first two years of our stay, from 1989–90, and just kept on doing it. I use whatever recording devices are to hand, from Dictaphone to DAT recorder for sound and Hi8 to mini-DV for picture. However, for *This Our Still Life*, I confined my selection to just a Super 8 or a 35mm digital Sanyo pocket camera. I have also kept a written journal of prose poetry and tend to collect most of Eden's drawings and paintings that she makes. I collect the memories. The house itself is both a mnemonic and nostalgia vessel. When I'm there alone, I'm usually overwhelmed by a sense of melancholy and palpable yearning for the past. The emotion is quite potent, and this is something I tried to convey in the film.

A portrait of a family busying itself with simple living, the way of life portrayed in the film is very much at odds with the modern world. Does your Louyre hidey-hole represent something of a sanctuary for yourself, Eden and Leila?

Louyre as bolt-hole, hidey-hole and safe haven. It is an antidote to a life back in the UK. Our existence in the French Pyrenees is very self-contained and hermetic. Time slows down. The house is up a track, five miles from a village, which no longer has a bar or a shop. Our letterbox is a mile from the front door. We hear only the sounds of the forest and the stream. Sometimes it's terrifying. We have had friends running for their lives when left alone up there. The wild boar and deer also run for their lives in the late summer when the hunt starts. We can hear the sound of howling dogs and intermittent gunshot. The Foreign Legion do some of their training in the forests opposite. The house has remained untouched for a hundred years, and it is in the shadow of the Mountain of Fear (Montagne de la Frau). We have a compost toilet and only intermittent running water. At night we have the

Herzogian terror that is the great out-of-doors. I love it.

Drawing is an important means of expression and communication for Eden. This may be difficult for you to talk about as it is quite an emotive issue, but how has this process of drawing and creating together furthered the bond between you both as father and daughter? And how much joy does it bring you to see Eden so happy with the results of your endeavours?

The drawing and painting is therapy for the both of us. It is the glue that holds us together. The collaboration has become vital. Eden is very uninterested in television or reading books, and finds it hard to walk long distances. Sometimes you can feel very trapped in her company. She is severely disabled and has a tendency to switch off – she rolls her eyes to the back of her head and literally zones out. It's a comforter for her. She can disengage from the world quite easily. I sometimes envy her this 'ability', but it has always been in mine and Leila's nature to motivate and inspire her. We have made several films together as well as some larger 'art projects'. With support, she is game for anything, and luckily she has always had a dark and sometimes wicked sense of humour. I love it when she laughs. I love it when she is happy. She is very happy drawing.

When we first started drawing 'Still Life' together (maybe ten years ago), I noticed that as well as being attentive to the task in hand she was also incredibly attentive to what I was doing, the marks I was making and how they corresponded to the objects in front of us. Leila would join in and so would friends and family. The sessions would last at least an hour, and Eden found in herself the ability to really focus. More importantly for me, I found her drawing skills compelling. Idiosyncratic and glorious. She has an innate ability to position things on the page and deconstruct what she is seeing in a remarkable way. She then insisted that I help label the drawings by spelling out for her the things that she had been drawing. She would write what I spelled. It was through this process that our more recent collaborations have grown. Eden's work is now being 'collected' by private individuals and shown in galleries across Europe, and she is 'happy, happy, happy'. We have been on an incredible journey together, and she has even spoken about her work at Tate Britain, with me as a translator. My joyfulness is as BIG as a mountain.

Landscape is an integral part of your work, and This Our Still Life *and* Swandown *are no exception. How do you work to incorporate the environment and the life that surrounds you into the fabric of the films? It feels incredibly organic.*

Landscape is vital to my practice. It always has been. I was very influenced by land artists such as Robert Smithson, Richard Long and Hamish Fulton when I was at art school, as well as Joseph Beuys and Stuart Brisley. But it was Werner Herzog's *Aguirre, the Wrath of God* that really ate into me. I wanted to be in the landscape, at one with the landscape, fuck about in the landscape and get fucked over by the landscape. Endurance and suffering seem to coexist in much of the work, but are always contextualised by the topographies in which I am working. I think this is why I have such an affinity for much of Iain Sinclair's writing. There is rarely a script, just some ideas that fit a theme. And even if I'm working on narrative films with scripts that I have laboured over for years, I invariably look to improvise the minute I am on set. I embrace happenstance and serendipity and then reverse engineer meaning into the finished works. The manipulation, mediation and editing of materials are key.

Swandown *marks a collaboration with long-time cohort Iain Sinclair. How did the film come about, and what kinds of themes and ideas did you wish to explore in the advent of the London Olympics?*

Iain was driven by a desire to politicise his stance against the corporate hijacking of the Olympics and their riding roughshod over his beloved terrain. I was driven by the ridiculousness of attempting to pedal a swan-shaped pedalo from Hastings to Hackney. The film is a mixture of both, but more importantly a celebration of endeavour and literature. Thematically, everything was up for grabs, which is why Ophelia features, as does Leda, Virginia Woolf, Ezra Pound, Alan Moore and Stewart Lee! We had walked the route maybe two years before we were commissioned to make the film. We knew the geography but the research also brought us closer together. We'd present work-in-progress 'performances' around the country, assuming that the project was sheer folly, but quite quickly we found that people really supported it. Lisa Marie Russo and Cornerhouse in Manchester were fundamental to the film eventually getting made. Iain is a man of enormous generosity, especially if he likes you. He also has a ceaseless imagination, which might be seen as Tourette's. He walks every day. He is a kindred spirit, and for me his agitation of mind and deftness of pen set him apart as the UK's greatest living writer.

How did Jem Finer become involved? The music is perfect for the film but also works as a record in its own right.

I met Jem in Moscow many years ago when we had both been commissioned to make work in Star City. Jem is a very modest man, and it was only towards the end of the residency that I found out that he was the same Jem Finer from the Pogues, a band that I had adored throughout the seventies and eighties. He is a remarkable musician but also an artist, scientist and fiddlesmith. He was developing *Longplayer* at the time we met – a piece of music that is scheduled to run for a thousand years. It was the sheer intellectual and conceptual brilliance of the idea that completely beguiled me and made me want to know him better. We have performed live together using film projections and sounds, and produced an album called *Visionary Landscapes*. Last year saw its ten-year anniversary release, so it was always our intention to produce a second album. We called it *Visionary Seascapes*, and in a decade we hope to produce a third album called *Visionary Skyscapes*.

The film is initially quite jolly, but once Iain departs it takes on a much more melancholy tone. How much did his absence influence your mood and the direction the film would go on to take?

Although I did miss Iain, for the last leg of the journey there was a little artistic licence or reverse engineering afoot during the edit. In reality, I had invited several pedal-philes or guests to join me for the final few days pedalling, including Iain's son, Will, who dressed up in Iain's damp clothes and regaled me with hilarious childhood anecdotes about his father. There were also several female friends and writers who really expanded on some of the themes that we had been exploring. But ultimately, in the edit it felt as if the film had run its course and needed a slightly more melancholy finale. I liked the way the film drifts off into the gloom, and the voice-over was designed to illustrate my feelings as the odyssey reached its conclusion. However, there is also a little guilt in my voice for having had such a jolly time in London without him.

You seem to be able to work without compromise and attain the necessary funding to fulfil your pursuits.

I lurch from one artistic endeavour to another. There are always plenty of plates spinning. Eden helps to keep me focused and rooted, and in many ways has prevented me from having pursued a 'proper' career in either film or 'the arts'. Yet it is these very 'restrictions' that have inspired me to turn the gaze back on myself. My work is very autobiographical – a psyche and its geography, and therefore not always dependent on big budgets or the industrial process of movie-making. I cannot not make work, and therefore I blunder on regardless in a somewhat shoddy and ramshackle way. However, there is now enough of the 'stuff' behind me to count as an oeuvre or body of work, and thematically much of it 'belongs'. I cut the cloth accordingly, which is why it might look as if it's uncompromised, whereas in truth it's just an approximation of the work that I really wanted to make. I have also been supported over the years by a loyal and gifted cohort of collaborators who invariably give of their time and creativity for no financial reward. Without them, so much of what I have achieved would not have been possible.

Gideon Koppel (photo: Dave Swindells)

Gideon Koppel

Gideon Koppel grew up in Liverpool, studied mathematics and was a postgraduate student at the Slade School of Fine Art, in the Experimental Media Studio. His work is exhibited in a wide variety of forms, from the film installation for fashion label Comme des Garçons to the controversial and never broadcast BBC film *Ooh la la and the art of dressing up*, which explores the psychopathology of celebrity.

Sleep Furiously (2008) was a major critical discovery. A meditative study of a small farming community in mid-Wales, the film observes the rhythms of country life and considers the likely impact of modernity. Koppel's interest in the eccentricities of life is simultaneously affectionate, moving and humorous. No follow-up feature has been forthcoming, after Koppel's relocation to Paris to teach. And we can only hope that the Markeresque short *A Portrait of Eden*, a quietly hypnotic study of Eden Kötting, is not the last we will see of this excellent film-maker's work.

You've described Sleep Furiously *as being influenced by conversations with the writer Peter Handke. What form did these conversations take, and what were some of the primary topics?*

A few weeks into the filming of *Sleep Furiously*, I was reading Peter Handke's play *Kaspar*. The world of Kaspar had a particular resonance for me at the time: exploring relationships between external and internal landscapes; questions about belonging; a sense of what is 'possible' rather than what 'is', or 'was'; Kaspar's struggle for language, for words – his cry 'I want to be someone like somebody else once was.'

I wrote to Peter, describing the film I was making and asking if I could come to Paris to talk with him about it. One month later, over lunch, we talked. We talked about all kinds of stuff, but I remember coming away thinking differently about stories – what a story could be. I really enjoyed the idea of a story as an evocation of a moment, a place in time, a gesture . . . But perhaps most important was Peter's response to the uncertainties I expressed about what I was filming and how I was filming it: he said simply and emphatically, 'Follow your instinct.' Peter's words were and remain very important for me. And the conversations continue.

What is your direct relationship to the community in which you filmed? And how did this impact on your decision to film there and the way in which you chose to represent it?

I guess I should start answering this question by saying that *Sleep Furiously* is not intended to be a film 'about' the community of Trefeurig – I didn't really set out to 'represent' Trefeurig. In that sense, I don't experience the film as a 'documentary', or at least what 'documentary' has become associated with now. The writer and psychoanalyst Adam Phillips viewed two rough cuts of the film. Of the second, he commented that he felt there was a more developed emphasis on 'aboutness'. I enjoyed this term Adam coined, and recognised my resistance to the demands for 'aboutness' and my interest in the qualities of evocation.

I wanted to make a film in which moments of intimacy and human gesture became juxtaposed with the infinite space and time of the landscape. I think about the landscape of the film as an 'internal landscape' – it has a quality of childhood about it . . . I suppose my own childhood, although I tried to evolve a film that touches on more universal sensibilities. But it is not stuck in childhood – there is a development in the film which I perceived as a passage from nature to culture. Having said that, my relationship with the community of Trefeurig is rooted in my childhood: we used to go on family holidays there and I often 'worked' on one of the local farms with Edwin and Eleanor Hughes. I smile when I say 'work', because all I did was tag along with Mr Hughes, but it felt like work and I discovered a deep sense of contentment and satisfaction in that experience.

When I was twelve or thirteen my parents moved permanently from Liverpool to a smallholding in the area. Without having had any farming experience, they kept cows, sheep, goats, chickens etc. I was roped into helping look after the animals. My parents, both artists and refugees, found a home and a sense of belonging in this beautiful but sometimes harsh environment. So Trefeurig became – and in part remains – my home too.

Before I even viewed Sleep Furiously *I was immediately drawn to the title. It seems so incongruous and yet after seeing the film it seemed so apt in its capturing of an environment and a community in what has been described as 'quiet uproar'. Did you wish the title to reflect this, and is the phrase 'quiet uproar' one that you feel appropriate in terms of describing the changes that are afoot in rural communities?*

This is such a difficult question, because at the moment I still lack the confidence to really play with the significance of titles. It seems to me that a title is like the outline of a drawing or painting, which in turn makes me think of Marion Milner's book *On Not Being Able to Paint*. Here Milner describes 'the outline' as that which separates the external realities of the world from imaginative experience, and in that sense 'the outline' becomes the containment of what might otherwise be an unmanageable madness. I suppose what I am saying is that for me the title can generate boundaries in which the film evolves as an autonomous world with its own logic, moralities . . . *Sleep Furiously* had a working title of *The Library Van*, which I liked for its direct simplicity. For me, this title suggested the possibilities of the van as an actual and metaphoric vehicle of stories, but I feared it might reinforce the film being perceived as a documentary 'about' a library van.

I used the cutting room as I would a studio space – covering the walls with images and text. My eyes and my mind could wander away from the screen I was working on to these associative elements I had found throughout the film-making process. One of these elements was a large graphic of the Chomsky phrase 'colourless green ideas sleep furiously'. At one point I removed this sheet from the wall and placed it directly under my monitor. In this act, 'sleep furiously' became the title of the film.

Acting as your own cinematographer you opt for long, unhurried takes, with your camera remaining static as it observes life passing in and out of the frame. What was the defining principle behind this aesthetic choice?

When I composed pictures in the viewfinder I was thinking about using the frame to create a stage. In that sense, every environment becomes a theatrical set in which a drama could – no, would – take place . . . a story would unfold. This space within a frame also offered a containment of time, rhythm and ritual – three dynamics that are very important for me – perhaps the essential components of stories.

The camera becomes a microscope through which I can explore the world – in doing so, everything I observe becomes to different degrees fictionalised. By that I mean the composition suggests relationships between objects that are not otherwise there. Imagine looking out over the valley, the fields, fences and houses, the sheep and the tree are just a part of that continuum. But through the camera, they can be brought together – perhaps it is the lens making the tree and the sheep appear on the same focal plane, or they are isolated, contained within the frame as in a way to highlight their presence above all the other objects in view. Either way, there is now a suggestion that the sheep and tree are in some sort of communion.

Perhaps this might be saying the obvious, but *Sleep Furiously* is a fairly accurate translation of how I see and experience the world. That is to say, the images on screen are very close to the images of my mind's eye – a quality of contemplation and gaze that, to my great frustration, did not help my childhood ambition to be a good goalkeeper.

It is perhaps unavoidable that some moments in Sleep Furiously *evoke a bygone era, but the film, because of the issues it seeks to address, never settles for mere nostalgia. Was this, and overtures towards sentiment, something that you were keen to avoid?*

Almost every story in *Sleep Furiously* suggests both beginning and ending – the circularity of life. The owl dies but then becomes something else – a sculpture; the piglets are cute and loveable but will be equally appealing when unrecognisable – grilled with a little salt and pepper. I guess that the paradoxical and contradictory in life, however difficult, are important for me. So it is not that I set out to specifically eliminate sentimentality or nostalgia. My intention was for the film to create its own moral constructs rather than use assumed values.

Sound as well as image seems particularly important to you. This is a film that could be experienced with one's eyes closed and it would still be possible to take enjoyment and enlightenment from it. Was sound design something to which you paid particular attention?

I trained for three years as a sound recording engineer at Utopia Studios in London, working on all kinds of music projects, from the Queen soundtrack for the feature film *Flash Gordon* (1980) to *Neutronica*, an album by Donovan. It is funny but I wasn't interested in the music bit at all. However, I was really curious about sounds and used studio 'downtime' to make sound montages. That later developed into a fascination with the juxtaposition of sound and picture. Jean-Luc Godard's *Prénom Carmen* (1983) and *Passion* (1982) had a big impact. I thought it was magical to be immersed in an image of the sea at night-time while hearing the sound of a train, then propelled into an acute sense of the infinite as the sound of the train was suddenly replaced by the distant waves.

I think about the microphone like I do the camera – as a kind of microscope on the world. Not merely to record sounds that accompany or illustrate the image, but to create another dimension to the picture. This approach was developed in post-production by a sound supervisor who created movements of sound that evoked the character-like presence of 'the land' and the ever-changing light, skies and weather. We talked about juxtapositions of scale – for instance, rather than losing the tiny figure walking in the vastness of the landscape, she is given a particular presence as the sound of her footsteps cuts through the gusts of wind.

I remember that my original notes for Joakim [Sundström, sound editor] included a quotation from John Banville's novel *The Sea*. Banville describes silence in terms of sound and questions whether this is a quality he brings to the environment or something which has its own presence. Throughout *Sleep Furiously* I am asking the audience to listen to the silence – a silence equivalent to the stillness of the camera.

Could you talk about the score and your collaboration with Aphex Twin? I think I'm right in saying that this is the first film with a soundtrack by him.

I've seen all kinds of stuff on the Internet from Aphex Twin aficionados about this. The soundtrack for *Sleep Furiously* isn't an original score – it's made from existing Aphex Twin tracks – so in that sense it wasn't a collaboration with Richard James [his real name].

This music naturally found its way into the film from very early on in the editing process. It is not an accompaniment, but becomes a form of voice for each of the main characters. I sent Richard a DVD of a rough edit of *Sleep Furiously* – he really liked the film but was irritated by the way I had edited the music: cutting tracks short, repeating sections . . . We were both sorry that there wasn't time for him to compose a specific soundtrack. The music is such a vital part of the film – I am really grateful for his generosity and support.

Do you see the film, unique as it is, as existing in any sort of documentary tradition? Serge Lalou (Être et avoir, 2002) is an associate producer and Raymond Depardon comes to mind. Interestingly, Mark Cousins, who has been a passionate support-er, located Sleep Furiously *in the tradition of Humphrey Jennings. Elsewhere, the film's psychogeographical bent has evoked Chris Petit and Andrew Kötting.*

Mark Cousins provoked me to look again at the work of Humphrey Jennings, and also introduced me to a wonderful film – *Farrebique ou Les quatre saisons* (1946) by Georges Rouquier. Another writer on film, Neil Young, equated *Sleep Furiously* with the work of James Benning. I hadn't heard of Benning, so eagerly went to see *RR* (2007) at the BFI Southbank. What a revelation – it is one the most powerful pieces of cinema I have seen for years.

I guess that with Serge's involvement the comparisons with *Être et avoir* are inevitable, but the [Nicolas] Philibert film that resonates with me is *La ville Louvre* (1990). Kötting's *Gallivant* (1996), Dvortsevoy's *In the Dark* (2004), and above all Chris Marker's *Sans Soleil* (1983) are all contemporary 'document-aries' that are important for me.

But as to *Sleep Furiously* existing in a documentary tra-dition? It seems to me that since the 1920s film-makers and artists from Vertov to Chris Marker have used notions of 'documentary' as a way of qualifying work that did not have 'screenplay' scripts, that are open-ended . . . what might be called ciné poems. I use the word 'documentary' cautiously, because unfortunately what was once an idiom of film-making and art is now often conflated by both broadcasters and academics with factual television programme production. That is to say, polemical themes and journalistic structures prevail over visual observations and lyrical stories. The camera is used more as a recording device than as a kind of microscope which contains, discovers and evokes dynamics of the world that otherwise pass by unnoticed.

The overall impression I was left with was one of tranquillity and disruption. How are others responding to the film? And as your first feature, how gratifying is it to experience such positive audience and critical responses?

It is funny because a lot of my work has never been seen publicly. *Ooh la la and the art of dressing up* was the last film I made for television. Set in a world of high fashion – Julien Macdonald and Givenchy – it is a modern-day Faustian story which explores the psychopathology of celebrity. BBC Wales really hated it and it was never broadcast.

So the positive response to *Sleep Furiously* is all the more gratifying, especially, as you say, since it has come from audiences and critics all over the world. Most people seem to be genuinely touched by the film. But perhaps the greatest reward for me is that against all odds for a £200,000 film it has been seen in the cinema. That was my and Margaret Matheson's ambition right from the outset, right down to shooting on film. I love the sense of occasion and the spectacle of cinema – sitting in a dark space, eating chocolate peanuts and raisins while gazing up at vast photographic images, cloaked in a world of magical sounds.

Although *Sleep Furiously* is an unusual film, I think that it has a haunting beauty and speaks to something universal. Unlike much of contemporary culture, it is neither sensationalist nor prescriptive, so it offers space for people to think and imagine for themselves.

John Maclean

John Maclean

After leaving art school, John Maclean performed with the Beta Band, then with the Aliens – for both of whom he made films. His first short film, *Man on a Motorcycle* (2009), was shot on his phone. This was followed by *Pitch Black Heist* (2011), which won the BAFTA award for Best Short Film. His first feature, *Slow West* (2015), won the Grand Jury Prize at the Sundance Film Festival in 2015. All three films starred Michael Fassbender.

You were originally involved with the Beta Band. How did you move from music to film?

I went to art school and studied painting, then joined the Beta Band when I finished my Masters. Straight away, I said I wanted to work on the music videos and make them quite creative, not just performance pieces of the band playing. So very quickly they became like short films – with no budget, filmed with my own camera. It was a great way of learning how to make and edit a film. I made about twenty-five of these short films, and was starting to tell stories.

Why did the band break up?

We had reached a kind of creative lull. We really wanted to keep pushing forward, to re-invent – and it was becoming more and more difficult. So, we all thought it was time to quit and try other stuff.

What instrument did you play?

I played piano and keyboard, but I also used samples and beats. I was interested in hip hop and sampling, which I saw as musical collage and montage. It was all very much feeding into my work on the album covers and videos, rather than my skill with any particular instrument. I began to enjoy making the videos more than being in the studio.

After the Beta Band broke up, were there any other music projects?

I got together with one of my oldest friends Gordon Anderson, who's very talented, for a three or four year stint in a band called the Aliens. However, at the same time, I was trying to write, and began writing screenplays, at first very unsuccessfully, but I stuck at it.

The band split up around that time and I met Michael Fassbender. I first met Michael when I was playing music with the Aliens, because Michael's manager – a guy called Conor McCaughan at Troika – was looking at managing bands, trying to suss out the music industry. Conor watched the short films I had done for the band, and he showed a few of them to Michael. Michael saw something in them that interested him, and when we met, he said, 'Do you fancy doing something?'

He was doing *Inglourious Basterds* (2009) at the time, and didn't necessarily need to offer me his time, but I got one day with him and decided to make a film on my mobile phone. It was a film about a motorcycle courier in London. I had my friend do four days of filming with a helmet on, and then he takes his helmet off and it's Michael. So that's the kind of thing I learned by making no-budget films – how to cheat. There's a bit of dialogue, there's a story, there's a narrative, and it's called *Man on a Motorcycle*. It's a day in the life of a London motorbike courier. One of the last truly dangerous jobs left in the capital. I shot that on my mobile phone and it kick-started my film career.

Then someone gave you the money to make the next one?

Yes, I sent *Man on a Motorcycle* out to festivals – and for eleven or twelve months every one rejected me. But then, suddenly, it got into the London Film Festival. Philip Ilson, the nice chap that does London Shorts, saw something in it, and Film Four sent along someone to see if it was any good. He reported that it was, so Film Four said, 'Do you fancy doing something?' and that became *Pitch Black Heist*.

So then I got back to Michael. I had made sure that our one full day of filming together had been fun. I didn't want to get involved with big film crews, and have him waiting around; I wanted it to be more like guerrilla film-making. So it was just a mobile phone, him riding a motorbike, and me on the back. We didn't ask for permission, we just filmed in the street, then jumped on the bike, and went to the next location – it was quite exciting.

So he said, 'Let's do something again,' and I said, 'What? Three days of filming?' and I made sure, again, that they were three great days. It was easy and fun. I wasn't paying his full fees, so I made sure the food was excellent, and that seemed to work – I got my feature, and Michael said, 'Let's keep going.' We had three days, but they were very light days. I had learned through my Beta Band videos to thoroughly storyboard, and that was the only way I was able to construct the right footage – not because I shot lots of coverage, but because I storyboarded and only filmed those short sections, almost editing in camera. We shot on 35 mm so this helped keep stock down, but now if I shoot digital, I still pretend it's film and only shoot what's needed.

Pitch Black Heist *always seems sure of exactly what it wants the audience to see in order to make it work.*

When watching a lot of the history of cinema, if you look at the masters of economy like Bresson, you learn quite quickly that there's no shot that's just pretty or purposeless – everything is part of the story. It's a similar process with the script – it's about using the fewest shots to tell the story, the fewest words of dialogue to convey the message. So that's where I see beauty in film, I see it as economy. Other people see beauty in film as the opposite: they stretch things out, and use longer, more fantastic shots.

When you see stacks of boxes in the warehouse in the opening shot, it looks like the art department has made them. Then you realise why they have that handmade look to them – it's a rehearsal. You realise that everything you're seeing is there for a reason.

I saw the boxes as an aesthetic thing, almost like an art installation, but also as something some crazy guy, organising a heist, has built so that the two criminals can practice; the beauty is in the practicality.

When the two characters go into the dark towards the safe, did you record the dialogue there?

No, the sound man wanted to do it in a more enclosed, comfortable environment. We actually ended up recording it in one of the actors' sitting room, and I quite liked the idea of doing that section in a completely different place. It was pretty much just Michael and Liam [Cunningham] speaking into the microphone, but Gernot Fuhrmann, who did the sound design, really helped create a sense of distance – the characters moving away from the microphone, and then moving back. All of that was part of the sound design. We drew up a plan of the place to make sure we knew where the characters would be going in the dark.

In the old days, studio chiefs would go crazy if there was a black screen.

Someone told me there was a rule that you couldn't have black that lasted more than forty seconds.

So how long is that section?

About three minutes. I've seen the film a lot in cinemas in differ-ent film festivals and there are two interesting things: firstly, the audience are very drawn to the black section, almost more than the rest of the film; and secondly, you can really tell which cine-mas go overboard with the emergency lights. Sometimes, when the cinema goes black, it's really amazing, but other times, you're suddenly aware of all these emergency lights – everywhere, all down the sides of the cinema.

I thought that when Michael Fassbender sings the cheesy song – it's like in a Wong Kar-wai film, it exactly fits the moment and the emotion.

The song is a B-side of a 45 vinyl – I collect vinyl – the A-side is very much easy listening, and I don't think anyone really knew about the song on the B-side; but I thought it was a beautiful song. We spent a long time tracking down who had the rights, and at the time, the producers said, 'We're going to have to do a shot without the singing, in case we don't get the rights.' So we did this half-hearted shot that was awful; the camera didn't really curve round in the right way and I said, 'That's it,' be-cause I knew that if we got it right, they would slack off getting the rights to the song. I wanted it to be that we *had* to get the rights. When we shot the version with the song included, it really worked – Michael did it great. I knew we'd get the rights eventu-ally, but it was a battle.

That section probably wouldn't have worked if the song had been lip-synced at random, because if you had tried to have the actors move their lips without any music, the song wouldn't have been picked up so precisely by the other character.

Yes, it's also a story point – SPOILER ALERT! – about them being father and son, that's why they both know the song.

They're father and son?

Yes, some people get the twist at the end that he's Michael's dad, and some people don't. Michael's dad has left him when he's a child, so that's why Michael leaves him at the end, and gets his revenge as the alarms go off. There are clues earlier, when he says his name is Michael, and then, at the end when the father says, 'Michael, Michael,' and Michael says, 'Too late.' That's why the song is so important: it's something they both know. That part of the story is really something I wanted to keep at the back of the film, rather than foregrounding it.

Robbie Ryan shot the film. What did you think of his work?

Well, great. I fought hard to get him on board. I wanted him to do all the things he wasn't known for: at the time, his stuff was very much hand-held, shallow focus, and quite intimate – he excelled at that. I wanted to make films using a very deep focus, films with no hand-held set-ups. But Robbie is incredible and constantly exceeded expectations.

Once Channel Four saw Pitch Black Heist, *did they immediately say they wanted to do a feature with you?*

Yes, they said, 'What do you want to do next?' and I said, 'A feature film.' There were a couple of reasons why: firstly, I knew I could get Michael for a feature, I couldn't just keep doing shorts with him. Secondly, I think I felt quite confident. Everything had happened so quickly. At first, it was just a mobile phone, then it was a short, then a feature – I felt I was ready.

This was before winning the BAFTA award?

Yeah.

When you were writing Pitch Black Heist, *I assume one of your main concerns was how long you could keep the audience wait-*

ing before they feel they've been waiting too long?

A bit of that was worked out in the edit. I think in the earlier drafts, there was quite a lot of talking; I was influenced by the work of Harold Pinter – particularly plays like *The Dumb Waiter*. I'm not a huge fan of dialogue in film; what I mean is, I love dialogue, but not a lot of it, it has to earn its place – I want the lines to be memorable. So as the drafts proceeded, the dialogue got shorter and shorter, until the actors only said what was needed to push the story along. For the rest of the film, I wanted action, such as playing pool, drinking, and arm-wrestling. From the beginning, I knew that Michael was going to be the quiet one and Liam was the talker. Like with *Slow West*, the dialogue got stripped right down until it was just what was essential. Then when you're editing, you instinctively get a sense of pace, you know when to end a scene.

In the kind of situation you've set up, the two characters don't know each other, so what would they talk about?

When writing *Slow West* it was the same, every time Michael even asked a question, it became loaded or out of character. He's the kind of person who quickly answers questions – he doesn't ask them – it's the Clint Eastwood thing. In the same way, in *Pitch Black Heist*, he's not going to turn around and ask, 'So where are you from?'

When you create a character that says very little, every time they do say something, it becomes very loaded. If you want to create a sense of mystery around a character, the less they say the better.

I was watching a lot of heist and noir films. I think the main influence was *Rififi* (1955) – especially the middle section, where there's half an hour of silence – they can't make a sound without the alarm going off. I think Polanski said something like, 'Short films shouldn't have dialogue.' I see what he means because when you get two people just talking, suddenly it becomes a bit like *EastEnders* – in a short film, there isn't enough time for that.

Short films do need to have a narrative to them. Then you can get away without having too much dialogue.

I was very conscious of trying to make the film look different. At the time, a lot of short films were incredibly shallow focus, incredibly hand-held. I remember being at festival screenings and my film was the only one that used a tripod. No one uses a tripod any more. It was going against fashion; everyone was using the Canon, which seemed to have very shallow focus – you can have someone's nose in focus and their eye out of focus. I was conscious of trying to do something very different. All the films I love are deep focus. For *Pitch Black Heist*, it was all about noir films like *The Third Man* (1949), *The Killers* (1946) or *Double Indemnity* (1944).

I think it's about moving the camera only when it needs to be moved. That's something I want to improve on, to keep working out – building up the complexity of starting to move the camera, but making it purposeful. Like Spielberg in *Jaws* (1975), when the camera moves, it's deliberate and subtle in order to show economy: showing three people moving around, and having them all do their bit in one shot, without having it look like a trick shot/one shot. I watched *Brute Force* (1947) recently and everything was framed really amazingly.

Can you describe the conception of Slow West?

There was a novel that had two cowboys in a cornfield and it was just that one image that sparked me writing. There were actually four separate sparks – but I never really associated agriculture and cowboys, and that got me thinking about Merchant Ivory films – they're set in Britain at the same time as Westerns.

So I started writing about an aristocrat in Britain who went out to be a cowboy. And that's still there in the backstory. And this very interesting time-link thing got me thinking about migration, about writing a film where no one was really American, everyone was from all over the world. So these were the sparks.

I was working with Kate Leys, who was the script editor; she very much drew the story out of me, in a therapy-style way. So the main character did become me, to some extent. And, in a way, the heart of the story is a young boy who liked an older girl – like I might have when I was a kid – so that was another thing that came to the table. It was having all those ideas and trying to simplify it.

Was it difficult finding a narrative skeleton for something that was longer than a short film?

The structure was very much hauled out of me by Kate. I spent two months getting the whole story on to one page. Then I went back to Kate and she said to take each sentence and blow it up into a scene. That made it easier than what I'd been attempting before, trying to write the whole script one page after another.

It took me nearly two years to write it, though it wasn't two years sitting at my desk – I was watching a lot of films, reading a lot. And most of the books I read were by the authors of that time, not revisionist – Nathaniel Hawthorne, Mark Twain, Ambrose Bierce, and *The Little House on the Prairie*, which was the most informative one. And then the writing and the daydreaming and coming up with scenes.

Did the fact that the film is a road movie provide a skeleton?

The film is episodic, so that helped because, in the end, I wrote maybe twenty scenes that were sort of an odyssey thing, then realised that ten of them were less relevant, so they got dropped.

The other thing that transpired was that I was reading Bruno Bettelheim's *Uses of Enchantment* at the time, and the film started feeling like a fairy tale, it started feeling like the characters were archetypes. I didn't want them to be particular people; I definitely wanted them to be familiar traits.

In terms of the structure, I said: let's look at a map. I thought if they have to go from there to there, and they go twenty miles a day, and the journey's over five days . . . but, in the end, I just forgot all that and just made it like going down the yellow-brick road. It's interesting that one producer said, 'They've obviously been together for weeks'; then another producer said, 'Isn't it a few days?' I quite like that ambiguity.

And then, shooting it in New Zealand instead of America – it all added to this disorienting, other-worldly atmosphere. So, rather than thinking: they slept here, they wake up, they must be hungry, they eat three times, it's night again . . . in the end, in my mind, it did have five days, so there is five nights.

And, after I had written it, I drew a map which was very much: they're in a forest, then they go through a canyon with rocks, then they're on the plains. The whole cast and crew got the map, and everyone was very happy about that because it really helped. It was probably the most useful tool because when we were in the forest, the AD's always asking, 'Are they coming out of the forest or going in?' And I'd point and say, 'Look at the map. We're here now.'

I was watching a lot of films and halfway through – thinking about my film – it struck me that the characters had to move from right to left on screen. You couldn't have them go the other way because it would look like they were heading east.

I watched a lot of films and not that many go from right to left – maybe because you read that way, left to right. It has the effect where it feels like you're going against the tide. I think I may have read somewhere that when you shoot people going that way, from right to left, it's good for stories about adversity because it seems tougher for the characters to be going that way. And films like *Stagecoach* (1939) and *The Iron Horse* (1924) – films where people are talking about expanding into the West – do go that way, from right to left.

Anyway, it was an awakening. So that's why I shot it, going right to left. I think it had to be that way – no one's picked up on it or said anything.

Why was it shot in New Zealand instead of Colorado?

Quite early on when we were considering finance, Robbie Ryan had just come back from shooting an ad in New Zealand and he suggested that I go and have a look there.

And Michael was only available in the winter. I would have preferred a summer shoot, because Colorado would be tough in October, November and December. And there was the logistics of the distances in Colorado.

So I went out to New Zealand and once you're in a forest there, the trees are very similar to those in Colorado. However, because it says 'New Zealand Film Council' at the start of the film, people have talked about it as a New Zealand western. It's frustrating because I did want to hide that aspect of it; I wanted people to feel that it was a Western. But I think once you're in it, you don't think it's New Zealand. But, at the time, I did want it to be Colorado.

Some of the reviews have said that it adds to the disorienting effect of the film, and even if I had shot in Colorado, I wouldn't have shot the landscape anyway. I was more interested in the characters. *Slow West* is 1:66, it's not widescreen. So I tried very much to keep the landscape out of it.

You said that there were things about the boy that were personal to you, but the film's about the man, isn't it?

The idea that developed while I was writing is that there is a switch from someone who is the archetypal mentor to the ar-chetypical, ignorant student. The student becomes the mentor. And the mentor hasn't realised that he's been living his life in an incomplete way.

When I imagined it on a bit of paper, it was quite even between them. It wasn't that it's a film about someone and then it becomes a film about someone else. It's about both of them, and then it becomes about both of them, but they shift – the one you expect to have the least arc has the bigger arc, and the one you expect to have the big arc doesn't.

That's the mechanics of the film.

What was it like working with Fassbender longer than one day, or three days?

It was just the same. Once you establish a working relationship, then it feels the same.

I like to shoot very fast. If I feel that I've got it, I like to move on – which worried Robbie Ryan. I know Michael would do it again and again until it was perfect; but, at the same time, he'd like to record the first time as well. And, I think with him, you have to have a good reason to do it again. So either he'd want to do it again, or I'd want to do it again. We had that in common.

I feel like all the characters in the film have quite an even amount of screen presence. No one's really an extra, everyone who is in a scene has an even share of it. And everyone has a full back story.

What about Kodi Smit-McPhee. Given the number of films he's done, especially The Road (2009), *he must be very confident.*

He's incredibly confident, but he's also incredibly sweet. He's not lost any of his appetite to learn. It's an unusual combination. He throws himself into the part; he's not fazed by working with major stars. He's very smart, he's very well read, and that helps. He's interested in everything.

When we were setting up the film, I was thinking: how am I going to find a seventeen-year-old, especially because he has to play a Scottish aristocrat. Many Scottish actors come out of Glasgow and immediately have more of a working-class accent.

I wanted someone quite posh-looking and I had quite a definite idea about what he physically looked like. He had to be fragile, yet active – which Kodi is. So, when I first saw Kodi, it was a relief to know I had found someone who I had imagined.

What about the film's music and sound design?

I collect records and I've got a huge interest in many styles of music, from Alan Lomax field recordings to the Wu-Tang Clan, Neil Young to Trinidad steel drummers.

I think people expected me to have Beta Band songs all over the film. But the music has to be right. It has to be used as sparingly as possible. I did get into TV shows like *The Wire* that only has music that's coming from source in the scene. There's music in the jukebox in the pub in *Pitch Black Heist*, so to have a musical score would have interfered and reduced the power of the moment.

It's about being careful with the music. A lot of short films have a lot of slow techno piano music – there's definitely something to avoid there, unless your film is about a slow techno pianist.

And when it came to *Slow West*, I was listening to a lot of Moondog. Moondog is a New York street artist from the fifties till the eighties who mixed a lot of European classical influences with Native American percussion influences. It's amazing stuff. He was called the Viking of Sixth Avenue. He'd live on the streets and do these incredible songs. And because *Slow West* is supposed to be a mixture of this classical European character meeting native culture, it fit perfectly.

So, while I was writing, I was listening to a lot of Moondog and thought I'd just have Moondog on the soundtrack, but then, when I was editing, it always just felt like records on top of the film, it never felt authentic; it made it feel like the fifties or sixties. So I just edited and edited without music, which worried everyone. And, then, at the last minute, I realised I had spent my tokens for European cast and crew, and if I was going to get a composer, it had to be from Australia or New Zealand. I realised my records wouldn't work and that the score had to be composed.

I knew it had to be classical and I knew it had to be very European; I knew it couldn't be Morricone, in any way. And I started thinking that it had to be a waltz 3/4 time. So See Saw – the production company who we were working with – was working with Justin Kurzel on *Macbeth* (2015) with Michael in London. And his brother Jed was over to do the *Macbeth* theme and so he said, 'Jed's over, so why don't you meet him.' So I did, and said, 'I'm looking for a waltz 3/4 time. I want melodic, I don't want drone. So, here's the film, see what you can come up with.'

And four days later he had done it – an amazing piece of music. I didn't even have to change it. As usual, I said I only wanted ten minutes and he did such a good job, I thought: maybe just another bit, and then another . . . In the end, there's about half an hour of music – five or six pieces.

And, for the rest, my friend Gordon [Anderson] – who I was with in the Aliens – did two pieces. He's constantly making four-tracks, he's a compulsive music-maker. So, I'd heard a few of his pieces and said to him, 'There's one shot of horses riding across the screen that needs something.' And he provided a beautiful piece of music.

And then another friend, Bryan Mills, who's a musician, did another couple of tunes. Bryan is also in the film as The Minstrel, a banjo-playing outlaw in the bad-guy posse.

I was aiming for as close to no music as possible, and, in the end, there's less music than people think there is. And whenever there's dialogue, there's no music.

And then I worked quite closely with a brilliant sound team. I wanted them to get creative – I didn't want fifty layered sounds, I wanted three big sounds. I talked to them about Cypress Hill, the hip hop group; their sound is so chunky and clear and simple.

I wanted to make sure the sound was always chunky because there is a tendency these days, with Pro Tools, to layer and layer and layer until you get mushy sound.

I wanted wind, crickets, creaks, and drips – I wanted to make sure the audience could hear the drips.

That's very much Sergio Leone's sound design.

So the sound definitely took over when there was no music. I think the audience these days is much more intuitive about being manipulated: strings when someone's upset. That can really get in the way of a film working.

Has the work with Robbie Ryan evolved over the two films?

Robbie's very much someone who thinks about story and thinks about the few things I've given him that restrict him – like: don't go hand-held or deep-focus. But the rest of it – between him and his lighting crew – sort of takes care of itself.

In the end, we've developed a short-hand where I'll say, 'Let's Bresson it,' which means go three-quarters down from a three-quarter angle, or, 'Don't Wes Anderson it,' which means don't make it symmetrical.

On *Slow West* I wanted a Golden Rule type of composition – and the rest of the time, it was just letting him do his thing and I didn't look through the camera very much.

That's the beauty of film-making right there. I try to achieve my vision, the film I have in my head, but collaborate with great artists, from the costume to the scheduling to the lighting, and the greatest thrill is my expectations being exceeded.

Harry McQueen (photo: Sam Churchill Photography)

Harry Macqueen

In many ways Harry Macqueen is among the most interesting figures in this book, though some readers will not yet have had the chance to view his debut feature, *Hinterland* (2014). Premiering at Raindance, the film is an affectionate homage to Chris Petit's *Radio On* (1979), retracing a similar journey but replacing Petit's (dis)interest in the thriller genre with an engrossing and idiosyncratic 'meditation' on friendship and sexual attraction.

As a trained actor – he takes the leading role in *Hinterland* – Macqueen's story has echoes of Peter Strickland's, in that he eschewed more traditional industry routes, instead investing a £10,000 inheritance and making many personal sacrifices – and imploring others to make them too – so that *Hinterland* could be completed. It's an honest, touching work that deserves to find a cinema audience.

You initially trained as an actor at the Central School of Speech and Drama. What precipitated a move into directing?

I definitely consider myself an actor foremost. My move into directing is still a very new one and, having had no formal training, it feels a little like I'm intruding on someone else's party. Acting is great when you are lucky enough to be doing it but hugely frustrating when you're not. It's far more disempowering than most of the other creative arts, for the sole reason that you need to actively be given a role in order to work. Making the film was, in one sense, a way of getting some of the control back. But it was also a vent for creative expression. I had some time off between a few acting jobs, and for various reasons suddenly found myself with no fixed place to live. It was this period of flux that enabled me to think about making something, and my situation facilitated that to a degree. I had always seen myself attempting to write and direct eventually, but I hadn't expected it to happen so soon in my career as an actor.

Hinterland is, by all accounts, a labour of love. Can you talk about how you accrued the £10,000 to make it? And what hardships and sacrifices did you have to endure during the pre-production and shooting stages?

It was a huge labour of love, and it is important to always love and believe in what you're making. This is especially true when you're doing it on such little money. I inherited £10,000 in a will and, as temping as it would have been to spend that money at the local pub, I wanted to put it to good use. An investment, if you like, but also something that would hopefully have made the person who left it to me proud.

The process that actually led to getting the film made involved a lot of sacrifices at all stages, though I suppose it always does. I lived on friends' kitchen and living-room floors and sofas for over a year. I even ended up staying in the DoP's garden shed in order to afford to finish it. Naturally, there were a lot of sleepless nights and worry in there too. It was all-consuming, but I guess that's the nature of the beast.

Did you attempt to go a more traditional route for funding, such as the BFI Production Board or Microwave?

I didn't. Quite honestly, I thought every single one of those organisations would have laughed at me if I had approached them. I have no background in film-making at all and, as such, would have been an unlikely person for them to back. Also, I didn't feel comfortable taking money from people whom I had never met, so, on an ethical basis, that ruled out crowdfunding.

I was keen to have as much creative control as I possibly could, so making the film on a £10,000 budget became a personal goal, not to mention a significant challenge. I vaguely remember thinking that if I could prove I could make it on that sum, and without any help, that might put me in a stronger position if I ever wanted to make another film.

Could you talk about any directors who inspired you? Chris Petit's Radio On *seems like a clear influence.*

I am very good friends with Chris Petit's son, Rob – who is an amazingly talented film-maker in his own right – but I'd watched *Radio On* many times before we met. It is such a brave and unique film – certainly within the landscape of British independent cinema. There are a few nods to the film within *Hinterland* – more as a thank-you than anything.

The first professional acting role I ever got was a tiny part in *Me and Orson Welles* (2008), which was remarkable because Richard Linklater has always been a hero of mine. His set was fun and mostly laid-back, which is certainly an atmosphere I tried to emulate when I was making the film. As an actor, that sort of environment can be so helpful. The idea that it should always be fun is an important philosophy.

I am a huge fan of directors like John Cassavetes, Béla Tarr, Ingmar Bergman, Andrei Tarkovsky, Akira Kurosawa, Wim Wenders, Michael Haneke, Steve McQueen and Joanna Hogg, to name a few. Anyone brave enough to try something new with the medium, I guess that's what I mean. Kelly Reichardt was a constant reference point when we made *Hinterland*. If I could work as an actor with a director of her calibre, or make films anywhere near as good as any of those film-makers, I would be very, very happy.

What was your approach in terms of your visual aesthetic? You have the beauty of Cornwall to back you up, but was it also a case of necessity being the mother of invention?

I worked hard with my incredible cinematographer Ben Hecking to make the visual aesthetic of the film as evocative and meaningful as we could, at least on the budget we had. I was interested in developing a counterpoint between the city and the countryside, and I hope they exist as two characters in the film. Contemporary life inside and outside a city in Britain is a very different experience, and I felt that was important to explore. When Harvey and Lola are out of London, there is a freedom implicit in their adventure that isn't so apparent in the urban scenes that bookend the film, where high-rise buildings and neon lights surround and enclose them.

But you are right, there was certainly necessity too in the choice of locations. The bottom line is that I wanted, if possible, to make a film as visually beautiful as it was emotionally powerful. I was confident we could make a lovely looking film by shooting cleverly with what that part of the countryside gave us. It is effortlessly dramatic and awe-inspiring, especially along that coast. I also hope the way we shot London feels fresh.

I enjoy films that place their characters in a specific space and allow the action to control movement within the image – sequences where the camera acts as a passive observer. *Hinterland* was mostly an exercise in trying to capture arresting compositions in which the narrative unfolds. That said, we couldn't afford any kit, so there was no chance of a long dolly shot or the use of a Steadicam.

Can you talk about the casting of Lori Campbell? She has an engaging naturalism and is incredibly confident, considering it's her first screen role.

One of the main challenges in making the film was always going to be casting the part of Lola. Harvey was a different task and I only took on the role by necessity, much later in the process. I knew what Lola was on paper and I also knew that I had never met anyone like her. She wasn't directly based on an actual person, and given the specificities of the role I was worried it might be an impossibly difficult task. I was living with my friend Rosie

Morris (who ended up being the script supervisor on the film) when I was writing the screenplay and was telling her about it one day, when she said I should get in touch with her friend Lori, to see if she was suitable and would be up for playing Lola. When we met I knew instantly that she was right.

Music is incredibly important to the piece and I wanted to find someone who was a musician first and an actor second. It took a bit of persuasion, but thankfully she was brave enough to trust that it might be a project worth throwing everything into, even though she had never acted before. We lived with each other for a while so we could workshop the characters and get to know one another, and I think the result of that experience is one of the things I am most proud of. Their relationship has a truth to it that really drives the film. She's absolutely great.

Hinterland is a film about friendship, but it's also tinged with melancholy and regret, especially in regard to a love affair that never quite blossoms. What other subjects were you keen to tackle, and how hard was it to achieve the film's bittersweet sensibility?

Broadly speaking, I wanted to explore love, but those instances when it doesn't quite work. *Hinterland* is very much a film about what isn't, or can't, be said. That inability we sometimes have in vocalising our feelings when perhaps we really should. In this case, it is within the context of two people trying to find out what they are about and where they are going.

Individually, both characters are experiencing a period of ennui that most of us go through – particularly at that age – albeit for different reasons and in separate ways. Maybe what both of them really, truly need is each other, and we will never know if they succeed in achieving that. Hopefully, within this sentiment lies some sort of resonant and beautiful truth for the people watching it.

I think the film also explores nostalgia and the idea that

revisiting a place in a new context can be a difficult experience. The two characters are affected by the same problems my friends and I face, from the impossibility of affording a home to disillusionment with mainstream politics. The abandoned hotel we see is an example of that state of affairs. It used to be glorious, now it's a metaphor of the 'boom and bust' culture we live in.

I think the bittersweet nature of the film comes directly from its naturalism. We never worried about how long something was taking to say or do, only that it was natural and organic when it happened. The spaces and silences in between words, the unnoticed glances, the mutual acceptances, the stillness and quiet are all vital to generating that feeling. The vast majority of the film is spent with Harvey and Lola in each other's company, but when we occasionally see them alone we understand even more about their inner workings – their thoughts and feelings.

What now? Given that you have retained a spirit of independence, are you finding that people in the industry and audiences are receptive to the film?

I have been incredibly humbled by the response to the film so far. Some wonderful people who I really respect professionally have been immensely supportive and have gone out of their way to make others aware of it. Our UK premiere was at Raindance this year [2014], and there are more festivals on the way. The most important thing for me is that people get to see it and, with a bit of luck, appreciate it. We are in talks with a few distributors, so we'll see where it goes.

I am keen to explore other avenues as well, and have been working out a way of potentially touring it regionally, or something like that, if there's interest. We are just about to make the film completely carbon neutral, which I want to promote as something people should be trying to do too.

As with any creative enterprise, the main goal is to try and get it seen by as many people as possible and hope that they engage with its message. If that happens, in whatever way it does, then great.

Steve McQueen (photo: Thierry Bal)

Steve McQueen

A graduate of Chelsea College of Arts and Goldsmiths, Steve McQueen's first success came with his 1993 short film *Bear*, which featured an encounter between two naked men and whose themes explored violence, homoeroticism and race. In 1999 he was awarded the Turner Prize for his video art, which often drew on cinematic signifiers, most notably in his film *Deadpan*, in which the façade of a house falls around him, echoing the same stunt employed by Buster Keaton in *Steamboat Bill Jr.* (1928). McQueen continues to produce video artworks alongside his feature films. His most recent gallery exhibition was *Ashes* (2014), featuring footage from 2002 of a Grenadian man who has since been killed, and with a voice-over (from people who knew him) of the events that led to his death.

McQueen's feature debut, *Hunger* (2008), follows the last stages of Bobby Sands's hunger strike in 1981. Eschewing a conventional historical account of the Troubles, the film reveals in harrowing detail the gradual decline in Sands's health as his body gives up on him while his mind remains resilient. It also lays bare the day-to-day conditions in the prison holding the hunger strikers. Acclaimed for its bold approach to the events and for the director's stark visual style, the film also marked the first collaboration between McQueen and Michael Fassbender.

Shame is another uncompromising character study, this time of a seemingly successful Manhattan businessman whose addiction to sex is all consuming. Fassbender plays the central role with bleak abandon, while Carey Mulligan gives an equally raw performance as his sister. McQueen continues his partnership with cinematographer Sean Bobbitt, who captures Manhattan – both on the ground and high above the city's streets – as a world of reflections. It is a beautiful yet brutal drama.

After his success in the art world, as well as a royal honour (he was made Commander of the Order of the British Empire in 2011), in 2014 McQueen received the highest American accolade, an Academy Award for Best Film, for his third feature *12 Years a Slave*. The story of Solomon Northup – a free black man from the North who was kidnapped and sold into slavery twenty years before the American Civil War – McQueen's is one of the few films to deal directly, and seriously, with this period in American history. His next project is a film about the life of the black American singer, actor and activist Paul Robeson.

Do you regard your work across all platforms as a dialogue?

It's not a jigsaw puzzle. It's just a response to life. Life happens while you're making plans. It's a sphere, it's not linear.

Did you always plan to move into narrative film-making?

What happened was the subject of the hunger strike and the story of Bobby Sands came to mind. But it's not necessarily about the medium for me. It's more about ideas, and the ideas themselves then raise the question of what medium they need to be in. So that's what happened in the case of *Hunger*. It became about storytelling. It needed to be a feature film.

Your films deal with hidden, forgotten or secret histories and lives. Do you see your new installation in London, Ashes, *in the same way?*

I don't think Ashes' story was hidden. It's a story that happens every day. But in terms of the features, yes. They deal with issues that aren't or haven't been talked about – slavery, the hunger strike and sexual addiction. I think artists are drawn to things that aren't being spoken about. It's like sprinkling flour on an invisible subject matter and making it visible.

Both 12 Years a Slave *and* Hunger *sidestep engagement with the political issues surrounding their subjects, and seem more concerned with the idea that these subjects should not be forgotten within an historical context.*

Sidestepped? I was confronting it face on. I wasn't engaging in any academic pursuit or distinction. It was much more of a discussion about the characters in these films. Politics will take care of politics – my interests in the immediate everyday lives of people were more my concern.

What drew you to the story of Bobby Sands?

I grew up with that narrative. I grew up in the 1980s. He appeared on TV and I remember asking my mother who he was. Then the following day I saw him on TV again and there was his name with a number next to it. I didn't understand it and my mother said it was the number of days he had been on hunger strike. I didn't understand what she meant, but later in life I equated it with a child who's been told they can't leave the table until they've finished their food, resulting in their being sent early to bed hungry. So these things ended up staying with me.

What was the attraction of Solomon Northup over other slave narratives?

You start a narrative at the point of interest where you can tell a story and say what it is you want to say. That's why I told the story of Bobby Sands from the point he was in prison. Solomon's story is so complete. He's someone who survived slavery – 99.9 per cent of people didn't. It's the only slave narrative of someone who is kidnapped, sold into slavery and ultimately survives. There are many slave stories but this is the only complete narrative that ends with emancipation.

What was interesting for me was that Solomon's story was a detailed description of that world – a first-hand account of slavery told by someone who was subjected to slavery. It was a parallel to Anne Frank's diary, revealing this world to us.

It's an important story that needed to be told. There hadn't, for me, been a film about slavery that dealt in a real way with the issue of slaves and slave owners and how they lived and interacted.

You've said that you saw the story as being like a Grimms' tale or Pinocchio. *What did you mean by that?*

When I first read the book I thought it was like the tale of Pinocchio. You had these two men, Hamilton and Brown, luring, seducing someone into a circus. It had this classical fairy-tale air that is dark. I think that's why it's an amazing story.

Duration is a fascinating aspect of your feature work. There are shots in all your films that continue for a lengthy period of time, allowing us to observe a character in a given situation or to witness in real time a dialogue between characters. How early in the process do you think about how you would shoot such scenes?

Very early. It's like composing music. Most of the time when we speak it's bullshit. The first time we open our mouths it's small talk: 'Hello. How are you?' We never just hang out with analysts to analyse ourselves. But most of the time when people speak in film it's descriptive or giving audiences some background to the character, which would never happen in real life. It's when we're having an argument in our own heads that what you could call a kind of reality is actually occurring. That's what I want to portray. I want to find and portray a reality that is recognisable to the viewer. I want to hold up a huge mirror where people see themselves reflected in it.

That's why I have that central scene in *Hunger*. I wanted to push it to the extreme. I wanted to push the language to the extreme. I'm after the moment where I can illustrate the space between the words. For example, when I was interviewing the people who had been on the hunger strike I would ask for details. I wanted to know if it was raining on that day and if so, what kind of rain? When did you get used to the faeces on the wall? Was it cold? And how did you react in the cold? These things aren't mentioned in history books, but they can have a huge impact on the outcome of events.

These observations – the visual aside or the pauses in certain scenes – that populate your films have a fascinating impact on their tempo. How early do you discuss each project with your editor Joe Walker?

From day one. I'm there with him for every cut. Every sound. I'll meet with Joe early and we'll start discussing the edit. Then we will begin to assemble things while I'm still shooting. I don't just come in and look at a rough edit. I'm there for everything.

When did you and Abi Morgan decide that Shame *would be set in New York?*

Abi and I were talking about the idea of sex addiction when the press surveillance story broke in the UK. There was also the Tiger Woods incident. People weren't trusting journalists or newspapers. They weren't trusting people asking questions about private matters. The door was firmly closed on this. At the same time we were discussing that in New York there were these analysts dealing with sex addiction, and we agreed that this would be the best place to set the story. After all, this is the city that never sleeps and so an addict in this environment would feel like a kid in a sweet shop. It was also around the time of the start of Grindr and websites that facilitated these situations. For me, that was key to where the world of the film should be set.

Do you see Shame *as a modern take on the morality tale?*

Morality doesn't interest me. I wanted to make a film about sexual addiction in the same way that Billy Wilder made *The Lost Weekend* as a film about alcoholism. Before that film it hadn't been represented as a disease. It was just seen as a weakness. They just didn't take alcoholism seriously as an illness. Likewise, *Shame* is not a film about a person who is promiscuous. It's about someone who is hurting themselves, damaging themselves through the pursuit of sexual gratification. It's just been exacerbated through access to the Internet. It's not about morality. It's about an illness. Morality is for everyone else's judgement.

Can you talk about the process you work through with actors?

I love rehearsals. It's there that you find things out. I find camera angles you've never thought of before. When you're writing on a piece of paper you're living it in your head. You can't see it. When you start rehearsing you begin to see how things play out in reality.

On *12 Years a Slave*, there's a scene where Epps wakes Solomon up and is talking to him about a meeting. At one point he puts his arm around Solomon as though he's a friend. It was a subversive moment, including what appears to be a friendly gesture in a scene that is extraordinarily threatening. It's almost a gesture of love accompanying words that are completely different in tone. That was worked out in rehearsals. I just asked Michael to put his arm around Chiwetel to see how it would look and suddenly we had our two-shot.

The response to 12 Years a Slave *has been astonishing. Are you surprised by the way people have reacted to it?*

It's incredible what can happen with a film like this, but it shows that art can affect the everyday. It's clear that people really have an appetite for this subject and want to engage with challenging stories. I hope they continue to do so. It has been humbling to see this.

Christine Molloy and Joe Lawlor (photo: Ronan Delaney)

Christine Molloy and Joe Lawlor

Over the past decade, Christine Molloy and Joe Lawlor have been contributing to their *Civic Life* project. With co-operation from local community groups, the project involves the production of high-quality short films for the cinema, shot on 35mm CinemaScope and making extensive use of long takes. In 2004, *Who Killed Brown Owl* won the award for Best British Short Film at the Edinburgh International Film Festival. In 2008, *Joy* won the Prix UIP Rotterdam at the International Film Festival Rotterdam.

An expansion of *Joy*, *Helen* (2008) is a hypnotic feature debut. Eighteen-year-old Joy has gone missing. Her college mate, Helen, who is a few weeks away from leaving her care home, is asked to 'play' Joy in a police reconstruction that will retrace the young woman's last known movements. Joy represents all that was missing from Helen's life – she had parents, a boyfriend and a future. Helen gradually immerses herself in the role, and by borrowing elements of Joy's life she begins to bloom. Remarkable for its examination of identity and representation, *Helen* is also distinguished by its casting from within the community in which it was set, as well as its stunning visual aesthetic and use of CinemaScope.

Growing out of their experience while shooting *Tiong Bahru* (2010) in Singapore, the pair's second feature is *Mister John* (2013), a beguiling exploration of identity and desire. Following the mysterious death of his brother, Gerry Devine travels to Singapore to help arrange the funeral and put business affairs in order. There he discovers an intoxicating world, far removed from his troubled life in London. But as Gerry is drawn towards his brother's beautiful wife and the sexual frankness of the local culture, he begins to realise that escape isn't as easy as it seems.

The interview was conducted in writing; the pair chose to submit their answers in unison.

Could you begin by talking about the genesis of Desperate Optimists [the name of their creative partnership] and your initial work in community theatre, experimental performance and online projects?

We both started to work together, in what can broadly be described as community arts, back in the mid-1980s in Dublin. Initially, the kinds of projects we ran were not art form-led. Instead, we allowed the interests of the given community groups we were working with to suggest the art form required. So, for example, some projects required writing to be the focus, whereas others were more visual arts orientated and some navigated towards theatre. The side effect of this is that we developed a very eclectic way of working before eventually specialising in writing and theatre. That said, we guess the art form that has inspired us the most has always been cinema. To our shame, long periods of time can go by now without us ever going to the theatre but we watch films pretty much on a daily basis.

How did this interest in cinema evolve to encompass the production of short films, and how was this production informed by other disciplines?

Because we didn't specialise early on in our various community projects, but instead kept things very open and fluid, we thought nothing of having live or pre-recorded film and video on stage in our subsequent theatre work. We liked sharing the stage with these other art forms and technologies in our live performances. They were a lot of fun to work with in creating more complex and layered approaches to narrative, performance and time. The audience reactions were not always much fun. We made very challenging theatre – maybe too much so. However, we noticed that the more we worked with film and video, the more we en-

joyed the film-making process. We recall on one of our last theatre shows that the moving image component was around 50 per
cent of the live experience. We calculated that it wouldn't be long
before our theatre work would be 100 per cent moving image
and 0 per cent live, and that this could be a real problem for a
paying public intent on seeing a live production. The writing was
on the wall in that sense, and it was an easy decision to make to
stop live theatre work and concentrate on the thing that made
us happiest.

In the late 1990s, when we began to move from theatre into
moving image, the practical reality of limited access to (then)
expensive technology and lack of money directed us to Internet
moving image projects to begin with, before we progressed to
video works and finally to short films on 35mm for cinema. One
of the things about this progression is that we were always interested in what was formally possible in the medium we were
working in. This clearly carries its responsibilities, but we also
enjoyed pushing the boundaries. Cinema, for reasons perhaps
beyond the scope of this response, is quite a conservative form
and one you have to be careful with in terms of how you push it.
That said, we love cinema driven by a formal bravery.

How did Who Killed Brown Owl, *the first film in the* Civic Life
*series, come about, and what decisions shaped your aesthetic ap-
proach and distinct take on narrative?*

The commission came from Enfield Council. Rather than spending the money on fireworks, they wanted to commission a film
project to celebrate the successful completion of the Council's
New River Loop Restoration Project. It was our desire to involve as many local people as possible in the project, and to
this end we held a number of civic meetings and ran a stall at a
local summer fete in an attempt to drum up local involvement.
Mindful that we wanted to avoid the pitfall of producing a tourist board film, we were nonetheless convinced we should strive

for something painterly, beautiful and elegant to match the setting itself – although we did undercut this Arcadian fantasy by lacing the film with a bit of murder, mayhem and dysfunction. Instinctively, we knew that video would never deliver the film that we wanted to produce, but we had no idea, never having worked with film before, if a budget of £20,000 would cover the dramatically cinematic ambitions we were beginning to develop.

There were two things that became clear to us very early on. Firstly, in order for the production budget to work, we would only be able to afford the equipment and crew for one day. Secondly, in order for the post-production budget to work, we would only be able to develop a minimal quantity of stock. The logistical constraints demanded by the limited budget began to force a set of aesthetic decisions on us that very much fell into line with our own desires about how we might 'stage' the film event itself and develop strategies for working with a cast of non-professionals. It became clear very quickly that the 'long take' would provide us with the solution we required, and it is this use of the long take, coupled with the challenge of working with non-actors and minimal rehearsal time, that has resulted in the distinctive approach to narrative and performance of the *Civic Life* series of films. One way or the other, given our background in experimental performance in which the 'liveness' of the event was always foregrounded, we're convinced we would always have been drawn to the long take.

Could you talk a bit about the actual process of going from making shorter pieces to the challenges and logistics of making a feature-length film? How did you find the transition?

To date, we have made nine *Civic Life* short films. All of these films have been made employing more or less the same rules. It was only after we'd completed the final film in the series, and were receiving invitations from festivals to screen all nine films together, that the idea of a *Civic Life* feature film began to take hold. A well-funded commission from the Liverpool Biennial and the Liverpool Culture Company allowed us to experiment with this. The resulting half-hour film, *Daydream*, was shot over four days and provided us with a very tough learning curve. A beautiful but deeply flawed film, *Daydream* provided us with the key to plan our approach to the shooting of a feature film. Indeed, if we hadn't made *Daydream*, we're convinced *Helen* would have been a disaster.

The realities of working with such a perilously low shooting ratio of only 1:3, and having only 30,000 feet of film (equivalent to only 300 minutes of exposed film in the can) from which to extract a 79-minute feature film, meant we had to find some new strategies. At the end of the day, this was always going to be the challenge of translating the *Civic Life* method from a short film to a feature-length film – the need to develop the narrative over time. The long take has always allowed us a tremendous sense of flexibility, enabling us to react on the day regardless of the many variables thrown up by our methodology. For a feature film that is ultimately dramatic in its structure, more has to be pinned down, and no matter how loose, fluid and open we might want to keep things as we are filming, the narrative structure has to work. Understanding how we might use cutaways and sequences that were freed up from serving the demands of the narrative – like the sequences in the woods – was central to making the transition to a feature-length film.

Did you cast from the local community?

Our cast for *Helen* came entirely from within the local community. As with all our *Civic Life* films, by and large, whoever turns up on the day is in the film. The exception to this is how we cast the title role. We knew it would be impossible without a more traditional approach to the casting process. We couldn't just take the first young woman that came our way and give her the part. In fact, we really struggled to get anyone even close to what we needed, and time was very quickly running out.

With only two weeks to go before we were due to begin shooting, we still hadn't found our lead. In the end, it came down to two young women. We were getting nervous, come early October, so much so that we actually approached the agent of a very talented rising star from Dublin and asked if we could arrange an audition. It went against all our desires to consider a professional, experienced actress for the part, but we seemed to have no choice. We liked this young woman very much and might have cast her there and then if we didn't have such thick skin when it came to wanting to do things our way.

We went back to our funders to look for their help, and the NewcastleGateshead Initiative put us in contact with Open Clasp, a local women's group. Annie [Townsend] came to an audition we arranged with them. We specifically recall taking Annie's photo, and the very strong way she had about her as she was being photographed impressed us. She appears vulnerable, but there's an incredible strength there. She also seemed to have a very clear and strong sense of how she wanted to be presented, which wasn't about what she thought we might want from her. We felt she had a very quiet, restrained but compelling presence on film. The Irish actress would have brought a lot of experience to the shoot but it was this quality, this rawness, which we loved in the end. We don't like to over-direct, so we pretty much wanted to let Annie interpret the role the way she felt it should be done. It was an act of faith that we believe paid off in the end. Annie will have to take all the credit for her wonderful performance though. She very much led the way and set the tone.

In many reviews of the film, it is your erring towards understatement and your sense of precision that have been singled out. Was this one of your objectives?

We're not sure exactly why we have arrived at such a particular way of filming and framing scenes, but we suspect that we like to keep the actual technical aspects of what we do very, very simple. For example, if there is a scene between people in a domestic place, we always try to work out the best way to film that scene and leave it at that. The idea of breaking down the shot doesn't come very naturally to us and, to be honest, feels like a very tedious task.

Filming the same scene from a variety of angles fills us with dread. When we've done it, it feels very mechanical and not something that we find interesting. Now this might sound like we're slackers but in reality we very much like cinema that has a certain theatricality to it, and one formal approach that can draw out this theatrical quality is to keep the cutting down to a minimum. Of course, if you're going to be so minimal with your shot list, you have to be very careful and clear about how you're going to set about doing this. Perhaps this is where the sense of precision comes in. In reality, it's probably just the perception of precision, as we don't imagine our methodology is any more precise than someone who likes very fast cutting.

It's hard to imagine the film without Dennis McNulty's ambient score. Had you worked with him before, and what was his brief on this project?

Dennis did a great job. We've known him for several years, since we were all commissioned to represent Ireland at the Bienal de São Paulo in 2004. We got on well and there was no doubt that we would end up working together.

We had asked Dennis to compose music for our short film *Joy*, a companion piece to *Helen*, which went well. His brief for the feature was very simple, but we talked a lot about certain sounds we wanted and the simplicity we were looking for, given the fact that we were also using voice-over in the film. We see *Helen* as a deeply emotional film, with the emotions simmering under the surface. Annie Townsend's performance manages to express that hidden turmoil in a very restrained and subtle way.

So we wanted the music to respond to that quality. We didn't want to force or drive an emotional response from the audience; instead we wanted the film to open up a space for them.

In the end, we worked on the edit almost to the point of locking it without ever introducing the music. We briefed Dennis by giving him a draft edit of the film, by talking to him, by sending responses back and forth and, ultimately, by trusting him to get on with it. The completed mix of the score didn't arrive in the UK until the week of the final Dolby mix. Our feeling was, if the music doesn't work we just won't include it. However, as we lay the tracks on the timeline, we knew that it would.

What was the genesis of Mister John? *Was it always your intention to shoot in Singapore? And what logistical challenges did this bring, or were these negated by your experience of working there previously on your* Civic Life *project* Tiong Bahru?

One thing that is important to us is to find personal relationships to the films we embark upon. Even in situations where it doesn't seem obvious, there is always a personal connection – often a family connection. *Mister John* is no different. The original starting point was Joe's brother. His name is John. He also owns a bar – but in Phuket, Thailand – and is married to a local woman. Since our first visit to Phuket in 1997 we've always been fascinated by John's life there and, like many starting points, you find yourself running with the ball to see how far you get. Sometimes the idea doesn't really sustain itself, but in this case it got stronger the more we developed the script. (We should point out that Joe's brother didn't end up face down in a lake. He is very much alive and happily running his bar, Blarney Stone, with his wife, Kai.)

As we were developing *Mister John* we were also involved in a community film project in Tiong Bahru, Singapore. We hadn't connected one place or project to the other in any way. It was only when our Singapore producer, Fran Borgia, asked if *Mister John* could be set there did we begin to wonder if a rewrite was even possible. An added motivating factor – but not decisive – was that Singapore had a small film fund we could apply to.

As we began the rewrite, we quickly realised that the film might benefit from relocation to Singapore because the country is a less easy place to read than Thailand, which has such strong associations with sex tourism. We felt it might frame the film in an unhelpful way. By contrast, Singapore is a bit of an unknown entity and that really suited the film. It has grown, socially and culturally, out of nowhere over the past hundred years and its identity is still being formed in many ways. This is reflected in the country's film industry, which declined after independence in 1965 and has only recently begun to gather momentum again. One consequence of this is that there isn't the same level of experience there. You have to work that bit harder to get the right crew and cast.

The film's theme of shifting identity is central to your work, specifically the idea of shedding one identity to assume another. What is it about this concept that fascinates you?

We probably need to climb on the psychiatrist's couch to answer this. We're not sure what lies deep in our psychology that draws us, almost unconsciously, to ideas of shifting identities. If we recall our own personal journey from Ireland to the UK in the late 1980s, and from the city (Dublin) to the country (Devon), the idea of the 'outsider' and questions about identity and belonging certainly informed our early theatre work. What has always intrigued us is not only the psychology of this but the potentially playful frameworks offered up by such a device.

This process of transformation contains in its DNA a sort of mystery. The mystery of who we are and perhaps our desire for who we want to be. Or, certainly pertinent to *Mister John*, the question of the identity we want to escape from. It allows characters to step into different worlds, another concept that appeals to us. In *Mister John*, Gerry's entry into his brother's world begins the moment he puts on his dead brother's clothes. Even if he doesn't realise this himself, from that moment everything changes. Sending a character on this kind of journey is something we've always been drawn to.

The film sees you working for the first time with a more established actor in the shape of Aidan Gillen. How did you find this experience, and what were the levels of collaboration in terms of establishing the character of Gerry? Gillen certainly communicates an almost unfathomable sense of sadness.

We had previously spent ten years specifically going out of our way to work with non-actors. So it's true there was a little trepidation about working not only with professional actors but also such established ones as Aidan Gillen and Zoe Tay, who plays Kim and has a big profile in Singapore.

Aidan was our first choice to play Gerry. We sent him an early draft of the script and he came back immediately to say he was interested in playing the part. We then met up to talk about the world of the film, the character and how we saw him. Aidan also had his ideas, and these just expanded upon ours. There were no rehearsals in advance of filming, just a lot of discussion. It is our belief that if the underlying thinking is right, then you have set something quite solid in motion for the days and weeks of actual filming. The music equivalent might be jazz. Our job, in many ways, is to set up a very strong structure into which someone (the actor) can play their role. As long as they are very sensitive to the structure, it will be very hard for them to play the wrong notes.

A strong structure will also, if we're doing our job well, free up an actor to play any given moment the way he/she thinks/ feels it to be right. A strong structure also opens up a space for the unexpected and for accidents. So there were narrative points that may not have been so apparent to Aidan, which he wasn't necessarily working off, that came alive for him when we shot specific scenes. It's nice when there are moments of surprise like that. So it was very much a collaboration.

We wanted Gerry's character to be slippery, as he moved from being himself to being his brother and back to being Gerry again, sometimes in the one scene. We think Aidan manages to pull this off with incredible skill and humanity.

You have established something of a signature relationship with DoP Ole Birkeland. What was the visual aesthetic you were seeking to capture here, and how much was the look of the film influenced by the exotic location in which you worked?

This is an interesting point as it led to a very challenging first week. Unlike *Helen*, *Mister John* was in every way a much more conventional film, in terms of the financing, scheduling, shooting methodology etc. We're not used to this way of working. With our *Civic Life* films and *Helen*, we had honed a much more idiosyncratic style. With *Mister John* we were looking for a challenge visually, and that manifested itself in a more conventional way of shooting, i.e. master shots and then breaking the scenes into mid-shots and close-ups, cutaways etc. We initially relied very heavily on Ole for this. He has much more experience than us in this regard. But by the end of day three we had pretty much worked it out.

As for the look, our approach was to keep it clean. Everything done in camera. Little or nothing to do in post. There was no attempt to 'exoticise' anything. That's just the environment. Our continuing collaboration with Ole working on 35mm film (anamorphic) as opposed to a digital format is a shared vision but the execution is all down to Ole's brilliant work. We're as passionate about film as he is, and felt that in this difficult tropical terrain it was the best and most economical and aesthetically satisfying way to go. Some may raise an eyebrow at the inclusion of the word 'economical' in the previous sentence, but it's true. We keep shooting ratios down very low and the lighting kit very simple. Digital video, even high-end digital video, would have struggled to keep up in the environments we faced, but also there's the more hidden back-end costs that we didn't really incur working with film. To put that into context, lest anyone thinks it's a doddle, it was a methodology and a relationship forged as a result of working on film with Ole for the past ten years. We're very disciplined with that format. We say this mindful of the way things are going in the industry, and that *Mister John* could well be the last film we shoot on film. We'll see.

There is a more pronounced humour at work in Mister John *than we have perhaps previously seen from you. The hostess audition scene conducted by Gerry's brother is priceless. Was the blending of the dramatic and the comedic something that you very much decided you wanted to explore?*

This goes back to the idea of slipperiness again. We recall a meeting with a sales agent. He had read a draft of the script and seemed to quite like it, but also felt he needed to apologise for finding it quite funny, quirky at moments. He wasn't sure exactly how to read it. In a world, and certainly an industry, that likes things (narratives, characters etc.) a little more black and white and a little more on the nose, this ambiguity wasn't necessarily a good thing. That said, we appreciate that this line is often walked by some film-makers. We very much appreciate such qualities in films we admire. The 'hard to pin down' aspect of them. Now, of course, this approach is not exactly going to win you any Oscars, and it certainly scared off that particular sales agent (even if he did like it), but we do think ambiguity is more true to life. Not black and white. Very much in the grey area. In our minds, humour was also present in *Helen* but it was so dark it was very hard for audiences to find. With *Mister*

John we felt it was both time to allow the humour to come out a little more, but also there was something in the material of *Mister John* that naturally allowed for it.

Carol Morley (photo: Paul Marc Mitchell)

Carol Morley

Carol Morley attended Central Saint Martins College of Art and Design, where she studied fine art, film and video. After a series of short films – often exploring girlhood, class and everyday moments, many of them inspired by newspaper articles – she directed *The Alcohol Years* (2000). Although the film initially recounts the film-maker's teenage years, mostly spent partying in Manchester at a time when the Hacienda was at the peak of its popularity, the film ultimately becomes a fascinating portrayal of that era and the many people Morley encountered.

Her first narrative feature, *Edge* (2010), explores the brittle psyches of a small number of characters who find themselves in a lonely coastal hotel in the dead of winter. This atmospheric drama hints at social neglect and marginalisation, themes that appear in much of her work.

Dreams of a Life (2011) is in many ways a breakthrough film. A powerful documentary featuring dramatic recreations, it details the life of Joyce Carol Vincent, whose body was found in her rented flat more than three years after she died. Contacting friends, associates and people involved in the story of her discovery, Morley builds a compassionate, complex portrait of Joyce while never judging those who lost contact with her. It is one of the outstanding British films of the last decade.

The Falling (2014) grew out of Morley's research into mass psychogenic illness, which was itself the starting point for her 2006 short film *The Madness of the Dance*. Set in a repressive girls' school in the late 1960s, *The Falling* is a haunting account of how a wave of hysteria affects a group of girls following a tragedy at the school. Featuring excellent performances by Greta Scacchi and Monica Dolan, as well as newcomers Maisie Williams and Florence Pugh, Morley's film is a mesmerising and unsettling drama that has been likened to *Picnic at Hanging Rock* (1975).

The Alcohol Years is a frank examination of a period in your own life. Did you feel that you had to start with yourself, and what you knew, before exploring other ideas?

At art college I'd been encouraged to tell stories about the world I inhabited. More than that, it was about how you told the stories, the form that you found for them. With *The Alcohol Years*, it started with trying to trace memories of events that had been lost in my memory to booze, but the film soon became about the possibilities of looking at myth-making and the possibilities of creating a portrait of other people in a city known for its pop culture. If I had decided to make a film solely about the music that came out of Manchester during the same period, I think it would have been a narrower overview, though it would have featured many of the same people.

I've always been fascinated by other people, and how we all construct our identities. In asking the people that feature in *The Alcohol Years* about myself, I think their guard was down about themselves, and you could see interesting ideas and feelings emerge that may not have come about if they thought they were talking about themselves. When you have a camera, it can also give you a different persona, one that enables you to ask questions you otherwise wouldn't, and to investigate more. After I made the film, somebody said that most documentaries purport to be about other people but are actually about the director. *The Alcohol Years* does the reverse of that. It seems to be about me but then becomes about the people I speak to. I see it as being in the tradition of Ross McElwee's film *Sherman's March* (1985).

Someone in the film tells me that I'm very manipulative, and I remember my editor saying to me, 'Of course you are, you're a film-maker.' *The Alcohol Years* is certainly the first film I made where I really began to understand the idea of just how powerful it is to be a film-maker and to construct a world. There's also a responsibility when dealing with real people not to judge or demonise them. You have to try to create a world where they can come across as close to the person they think they are, or at least as they are presenting to you.

The Alcohol Years felt like your accepting of the past and moving on. Dreams of a Life *feels in many ways like the start of something.*

There was a sense of real achievement, when I completed *The Alcohol Years*, that I had made something of that messy part of my life. I guess when you revisit a place in your life and you write about it or make a film about it and you make something coherent or structured, you can find it suddenly has value. If you take a disruptive part of your life and refuse to shrink from it, you find you can control it. That's powerful.

Dreams of a Life is an accompaniment to me. It will always be a part of my life, in so many ways. It's weird but I feel like I knew Joyce – there's a sense that sometimes things find you, rather than you going looking for them – and I feel that Joyce found me in order for me to make that film about her. So I guess it will always be an ongoing relationship as I'll never forget her.

Joyce's story mirrors that of characters throughout all your work, particularly female characters, whereby if they deviate too much from what is perceived as normalcy, if they raise their heads too high above the parapets of conventional societal behaviour, they are likely to suffer for it. Even if that means estrangement as opposed to punishment.

I haven't consciously set out to do that. But yes, I guess that's true. Take Muriel Box. This is a key figure in cinema who has pretty much been written out of history. She did so much for film in this country, but at one point her agent said, 'When I say you're a woman director, the film companies are worried about having you on board because of your gender.' This was the 1950s and 1960s. She directed her last film in 1964 and it was a critical disaster. However, in opposition to the film's values, one of her biographers has suggested the film's critical failure may be more to do with the fact that the critical establishment – all the people reviewing the films – were men. She put forward very powerful ideas about women and probably suffered as a result. She was a feminist, her themes were feminist, and she set up the first feminist women's press in this country. But her films were not in themselves made in order to be feminist statements directed to a female audience; she just had things to say to everybody, and about everybody, and the ideas she presented were complex and entertaining, but probably threatening to the status quo.

I am interested in male psychology, but there is a lack of complex female characterisation, so I'm always going to be drawn to that. I didn't necessarily set out with a conscious agenda to do that, but I just find that it's something I need and want to do, and by the very nature of doing that it's something political. You don't want it to be, because it shouldn't be. I don't necessarily look at an image I'm shooting and ask myself how this is going to be perceived in gender terms. But if you give someone the opportunity to tell the stories, then it's going to be from their perspective and they're going tell the stories they want to tell – this is why it's so important ideologically to have a truly diverse range of people making films.

So women being silenced, or women not being seen to have a voice, is definitely a part of what I've been making. And, sadly, it's part of many women's experiences.

Your 'voice' is incredibly strong in your films – the way you are present through other people's recollections of you in The Alcohol Years, *or the passion with which you explore Joyce's story in* Dreams of a Life. *Yet where some film-makers might feel the need to literally be heard throughout their films, talking to camera or being the audible interviewer, you have chosen to remain quiet.*

A voice is generally a commentary in documentaries. I have no desire to impose a narrow viewpoint with my films. If my voice were present in my work, that would be the front line of how an audience would receive my film. I would rather explore the idea that testimony is contradictory. It can be authentic but it can still be at odds with other interpretations. Truth, on the other hand, is a difficult thing to define. Authenticity is more about who someone thinks they are and how they're going to present themselves or their story to you. It's not dishonest. It's just who people are.

If you make a film about a building and have a commentary telling people about it, then the audience's view of the building is filtered through everything they've heard and not necessarily what they've seen and judged for themselves. Now you have the same film but with no commentary and the audience is left to decide the merits of the building. One person may hate the look of the building but another might have lived in it and so there's an emotional response – an engagement that exists beyond what any simple narrative could convey. Obviously, the film-maker's voice still comes through strongly through how they've chosen to film and convey the building, but at least it leaves some space for the audience.

Ultimately, I think I've always avoided voice-over because I want people to place themselves within the film. It's why I never have names of people appearing on the screen. That doesn't happen in fiction films, so why does it have to in documentaries? You're expected to learn about the character as the film progresses in a fiction film. You might not even know their name by the end, but does that really matter when you've gotten to know the person? If using that documentary convention, I would have called Martin in *Dreams of a Life* 'The Boyfriend', but he's much more than that. And there's the fact that using that term in this instance wouldn't have been entirely accurate, and would have fixed his relationship to Joyce in a way that didn't reflect the changing status of it.

This idea of proscribing names or simplistic definitions to individuals becomes an interesting preoccupation within your work, particularly in the context of the way you employ print media. In The Alcohol Years *and* Dreams of a Life, *you also show the vapid way the media dealt with the mystery surrounding Joyce's death. Elsewhere, you employ newspaper stories to highlight patriarchal attitudes and how women are often represented in derogatory terms.*

I collect newspaper cuttings. What I find most interesting are the smaller stories – ones that present a situation in a very factual, superficial way but have no sense of what lies behind the story. These basic newspaper stories are presented so factually they intrigue me. The 'hows' are presented, but never the 'whys'. I am just fascinated by the lives behind those small stories, which is why they have cropped up, particularly in some of the shorts I've made. There's something evocative about them. I guess my work grows out of a fascination with things that really happened – real-life events.

I don't think that I set out to challenge ideas. I set out to tell a story that I think is interesting and important, but along the way I have often encountered problems in telling that story – purely from the point of view of raising money for the idea!

I don't consider myself as a subversive person trying to speak of subversive things, but I do feel I have encountered what you could call a subconscious antagonism towards the films that I'm interested in making. It's then that I am reminded that telling stories, and the form you want to use to tell them, is ideological. Making films is political.

For instance, with *Dreams of a Life* I was faced with questions at different stages over who would actually want to see such a film. Would audiences want to see such a grim story? Could they cope with a form that wasn't a traditional documentary? I wanted to create a unique form for Joyce and her life because I had no desire to wallow in tragedy. I actually tried to compare it to famous films in order to get some traction, and said to some potential backers that I saw it as *Citizen Kane* (1941) – unpacking one person's life from various perspectives. Having been turned down a number of times over many years by many people, it was heartening when the film eventually became financed and to see how audiences engaged so passionately with the film. It just shows that as a film-maker you must never give up on your stories, or your films.

Godard said that the important thing is not to make a political film but to make a film politically. I think that's important. My producer, Cairo Cannon, and I always end up working with a good balance of female crew because it's instinctive, and there are great women available who we make sure we meet, but also we feel we have a responsibility to make films in a certain way and address the balance of the way that films are made and who makes them. I think to be a woman and to make a film is political, no matter what kind of film you make.

From your early short films onwards, your interest seems to lie in humanising stories.

I am interested in heartbreaking stories that can be leavened with humour. Joyce's story has humour in it. She had a wicked sense of humour. Someone might look at a story and say it's very dark, but I think my role is to find the light in there. Finding the poignant and meaningful in everyday life – the struggles we face in life – is what fascinates me. I can't stand poverty-porn films, or something that focuses solely on the abject elements of someone's existence.

Cairo has been your producer since your early short films. How does the collaborative process work between you?

I tend to go off and research in a lot of detail and then start writing. Cairo will read some of it, but at this stage it's mostly a solitary exercise. In order to get anywhere I just have to knuckle down. However, looking at the larger picture, I'm not sure if I could have carried on making films without the support of Cairo, who is working alongside me for most of the journey. Anyone trying to make a film faces a difficult task. So to have someone along-side you from early on, with the conviction that your ideas and writing are sound, is incredibly important. It's easy to get turned on to other things in order to make money. Having someone you constantly work with – who can advise on the direction you're taking, providing a strong partnership and a belief in what you're doing – is essential. Otherwise, you just wouldn't fucking do it.

With Edge, *how easy was the move from fact-based film to fiction?*

We made that film for so little money – around £100,000. It came about because we couldn't get *Dreams of a Life* made. I knew how I wanted to make that film, with the re-enactments, which would cost money, so I decided I wasn't going to shoot it on a small documentary, talking-head budget. We decided to find another project and agreed that we would film the following January. We hooked up with Tyrone Walker-Hebborn, our local cinema owner, and raised the money for the film with him.

I actually find it easier making fiction films, in the sense that I'm not having to feel responsible for real people. With *Edge*, it was getting to grips with the idea of industrial film-making. There's more involved in the process of shooting with a fiction film. That said, I always feel that whenever anyone is in front of the camera, whether they're in a documentary or acting in a fiction film, you're eliciting some kind of performance. So that is exactly the same. The obsession with the image exists in both. And the need to tell stories is also there. Only the methodology differs.

You've approached the themes in The Falling *before, with* The Madness of the Dance. *Was the new film an extension of that project?*

Madness first came about when I was on the phone to a friend and she told me about a village in Africa that had a laughing con-tagion. This fascinated me, so I wanted to investigate more. I then contacted Simon Wessely, a consultant psychiatrist at the Maudsley

Hospital and professor of psychological medicine at King's, who agreed to meet with me. When I arrived at his office I saw these two massive boxes marked 'mass hysteria', nowadays called mass psychogenic illness. They were boxes of articles he had been collecting since the 1970s. He wouldn't let me take them away, but he let me stay for a couple of days to sift through the archive. I found so many cases that weren't documented, especially hysterias set in schools and institutions. That experience didn't just inform *The Madness of the Dance*, it made me realise that one day I just had to make a feature film about mass hysteria, set in a single-sex school.

Every project I embark upon starts with huge amounts of research, which informs how I approach a film as well as how it turns out. What fascinated me with mass psychogenic illness is the collectivity of the experience – a movement in a way – and how at the heart of an outbreak there is usually one influential person that everyone looks up to, often [someone] in personal difficulty. So, with *The Falling*, I wanted to set it in a girls' school and start with a collection of girls and then focus in until I ended up with this one influential person, which was the teenager Lydia, played by Maisie Williams.

While I was developing the film, the events at Le Roy High School in the USA took place, where sixteen girls fainted in a school. Erin Brockovich turned up and said that it was caused by a chemical spill that had happened forty years before – even though it was happening solely to girls. This was a perfect example of how mass psychogenic illnesses are not very well understood.

So *The Falling* grew out of *The Madness of the Dance*, but in all directions, allowing me to explore the structure of family as well as the dynamic of institutions and looking at adolescent girls; that was an in-depth and complex study. They're rebelling against their society while struggling with their sexuality and who they are.

What about the period in which the film is set?

That was down to the fact that mass psychogenic illnesses are always to do with the anxieties of the time, whether it's religious or societal or environmental. In the 1950s it would probably have been atomic in origin. Nowadays it might be contaminated food or chemicals, like in the case of the Le Roy school. I wanted to look at the 1960s because it was a time of sexual anxiety and of women's lives shifting, and ideas around female sexuality were in a state of flux. Many of the mass hysterias that took place during that period were of a sexual nature. I thought that was fascinating because women and sexuality in itself is often seen as really threatening.

I was interested in looking at a 1960s that wasn't swinging, that was inhabited by people still living in a 1950s atmosphere. For the teenagers, the Swinging Sixties was more a state of mind than something they could actively engage in. It was also easier perhaps to set it in a period where there were no technological interruptions! Teenagers today would be on mobile phones and computers, so I like the fact that we stripped away all the interfacing with technology and you're left with a more direct connection to the girls.

It was also important that I didn't make a film that was set when I grew up. I didn't want there to be any sense of nostalgia. I wanted the challenge of creating an atmosphere and landscape that were not familiar to me, and not just draw from my personal experiences.

Outside of the girls, you also explore the subjugation of women generally, as seen in the conversation between Monica Dolan's headmistress and Greta Scacchi's stern teacher, but also with Maxine Peake, Lydia's mother, a based-at-home hairdresser who offers a steady flow of women some cosmetic relief from their repressive lives.

It's 1969, so this older generation would have lived through the war. Maxine's character, Eileen, is agoraphobic – but 'Man' has just landed on the moon and I liked the dramatic irony of this.

It was an age when things were happening in the world, which helped change societies, but for many people that change was a long way off. If you were a middle-aged woman in the 1960s, what you were seeing in terms of change could possibly be seen as threatening. You were seeing what you weren't able to have or do.

There's also the judgement of the young on the old. Greta Scacchi's character – deputy head, Miss Mantel – did have a youth but the girls can't see that, and see her as never having lived. They see her as having a more restricted life than theirs, even though she has a degree of autonomy as a single woman and a schoolteacher. I remember reading somewhere that women often kept the kind of hairstyle from the period in which they felt most happy. Greta's character had kept her old-fashioned hairdo from the one moment of love she had experienced in her life, and there is a sense that all the older women in the film are somehow grappling with their lives and their place in society, and it's not just the young people.

It was interesting to see the photo of you as one half of the band TOT *in* The Alcohol Years, *because the way you dress is not dissimilar to the schoolgirls in* The Falling.

Oh fuck, yeah. I hadn't even thought about that. That's the advantage – or disadvantage – of you having watched all my films within a short space of time. That's really weird. Debby [Turner] and I did the school-uniform thing with TOT. I hadn't made that connection at all, but it shows that you bring things from your life with you into films. For instance, when I was growing up, my Auntie Sally was a hairdresser who worked from home, just like Eileen in *The Falling*.

Do you have an audience in mind when you make a film?

I wanted to create something complex with *The Falling*. A more open-ended approach allows audiences to ask more questions, about what they've seen, about themselves even. When I was writing *The Falling*, I wanted a certain mystery to remain in order for the audience to feel the power of engagement. I had these discussions with Chris Wyatt, the editor on both *The Falling* and *Dreams of a Life*, who has a theory that you only ever complete about 90 per cent of a film and let the audience finish it off – practically to try and not have everything answered and explained. If you allow complexity to thrive within a film, people can bring themselves to it and complete it.

Monica Dolan's school head, Miss Alvaro, is an interesting character. When she first appears she almost seemed cool in her nonchalance as she walked along a corridor. Then we see a shift and she's not that character at all.

It's because she's one of these people threatened by change. By the fact that the rebellion in her school will likely change her life for the worse as far as she's concerned, but also because her chance to be a part of it has long gone. The backstory for the school that I gave Monica was that the school was going to become comprehensive, so she always felt under threat of losing those grammar-school traditions. That was the era when so many schools changed from being grammar. She was railing against those changes, which weren't always for the best, certainly not in her eyes. Also, the idea of characters being seen in different lights at different points in my films is important to me. As Maisie Williams's character Lydia says at one point, we are all three people: the person you think you are, the person other people see, and the person you really are.

Can you talk about the music in your films?

I had the soundtrack for *The Falling* before I had written the script. Not all the songs I originally chose were featured, but most are there somewhere. For instance, the Mary Hopkin track was playing as I wrote. The other songs cropped up in the script as it progressed. I also assigned one song to each character in my mind. It doesn't necessarily work like that in the film, even though the songs are present, but when I was writing it was important to have them be there for someone. I began to understand characters through the songs they listened to.

What music we listen to in many ways defines us beyond words. It shapes our lives and how we live them. When I workshopped the characters with the girls, I would play the tracks. So, later on set, whenever I played the Mary Hopkin track they would cry because they'd associated the song with feelings of sadness. Playing the songs on set is a great way of getting both the cast and the crew in the right mood for filming. The soundtrack also came first on *Dreams of a Life*. Whenever I played Mahalia Jackson, you would get this incredible mood on set. So people can become more closely a part of the film and the story being told.

Tracey Thorn's involvement literally came from a dream I had one night during shooting, where she wrote the music for the film. I tracked her down and she agreed to do the music, which was brilliant. I gave her the instruments that were used by the alternative school orchestra in the film, and she used these instruments for the soundtrack.

With *Edge*, we had no money to license existing music, which is expensive. I had heard Alice Temple and wanted to use her songs, and she was kind enough to give us them. She returned for the closing track of *Dreams of a Life*. As for *The Alcohol Years*, I think Stella Grundy's voice and lyrics work so well, like an additional character.

Music is so important to both me and my work and I love what it brings to a film and how it can help shape it, even in the initial stages. You have to follow your instinct with so many aspects of the process of film-making, and music can really help that instinct surface and remain. What I'm working on next has its origin in a song. Music is not something you impose on the film in the edit, or at the end. It's the beginning for me.

Ben Rivers (*right*) on the set of *Two Years at Sea*
with Jake Williams (photo: Eva Vermandel)

Ben Rivers

Ben Rivers studied fine art at Falmouth School of Art, initially training in sculpture before moving into photography and Super 8 film. After his degree, Rivers taught himself 16mm film-making and hand-processing. His practice as a film-maker treads a line between documentary and fiction, often following and filming people who have in some way separated themselves from society. His raw film footage provides him with a starting point for creating oblique narratives imagining alternative existences in marginal worlds. *Sack Barrow* (2011) and *Slow Action* (2011) are two of his best-known shorter works.

The recipient of the FIPRESCI International Critics Prize at the 68th Venice Film Festival, *Two Years at Sea* (2011) is Rivers's debut feature. Extending the director's relationship with Jake Williams, who he first encountered in *This Is My Land* (2006), the film follows a man who has chosen to live alone in a ramshackle house in the middle of a forest. Jake has a tremendous sense of purpose as he works around the house and surrounding forest and moorland, largely existing on the land and with only an old radio for company.

Rivers's witty and beautifully constructed film creates an intimate connection with an individual who might otherwise be hard to get to know if we met him face to face. A beguiling portrait of a life lived without concession to consumer culture, it weaves an enticing story. Rivers has most recently completed *A Spell to Ward Off the Darkness* (2013), collaborating with Ben Russell.

Two Years at Sea is quite an oblique title. Can you outline its significance?

Two Years at Sea refers to the time Jake spent working for a shipping company, all the while saving his money to buy his dream property. He had been trying to get a group of friends to buy a property together, but he told me it was too difficult to get everyone motivated and come to a shared decision, so he ended up saving for his own place. He was working between Britain and India, where he bought loads of cassette tapes of Indian music, which is what you hear in the film.

In terms of foregrounding, could you explain your relationship with Jake Williams? What is it about him and his way of life that made you want to return to him for a feature-length piece?

This Is My Land was the first in an ongoing series of films I've been making about people living in the wilderness – a way of life I've always been fascinated by. I had been trying to find someone to film since 2005. Knut Hamsun's novel *Pan* sent me to north Norway to try and find a similar character living in isolation, but I couldn't find anyone. My friend then told me about Jake, and that's how *This Is My Land* came about. It was the first film I'd made that employed documentary techniques, filming an actual person in their everyday setting. It was a really important change in my film-making.

After that film, which was very observational, I began to play around the idea of what documentary means, incorporating more levels of construct into my work. Meanwhile, Jake had become a friend, and had also appeared in a road movie I made in 2009 called *I Know Where I'm Going*, where I travelled from London to the Isle of Mull, thinking about a post-human world. When I got the chance to make a feature-length film, it just made sense to go back to him. There was a nice circularity about it and I felt there was more to do at Jake's. *This Is My Land* was just a sketch of sorts.

His life is very inspiring to me and there are seeming contradictions within it that I find exciting; he is very ecologically aware and sensitive, and yet also has all this old machinery around; he really likes that landscape and environment, with its silence and birdsong, but also loves to blast music into the forest. The other crucial reason I went back was because my film-making strategies had changed and I knew I wanted to exaggerate elements of his life – to fictionalise things to an extent. Because we were friends, and Jake had liked *This Is My Land*, I knew he would trust me to make something that didn't reflect badly on his way of life. If I had tried to make this film with someone I didn't know, I think there would've been a much higher level of suspicion.

How did the shoot with Jake unfold in terms of the time you spent together, and how much direction – in terms of how he went about his day-to-day activities – did you give him?

I went up there five times over the course of a year, the first time by myself and then all the other times with sound recordist Chu-Li Shewring. We would spend about ten days there each time, although we weren't always shooting. There's plenty of time to sit around chatting and eating, or helping Jake out with jobs. I didn't have a script, just a list of scenes I had in my head, such as: waking up; shower or bath; caravan; lake/raft; cooking and walking etc. I have images in my mind but these are open to change as soon as I'm looking through the camera. This, to me, is one of the exciting things about film-making – how events can change your preconceived ideas. Each day, I usually had one or two goals, which we would try to achieve, although unexpected things can upset plans, particularly the weather.

Jake was an absolute professional. If I asked him if we could shoot something, he was ready and had no problem repeating things. Almost all the shots in the film are set up and directed, in that we spent a lot of time together and I got a sense of how best to shoot scenes. Then it's a matter of Jake kind of re-enacting himself for the camera, which he can do very naturally. Most action in the film is what he would normally do, apart from some of the more outlandish scenes, like the lake and the caravan up the tree.

It strikes me that an interest in figures who exist in some way outside of society, along with somewhat strange environments, is a recurring motif of your work. What is it about these topics that captures your imagination, and where did these interests first develop?

They began to formulate in my childhood, growing up in a small village in Somerset, next to a wood and a pretty ramshackle farm that's not dissimilar to the one in my film *Ah, Liberty!* (2008). The dichotomy of country and city has always been interesting for me because I enjoy both, and being in one makes me yearn for the other. One of the great things about film-making is that it is a vehicle to go places and meet people. I have enjoyed meeting all the people in my films and want to spend more time around them. The spark is often related to their way of life, in that they are doing things a bit differently, living in the wilderness and often fairly self-sufficient, but without being smug or judgemental towards the way other people live. As with Jake, there is usually a lot of junk and machine detritus around. Coupled with the surrounding landscape, this is an important ingredient for me – the totems of technological society left scattered and degrading, ready to be reused in some unforeseen way, or to disintegrate back into the landscape.

The film continues your tradition of favouring different film stocks and hand-processing. What is it about this approach and the aesthetic effect it produces that appeals?

I think it goes hand in hand with the kinds of spaces I was just talking about – places that are not sanitised. There is roughness, dirt and unpredictability. When I make films I like encouraging different ways of not knowing what the final film will be, and using film can foster serendipity, especially when hand-processing. I always like watching the footage for the first time, sometimes weeks after it was filmed, and seeing how the processing leaves its mark on the material, like watermarks or halos of light around objects caused by using developer too many times. For this film I really wanted to use Plus-X, one of my favourite film stocks, which Kodak announced the discontinuation of just after I began the film.

Two of the most striking elements of Two Years at Sea *are the incredible black-and-white photography and the sense of silence that pervades throughout. What was your thinking in these regards?*

The first time I went to Jake's for the feature I took both black-and-white and colour stock. I shot a bit of both, but it was very clear when I got home and watched the material that the film should be in black and white. There was something about trying to show the world in gradients of grey and not cluttering it up more than necessary with colours. There's enough going on already. I like thinking about the beginnings and ends of things – and humans – and somehow black and white fits with this. The film begins with the white of the snow and the white light of the projector, and ends with Jake's face disappearing into the blackness of the night and the blackness of cinema without light.

I love the silence of being in the middle of an evergreen forest, away from the noise of people. When I'm making a film, I think about sound as much as the images I'm making, so sound doesn't simply illustrate images but tries to get to a deeper sense of space. I'm interested in the idea of immersion in cinema, and sound can achieve this far more effectively than images. If an audience is willing, silence can be very powerful and you can then attune your ear to more subtle occurrences, like when Jake is on the lake. It's really quiet and the distant sound of the grouse becomes an event. I also like disrupting the silence in the same way Jake does, often by blaring out music into the forest, because sometimes silence is oppressive.

The ending also has something immaculate about it. How difficult was it to achieve?

This shot required four takes. That was more than any other. We made four fires and burned four tyres – all very bad for the environment. We had shot three versions, all slightly different in length, and I was getting very black from standing right next to the fire. It was around 2 a.m. and the three of us were feeling tired. As we sat by the dying embers with our whiskies, gradually dropping off to sleep, I suddenly had this urge to do one more take, which turned out to be the right move. That was the take that went into the film. Jake's face looks genuinely tired but also slightly amused. It's one of the most important shots in the film for me – one I had in mind pretty early on. In the end, it's all you need, a long look at Jake's face as it merges with the grain of the film.

As a film-maker whose work is considered to straddle the divide between fiction and documentary, and could be described as coming from a fine art and Artists' Cinema background, how do you feel about your ability to escape some of the rules of film-making and bring your own sensibility to bear on the medium?

Going to art school was a good start in terms of not learning the rules in the first place. I visited some film schools after art school, but when I asked if I'd be able to operate the camera and direct they scoffed. That put me off, so I never went. It seemed better to learn from watching many films of all types, to get a sense of the multitudinous iterations cinema can take, which I did when some friends and I ran a cinema in Brighton. Perhaps, most importantly, simply going into things and making mistakes can be the best way to develop, because sometimes those mistakes become very interesting tools. The collision between different modes of thinking and working always interests me – the spaces in between things.

How did you find the transition from shorter pieces to the feature-length format of Two Years at Sea?

It wasn't a big leap, as my films had been getting steadily longer over the years. The actual process of making a feature wasn't really any different, apart from having a sound recordist there the whole time, which I had only done on one other film. Otherwise, I worked the same way, only I just shot more.

Were you surprised by the fervour around the film? What is it you feel people are responding to? An alternative to the hubbub of modern living?

Perhaps it's that, a little quietness and reflection in times of insanity. Of course, some folk found it a bit slow, but I think when audiences were open to it, to immerse themselves in this world, then it could offer something different to the usual cinema experience, which is so beholden to plot and exposition. My film doesn't stand alone either, there are other examples of contemporary film-makers offering worlds that encourage more imagination on the part of the viewer, so that it's not just about taking in a narrative but asking for the audience to partake in completing the film. I was quite surprised it was released theatrically in the UK. And now it has been released in other countries. A black-and-white film with no dialogue.

Peter Strickland (photo: Marek Szold)

Peter Strickland

Peter Strickland's first feature film, *Katalin Varga* (2009), was made entirely independently over a four-year period. It went on to win many awards, including a Silver Bear at the Berlin International Film Festival and the European Film Academy's Discovery Award.

Prior to this Strickland made a number of short films, including *Bubblegum* (1996) and *A Metaphysical Education* (2004). He also founded the Sonic Catering Band, releasing several records and performing live throughout Europe. The band also released field recordings, sound poetry and modern-classical pieces in very limited vinyl editions.

Berberian Sound Studio (2012) saw him return to film with a very different but no less unique vision. A timid sound engineer, Gilderoy, arrives in Italy to work on a mysterious horror film, mixing bloodcurdling screams with the grotesque sounds of hacked vegetables. But as the onscreen violence seeps into his consciousness, reality and fantasy become blurred and a nightmare begins. Daringly original and masterfully constructed, this homage to 1970s Italian *giallo* horror is a cineaste's fantasy. A devastating assault on the senses, it is quite unlike anything else in recent British cinema.

The Duke of Burgundy (2014) explores the sadomasochistic relationship between two women, with each layer of the meticulously played-out scenarios revealing the true nature of their power games, wherein the sexual and emotional dependence of the characters is not quite so easily defined. At the same time, with co-director Nick Fenton, Strickland made *Björk: Biophilia Live*, a visually dazzling film of the Icelandic singer's end-of-tour concert at Alexandra Palace.

Katalin Varga, your first feature, was made over a four-year period. Can you begin by outlining how the film came about, and how somebody from Reading came to make a feature set in Romania?

I'd been making a nuisance of myself throughout the 1990s, but nobody paid much attention. There were some great times to be had making home movies on Super 8 and various projects with a small group of friends, but I was limited in terms of what I was able to achieve. Some ideas just need money, so when you find yourself with an inheritance from a close relative, you know you'll kick yourself for ever if you do something sensible. My family sold a semi-detached house belonging to my uncle in Aldershot, and my share went straight into the film. Those €30,000 lasted me up until the rough cut. Some very desperate, long and drawn-out times followed, but two Romanian producers, Tudor and Oana Giurgiu, put in the extra funds that allowed me to complete the film.

In terms of making it in Romania, I viewed it as a location first and foremost. However, if you come from Reading you want to get as far away as possible, and that was an undeniable driving force. That town is no place for dreamers and minstrels. I have no problem with people conforming and taking steady jobs, but when they have a problem with you for not wanting the same, that's when you know you're not welcome. I ploughed my way through one office job after another during the 1990s, and if you're stuck typing codes into a computer in sterile, unfriendly offices for several years, it's perfectly logical that you'd want to make a film in the Carpathian Mountains. Reading is somehow there in this film, even if by its absence.

In terms of narrative, the film is structured around fairly traditional themes of redemption and revenge. Why were these themes of such interest to you? And rather than being filtered though an interest in horror, were they more informed by art-house cinema?

It's always hard to say how ideas materialise. This stuff was just swimming around my head and I had to search for the most direct way to communicate that. In hindsight, maybe I was reacting against those inane funding application dictates to be 'groundbreaking' or 'cutting edge'. When there's so much chest-beating going on about having to be a trailblazer, you crave for something traditional, and the whole revenge–redemption thing was just that. Those themes that renew themselves again and again do require a simplicity and directness.

Somehow I felt cheated by other films dealing with those themes because they were so morally one-dimensional, and usually only from the victim's point of view. I wanted to challenge the audience, not by showing how brutal Katalin's assailant is but by how gentle he is, and that really disturbs some people, especially as I'm not wagging my finger. The presence of God is so central to society and folklore in that part of Europe, and if you choose to immerse yourself in that world and those stories, you have to face your own demons regarding justice and forgiveness. What fascinates me is how those themes weave around our faith, doubt and hypocrisy, and never give us answers.

The two main reference points, in terms of atmosphere, for this film were Laughton's *Night of the Hunter* (1955) and Paradjanov's *Shadows of Forgotten Ancestors* (1965). Two quite different films, but I grew up watching double and triple bills at the Scala Cinema in King's Cross in the early nineties and the programming was so askew that, as an impressionable teenager, I never properly discerned between trash and highbrow.

Hilda Péter and Tibor Pálffy are astonishing in the central roles. Both are acclaimed actors in their homeland, but how did you come to cast them, given that you're from the UK? And which particular qualities impressed you?

Hilda and Tibor were both acting in a local theatre in the east Transylvanian town of Sfântu Gheorghe. The scale of what I was doing back then in 2005 was so different. Obviously, I had hopes of making a film and finding an audience, but I still considered it an amateur project. With no disrespect to either Hilda or Tibor, both of whom I regard as modest, hard-working and very talented actors, it was just a case of knowing them through friends, and that was pretty much it. There weren't any casting agents, auditions or anything like that. I met Tibor, I liked his moustache, he liked the script, and I called him eighteen months later when I finally had everything ready for the shoot. I met Hilda, saw her perform in the theatre that night, asked her to do a film with me and she said 'yes'.

The location is essential to the film, with the landscapes inform-ing it as much as the narrative and the characters. How long was the location-scouting process, and how did the Romanian countryside inform the tone and approach you took?

Since the script had already been written, I had to find appropriate locations – and it was always that way round. Márk Györi, the cameraman, joked that you'd have to be totally incompetent to not make a beautiful film in Transylvania. Everything is there, even the thunder. We didn't need set dressers or art directors. However, finding the locations took several years. I started searching in April 2004 and we began shooting in July 2006. I'd have to count the stamps in my passport to tell you how many times I went there prior to shooting.

Once I found a place to shoot in, it was a case of repeatedly going back to get to know people. You can't force your schedule on them and you have to be patient. Things we take for granted in the UK, such as taking someone's phone number to make an arrangement, don't always happen. People can say, 'Just turn up, we'll be here – and if we're not here, we're not here.' You can't expect them to understand the consequences for the film if they're not there. Even when I arranged to visit someone 'high up' in a certain village, I had the wife saying, 'Come back another day, he's drunk.' Drinking is no joke in some of those places and alcohol becomes this malevolent spectre that can grip communities.

The film was selected for competition in Berlin and won a well-deserved prize for Outstanding Achievement in Sound Design. Do you feel that sound design is an underrated aspect of film-making?

I wouldn't say that sound is underrated at all, but maybe misdirected. There is a somewhat bombastic school of thought in which every sound, no matter how discreet, has a degree of horsepower to it, and that has its place with certain kinds of film. However, that kind of method is in danger of becoming generic, even though it's technically very advanced. With this film, we actually did very little regarding effects. It was a case of foregrounding certain background elements, and that alters your sonic perspective. It can be very disorientating and heady, but it barely involves any EQ, reverb or other effects. And it was a standard optical stereo mix due to the budget, but that's all you need. What's the point in 6.1 and all that sub-bass? You can evoke an incredibly wide sense of space with just mono, but ironically it's more expensive to mix in that than in 5.1 since hardly anyone uses mono now. If you listen to film or TV sound from the sixties or seventies – Daphne Oram, Delia Derbyshire, Alan Splet or Bob Bert – the ideas and sounds are just as fresh and relevant, but often done with very rudimentary equipment.

We had a huge amount of material to work with, considering that we started making field recordings in 2004, two years before shooting. A lot of music features in the film, but it's mixed in such a way that it doesn't sound like a hit parade. Often there is no distinction between music and sound design. I've been told about one scene featuring an avian cacophony being the highlight of the film's sound design, but that's a Nurse with Wound 'song' from 1982. Most of the decisions were intuitive and most of the work involved assembling and layering existing material, but it still took time – and after one failed mix we had to start again from scratch.

The score by Steven Stapleton [of Nurse with Wound] and Geoff Cox is similarly impressive. What kind of notes did you give them prior to the composing process?

That score was actually made for a film by Steven's wife, Diana Rogerson, more than a decade prior to *Katalin Varga*. I felt bad pinching someone else's score, but Diana gave me her blessing, as did Steven – and Geoff, when I met him much later. I gained permission very early on, in 2003, and that really helped the writing process.

Only two pieces were specially recorded. Both were by Roj [Stevens], who played keyboards in a band called Broadcast. No notes as such were given to him. I asked Roj to make a traffic report jingle, and for the second piece I called him up and played him a very intense prairie wind howl from *The Texas Chainsaw Massacre* over the phone. I asked him for something like that, but as the phone line between Budapest and Nottingham wasn't so good, he came up with a very different sound. That worked out even better.

Could you talk about how the idea for Berberian Sound Studio *took shape?*

It began as a joke when I made it as a one-minute film with the Bohman Brothers in 2005. Then it came to life again a few years later when I thought about the stories behind some of the *giallo* soundtracks. Some of those soundtracks were very advanced for the time with their use of drone, musique con-crète, free jazz and dissonance. The music of Bruno Maderna, Ennio Morricone and Gruppo di Improvvisazione Nuova Consonanza existed in the same high-art camp as Stockhausen, Cage or AMM, but then these guys were making money on the side composing soundtracks for B-grade horror films.

Berberian Sound Studio came out of that strange, sonic no-man's-land between academia and exploitation. What's interesting about so many of those horror soundtracks, along with their sound design, is that people who turn their noses up at that genre would probably love the music and sound taken out of context. The same goes for people who don't like 'difficult' music – in the context of horror, people *get* Penderecki. I think I remember Stereolab's Tim Gane saying in an interview how the horror genre can warm people up to sonic ideas they wouldn't find palatable in a recorded context. *The Texas Chainsaw Massacre* (1974) is a really good example of phenomenally crafted musique concrète that many people, sadly, wouldn't accept out of its horror context.

The script just swam around that idea, but also incorporating Foley and overdubs. I guess I was attracted by how something unspeakably horrific can be so ridiculous once you take it to a Foley stage. As an audience, you're caught between the sound of a woman being murdered and the sight of a man flapping cabbages. The two things are as far removed as you can get, and I wanted to focus on an innocent man surrounded by colleagues who have been doing this for years and who are completely blasé about the horror they witness.

I also wanted to make something visually quite innocent, but aurally very unpleasant. Perhaps, subconsciously, I was inspired by one or two videos I wasn't allowed to see as a teenager. I could hear the screaming and sound effects from a video my older brother and his friends watched on one occasion. I was too young to watch it, so I just stood outside the door and listened. That probably has a lot to do with how I got to this film.

I don't want to come across too art school, but when you deal with the illusion of violence you're inevitably making a reflexive piece of work that questions both an audience's consumption of it and how film-makers represent it. The main challenge was whether film-makers can responsibly portray violence without sensationalising it. It's a tough question: no matter how high-minded you are as a film-maker in terms of seriously portraying violence, you can't control the interpretation of your images once they reach an audience. In some ways, that's why I respect some of the *giallo* directors. There's an honesty about exploitation. When some directors comment on how they wanted to show how terrible it is when someone is tortured or whatever, it either smacks of bullshit or folly. That kind of hypocritical attitude is shown in the film, but I hope I'm being more satirical than didactic.

Without wishing to detract from the originality of the film, could you talk about some of your interests and inspirations?

In terms of film, the biggest influence was *The Cremator* (1969) by Juraj Herz. Superficially, there is no resemblance, but the way Herz edited some of the scenes in that film was a template for us. I also got into Peter Tscherkassky in a big way. I thought avant-garde film had lost its way in the 1990s, but Tscherkassky came along and completely split the atom. Both structurally and visually, we are paying tribute to those film-makers – or just plainly ripping them off, depending on your point of view.

We also took a few cues from some *giallo* films, but the film within the film fed more off the Gothic horror of Bava's *Black Sunday* (1960) or Argento's *Suspiria* (1977). Music played a big part in how I thought about the film. It goes without saying that Italian horror soundtracks were essential – Morricone, Bruno Nicolai, Riz Ortolani, Stelvio Cipriani, Fabio Frizzi, Claudio Gizzi, Goblin – but there were so many ideas in records by Luc Ferrari, the Bohman Brothers, Cathy Berberian, Katalin Ladik, Jean-Michel Van Schouwburg, Luigi Nono, Jim O'Rourke, Nurse with Wound, Faust, Merzbow, Trevor Wishart, early Whitehouse, early Franco Battiato, and Broadcast, of course. The influence of all that music is felt throughout the film. Even the studio photographs found in some of the Battiato or Gruppo di Improvvisazione Nuova Consonanza albums gave clues to the atmosphere and look of the film.

The design is impeccable. How did you achieve the look and feel of the film?

One of the reasons I wanted to write about analogue sound is because it was so incredibly visual, both in terms of the machinery and the performance aspect of splicing tape and looping it. You look at those old control rooms and they do have a very powerful, otherworldly feel: the racks full of oscillators, filters and oscilloscopes; the tape boxes and dubbing charts. There's a ritualistic and mysterious quality to it all and the film is meant to celebrate that. With digital, there's nothing mysterious about watching someone clicking on their plug-ins.

The studio itself is a composite of different studios I visited in Hungary and the Studio di Fonologia in Milan, where some of the most interesting music happened. Cathy Berberian, Luciano Berio, Bruno Maderna, Marino Zuccheri and Luigi Nono all made incredible stuff there. We threw in a long Luigi Nono sample into the film to make the nod more explicit.

Jennifer Kernke, the production designer, did a great job of assimilating all those influences and making something that took the best bits out of all the studios referenced. The only problem we had was sourcing the equipment. I wanted every piece of equipment in the mixing room to be the same as in the Fonologia studio, but it was a pointless exercise, even if one travelled to Italy. We ended up with some Brüel & Kjaer 1011 oscillators that were faithful to the original rack list compiled by an Italian acquaintance, but stuff like two-ring modulators and the General Radio 1398-A tone burst generator were bloody hard to find. Most of that equipment has disappeared. The curse of digital is that sound engineers now find it acceptable to throw an AEG Telefunken reel-to-reel into a skip.

When it came to the tape boxes and papers, we approached

Julian House. I was familiar with his record designs for Broadcast and other bands, but his own Ghost Box record label had this very arcane sensibility, which was tapping into similar territory. He instantly knew what was needed for the film and often led the way, pushing the design aspect more in the direction it had to go in. He had the idea of coming up with a fake title sequence for the film within the film, which I thought was brilliant. We spoke about the title sequence to *The Cremator* as a loose influence for what he would do, but otherwise he went off and did everything himself. I supplied him with some photos of two Slovak girls screaming, which was a salute of sorts to Herz's home country.

Julian designed the Berberian logo, the tape boxes and the dubbing charts, amongst other things. We could have used existing boxes but thought it better to make up our own brands from scratch, both for Gilderoy's home 'Shears Magnetic' tapes and the Italian studio 'Ventri Fonologia' tapes.

The dubbing charts are there for atmosphere and 'look' as much as information about the process of the film within the film. It took a lot of time to fill them in and it all had to be shot after the main shoot on a special 'paperwork' day several months later. It also took weeks to find the right paper to print Julian's template on, but it paid off. Even though it doesn't matter if one can't follow the charts, it was important for every single number and word to make sense for anyone who would know how to read them. I probably made a mistake somewhere along the line with the numbering, but the intention was there.

There is one abstract score included by a guy called Krisztián Kristóf, which was inspired by the notational scores drawn by Iannis Xenakis and Trevor Wishart. It goes back to the ritualistic aspect of sound-making. You look at these scores and wonder if there is some hidden pagan message within them. You can see why Joe Meek and Graham Bond lost it with black magic.

Sound and music have always been essential to you. Can you talk about your general approach to sound, and also how Broadcast came to be involved in the soundtrack?

The initial temptation with this film was to drench it in all manner of sonic effects and trickery. There would have been creative licence to do that since we're making a film about sound, but it might have been self-defeating. It felt more appropriate to hold the scope of the sound back and focus more on detail and perspective. When you're dealing with tape machines, headphones, loudspeakers and so on, there's a lot of fun to be had in constantly shifting the sonic perspective while remaining completely naturalistic. On one or two occasions we cheated, but as a general rule all the sound in the film, including music, is diegetic. Everything you hear is physically present – coming from a machine, instrument or whatever else is in the room. Since the narrative is a little askew, it's quite important to at least anchor the film in a sonic reality. Nothing comes from a character's head and certainly nothing is laid on the soundtrack by us, the sound team. There isn't a soundtrack as such, and the closest you get to being in Gilderoy's head is when he has his headphones on and we just amplify what's in there. But in general, we tried to be spare with the sound and not overuse effects. What took the most time was making the different sonic perspectives seem believable.

The screams took a lot of time as well, but most of that was done before the shoot. We tried to amass as many screams as we could from friends or some of the cast, and then sent it to various sound men I knew who could make everything more aggressive or abstract. Andrew Liles [sometime member of Nurse with Wound] gave me two CDs filled with treated screams, and after a while it started to mess with my head. I started to see how someone could go bananas listening to this stuff every day. Suzy Kendall – from *The Bird with the Crystal Plumage* (1970), *Torso* (1973) and *Spasmo* (1974) – came in to scream for the film and told me some very funny stories about her *giallo* days. She did all the screams for *The Bird with the Crystal Plumage*, so it felt like a blessing to have her with us.

Broadcast were my only choice for this film. They used to talk about Basil Kirchin and Bruno Nicolai in interviews – and just from those two names, all I had to do was join the dots. They knew all the influences inside out and had a way of summoning that sound from the past without falling into pastiche. Their former keyboardist, Roj, did some sounds for *Katalin Varga*, so he put me in touch with Trish [Keenan] and James [Cargill] around September 2009, but it wasn't until 2010 that we started to properly talk about the soundtrack and what should and shouldn't be done. I started off by talking about the more obvious references, but they quickly got me on the right track by playing me very obscure but beautiful records from that period. A few tracks were sent in advance of the shoot, but most of the music came in during the edit period. And it was a back-and-forth process right up until the very last day of sound mixing, but everything mostly took shape during the edit with Chris Dickens.

Speaking purely as a fan of the band, Trish's passing is a huge loss. It's not an overstatement to say that she was one of the most remarkably gifted musicians of my generation.

This is the first time you've worked with a 'star', in the form of Toby Jones. How was the experience, both for yourself and for Toby? He has an eclectic CV, but nothing he has done before approaches this.

Toby fully immersed himself in the character and got there pretty quickly in terms of the stillness within Gilderoy. It's a very hard thing to carry a film yet remain believably nondescript, but he pulled it off very well. He's not a broad-stroke actor. He did small things that I barely noticed on set, but when you see them on the big screen those little gestures reveal a whole inner life. He had already done a radio play that involved Foley, so this wasn't too unfamiliar for him.

As with anyone you work with, you have your good days and bad days, but that's not a big deal. In hindsight, I probably should've spent more time talking to Toby and the other actors rather than constantly trying to get the correct wave pattern on the oscilloscope. It doesn't matter now. On screen, Toby is more Gilderoy than the Gilderoy I initially had in my head, so I have nothing but praise for him.

I was intrigued by the device of the letters from home. It hints at a world beyond what we see on screen, and a strange relationship between the Toby Jones character and his mother.

The letters are an extension of the film within the film idea, in that once again you are denied the sight of that other world, but this time, instead of extreme horror, it's the tranquillity of Gilderoy's back garden in Dorking – which you only see once, in a photograph. The letters are there to set up Gilderoy's world, but also to offer clues to later scenes. Both the letters and Gilderoy's home recordings start to intersect with the horror film, but there's a loneliness and silence there for me that puts the whole film within the right frame.

Gilderoy himself is a composite of a few people I know, but he also harks back to the days of the garden-shed sound eccentric. I had this romantic idea of the artisan sound eccentric working away in the garden shed. Even if they didn't work in sheds, you can imagine that could be the only place where Vernon Elliott [British bassoonist, conductor and composer] or Desmond Leslie [film-maker, writer and musician] made their recordings.

I don't know why I chose Dorking. I just imagined there'd be many garden sheds there. The more I visited the town, the more it became the only place where Gilderoy could've come from. There were a few very pleasant moments of synchronicity there. The weirdest thing was when I went to photograph a garden shed. After making a few calls in Dorking, I found this man who agreed to have his shed photographed for the film. And after telling him a little about the film, it turned out he was a fan of the Ghost Box label, which made me feel it was right to make the effort rather than sourcing a shed image online.

What attracted you about the Biophilia *project?*

Initially, I'd never even thought about directing a concert film, which is strange, since I attempted both pop videos and commercials – mostly in vain. The producer, Jacqui Edenbrow, informed me that Björk was looking for someone to direct a concert film and it gradually progressed from there. There was a great appeal in working with someone as singular as Björk, but also it made sense to be a tailor for someone else's vision for a change. It can be exhausting pursuing what's inside your head all the time, and after *Berberian Sound Studio* I needed some fresh air. It was refreshing to step back and attempt to put myself in someone else's head – and if you have to put on a different head, it might as well be Björk's.

Can you talk about the challenges of shooting a conceptual concert film?

The basic stage set-up itself was an obstacle. It was in the round, which instantly meant sixteen cameras were needed. Placing them is a balancing act, as you want the best shot but don't want to disturb the audience or musicians. I was lucky to have a great team with vast experience. Jacqui Edenbrow had produced several concert films. Brett Turnbull has been shooting concert films for years, since his Test Dept days. Nick Fenton, the co-director, has edited several concert films too, so I was in exceptionally good hands. I'd be the first to admit how inexperienced I was. Finding archive footage to illustrate and bring to life Björk's lyrics and sonic textures was very time-consuming. You could spend at least a year going through archives, and again we had help in narrowing down the available footage based on our notes. But even when you have the footage, there is the task of finding those rabbit holes in the edit to incorporate it. The biggest personal challenge was in *Biophilia* clashing with production on *The Duke of Burgundy*. I remember flying to Hungary the morning after the *Biophilia* concert to prepare for the *Duke* shoot, and ever since then both films have shadowed each other, from post-production to actual screenings. Luckily, Nick took a huge load off my back while I worked on the *Duke* edit. He was on his own in the edit room a lot of the time, and all I could do was send notes or call him, based on each cut I'd receive from him. We spent some time together, but not enough. However, he's someone I trust immensely and some of my favourite moments in the film come from him.

What is the genesis – and the influences – behind The Duke of Burgundy?

Andy Starke, the producer, and I first spoke about remaking Jess Franco's *Lorna the Exorcist* (1974), but that idea didn't last long. However, there was something in making a film in the spirit of early 1970s Franco. I wanted to reinterpret elements from what has certainly been an overlooked, disreputable genre. Franco's films were a starting point to explore sadomasochism, which he dealt with a lot, but usually in a manner that embodied either a masochistic or sadistic fantasy, or both. As far as I know, I'm not familiar with a film that punctures that fantasy and presents the impracticalities of living out those desires, but more importantly how compromise can be reached between two lovers with different sexual needs. I'm not an agony aunt, but my guess would be that many couples are not sexually in synch, regardless of how relatively common or rare the desires are. There is an accepted compromise involved in which one person represses desire or the other person indulges a desire to keep the lover happy, which is part of any give and take in a relationship. But what happens when one person wants it their way all the time and the other is simply tired of putting on a persona for their lover? What fascinates me about that kind of ritual is how much it mirrors directing and acting, and I tried to play with that analogy.

Franco was definitely an influence, along with the films of Walerian Borowczyk, Jean Rollin, Just Jaeckin, Tinto Brass, Radley Metzger and Alain Robbe-Grillet. Some of those sexploitation films can be pretty hideous, but there is always something interesting to be found, even in the bad or repellent examples. What's interesting about them is that they only had to tick the sex box to keep the producers happy. Once there were enough titillating scenes in there, the directors were free to do what they wanted. They often abandoned all logic, and that's when it gets really interesting – sometimes even inadvertently poetic. Some of Franco's more fantastical early-1970s films are unlike anything else and evoke a wonderfully askew dream logic. They're just these very odd little portals that are hidden behind closed doors in world cinema. Franco was a cinematic outlaw.

However, all this was just a starting point and perhaps only a tonal influence for what is, I hope, a very different and tender film about the lengths lovers go to in order to keep each other happy. There were plenty of other influences such as Fassbinder, Douglas Sirk and, very specifically, Claude Chabrol's *Les Biches* (1968). In my mind, it's more of a melodrama than anything else.

It's a fascinating film in terms of sexual politics. Do you see it as overtly provocative, or do you regard it more as a study of a singular relationship?

I see the film as presenting niche desires to an audience who most likely won't relate to what they see, but hopefully by the end they see enough of themselves, or at least their struggles, in what might superficially be a polar opposite. From what I've seen in films, sadomasochism is often dressed up in an insular, sensational manner, both narratively and stylistically. I tried to avoid all the usual clichés but, more importantly, hint at the relative normality of it all, both within the world of Evelyn and Cynthia but also in the wider world, where there are waiting lists for bondage beds. It is absurd, but by normalising it you are inviting an audience to work harder at exploring the dynamics of the relationship, rather than writing the couple off as odd.

The highs and lows they experience are universal. The urination scene tends to provoke comment, but what's important is not the specific act but the manner in which somebody is asked continuously to do something for someone else that, at best, they have no interest in. As far as I know, water sports are not on the curriculum for most lovers, but you could replace that sexual act with something far more commonly practised or nondescript and you would find the same issues, if one lover had to do something they were not turned on by. What I like about the scene in which Cynthia urinates in Evelyn's mouth is that when you see it for the first time you understandably feel sorry for Evelyn, but after more is revealed about the dynamic between the characters you feel sorry for Cynthia the second time you see it.

What I found frustrating in other films exploring wayward desires was the psychology. Too often there is a backstory about something or other that happened during childhood. I'm not interested in that. I'm not interested in why Evelyn is a masochist, in the same way that I'm not interested in why Rocky Balboa is straight. What matters is how harmony or compromise can be reached with conflicting sexual desires. If you're getting into the arena of paraphilia or anything non-consensual, then that's a very different subject that this film doesn't deal with, but in my mind Evelyn and Cynthia are consenting lovers, only the line between consent and compromise is a little blurred on occasion, as it is with most couples.

Can you talk about the locations and the visual style you adopted?

We shot the film in Hungary, but it was important not to make the film specific to a country or time period. Hungary was chosen for convenience, as I spend a lot of time there and know people, but also because of its architecture and general ambience. Based on the architecture, it's often hard to pinpoint exactly where in Europe it is.

The first draft was relatively realistic and the characters had jobs rather than hobbies, but I found the social element got in the way. It was more effective to make the film absurd on a social and work level. It became a fable by the third draft, and then it became a matter of dressing that for the film. The main house we shot in was a derelict, stinky mess. Pater Sparrow and his team had to dress it from scratch and on a very low budget, but it was amazing how they could cheat things, such as stickers placed against the filthy tiles in the bathroom, and so on. For the more heightened scenes, when Evelyn is under her sexual spell, Nic Knowland [the cinematographer] tried to use mirrors and bevels, often with two pieces attached at different angles in front of the lens or pointing into a mirror. That allowed us to create in-camera superimpositions, which we worked through by trial and error. In general, we tried to find a heightened and tactile visual language that was quite languorous.

Sound once again plays such an important role in the film – far more complex than in most films. How early do you start to map out the layers of sound, and how much do they impact both the writing of the script and the shooting?

It all depends on the script. The only script that had the audio almost fully incorporated into the writing was *Berberian Sound Studio*, for obvious reasons. But even that changed during the sound mix. In all scripts, some scenes or sequences are either written with a specific piece of music or sound in mind, such as the suicide scene in *Katalin Varga* or the scream pull-back zoom in *Berberian*. However, a lot either falls apart or comes together during the sound mix. After *Berberian*, I wanted to make a much quieter film, and it's important not to draw too much attention to the sound if the subject isn't relevant to it. That's all I try to do in a sense – serve the subject or atmosphere of the film. There was a sensuality and decadence I wanted to evoke for *The Duke of Burgundy*, but hardly any audio indications were in the script. I think the only thing planned in advance was the Michael Prime recording for the moth sequence, which I had heard years ago.

The Duke of Burgundy was the first of my films in which the majority of sound was worked out only during the mix. We tried our hardest to be quietly sensual with this, a few anxious sequences excepted. A lot of the work was in taking sounds away. If you look at the WAV files in ProTools it's fairly barren, but that just makes each sound stand out more – and it's how you pair separate elements up, which hopefully gives a flavour to the film. I try as hard as possible to avoid library sounds for films and try to get as much as possible on set, or I approach field recordists for private audio. So, in a sense, the sound mix is more about compiling all manner of different elements in such a way that serves the subject matter. It is tempting to try something audacious during the sound mix, but that feels gratuitous unless the subject matter warrants it, as it did in *Berberian*.

Ben Wheatley (photo: Rook Films)

Ben Wheatley

Brighton-based film-maker Ben Wheatley is undoubtedly one of the most singular talents to emerge in recent British cinema. Incredibly productive and able to work within the confines of a minimal budget, Wheatley's films, made in collaboration with his partner, Amy Jump, are characterised by their rippling undercurrent of menace and distinctly off-kilter take on the British landscape.

His debut, *Down Terrace* (2009), went largely unseen on release but has steadily grown in stature. Taking the best elements of *The Sopranos* and giving them a very British twist, the film focuses on the kind of issues faced by all families, such as who grassed up son Karl to the local police, how will dad explain the recent profit drop to his bosses in London, can Uncle Eric dispose of a body without making a mess of it again, and what should mum make for tea? A British crime drama laced with blacker-than-black humour, *Down Terrace* also boasts inventive special effects, many of which were executed by the director himself.

Kill List (2011) made more of an instant impression. Eight months after a disastrous job in Kiev left him physically and mentally scarred, an ex-soldier turned contract killer is pressured by his colleague into taking a new assignment. As they descend into the dark and disturbing world of the contract, things begin to unravel. Described by Wheatley as an attempt to make a genuinely scary horror film, *Kill List* is incredibly disturbing. From the very first frame it unsettles with a sense of foreboding as it explores the darker areas of the human psyche.

Sightseers (2012) could be seen as *Carry On Camping* (1969) for psychopaths. Two new lovers journey across the

British Isles in their caravan, visiting the Crich Tramway Museum, the Ribblehead Viaduct and the Cumberland Pencil Museum in Keswick. Along the way they discover a shared disdain for dog owners, litterbugs and other caravan owners. Unlikely to be promoted by the British Tourist Board, the film presents a disconcerting picture of the British country-side.

A Field in England (2013) unfolds during the English Civil War and is perhaps the director's most fully realised work. A small group of deserters flees a raging battle through an overgrown field. They are captured by two men, one of them an alchemist who forces the group to aid him in unearth-ing a hidden treasure. All hell soon breaks loose as the film transforms into a psychedelic trip into magic and madness. *A Field in England* became the first UK film to be released simultaneously in cinemas, on DVD and Blu-ray, and on Film4 and VoD.

Wheatley also directed the inaugural outing of Peter Capaldi as Doctor Who, and is currently preparing an adaptation of J. G. Ballard's *High Rise*.

With Down Terrace, Kill List *and* Sightseers, *you take a unique view of Britain. You have an uncanny ability to make even its more mundane qualities seem strange and threatening.*

I work with what I see from where I am. I think we all have unique views in that respect. I guess it's in my nature, and the rest of the cast and crew, if I can speak for them, also have a bit of a bleak outlook.

I'm finding that you spend a lot of time planning what's in your work, but there are other meanings that slip in that reveal a lot about your character, which you might never have consid-ered, or wanted to keep hidden.

A Field in England *is your first period film. What challenges did this present, given your relatively limited budget? And what levels of research did you and Amy undertake? Was authenticity key to you?*

We researched the period but we're not historians. Authenticity was important and we came to the project from the point of view of wanting to do it justice. I appreciate that we may have made errors here and there, but we approached the material with respect and didn't change things just to suit the story. The budget didn't really affect the film-making. The script and budget level were developed hand in hand. A field, costumes for the characters, a tent – there's not a lot else needed to tell this tale.

What factors influenced your decision to shoot in black and white?

Black and white is beautiful. It's about texture rather than chroma – about the lines in the actors' faces as opposed to the colour of the sky. And, of course, it's in the past. They didn't have colour film in the past.

You have previously said that you've always wanted to make a horror film because you find so few of them to be actually scary. What aspects of the genre, if any, did you particularly draw on for A Field in England? *Though not a straight horror as such, it reminded me of the work of Michael Reeves.*

We were thinking about *Culloden* (1964), *Winstanley* (1976) and *Onibaba* (1964) in the early stages of development. We weren't thinking specifically about genre. I was happy when we were shooting the end of the film that it seemed to be like a cowboy film, and that Reece [Shearsmith] began to look like a refugee from a Jodorowsky movie.

I don't tend to think about other films that much, to be honest. If influences do come, they come in from the edges and we notice afterwards. Michael Reeves's *Witchfinder General* (1968) is set in a similar period, but I can't say it was a major influence. They do wear similar hats!

The film sees you working again with Michael Smiley, who featured in Down Terrace *and* Kill List. *His performance is full of menace and intrigue. As he's a natural performer, did you allow him to contribute a great deal to the character, or was his part very tightly scripted?*

This is the first film I've made that has no improvisation in it. We shot the script and in the edit maybe dropped a handful of lines. It's the clearest script-to-screen experience I've had. Having said that, the performances were free in themselves. Working with a cast like this, it's not really my job to tell them what to do. I'm there just to nudge them.

Reece Shearsmith is best known for his work on The League of Gentleman, *but he really impresses here in a more dramatic role.*

I love *The League of Gentlemen*. I remember it took me a long time to realise that there were only three of them performing in it – Reece especially is very hard to spot. He inhabits each role so totally. Michael Smiley introduced him to me. They had both been in *Burke and Hare* (2010).

We had him in mind for something, but we weren't quite sure what. Then Amy [Jump] wrote the Whitehead part specifically for him and we were away.

You blend the comic and the horrific seamlessly in your films.

I don't find it so hard, but then that probably says more about me than anything else. My attitude to violence on screen is generally to be true to it. Show emotion, show humour, show violence. Don't hide it from the audience.

Paul Wright (photo: Annika Summerson)

Paul Wright

While still studying at Glasgow's Royal Scottish Academy of
Music and Drama, Paul Wright won the Scottish BAFTA for Best
New Work for his short film *Hikikomori* (2007). His 2009 short
Believe, made while he was at the National Film and Television
School, won the Locarno Film Festival's Golden Leopard for Best
International Short. *Photos of God* was selected for the Berlin
International Film Festival in 2010, and in 2011 *Until the River
Runs Red* won the BAFTA for Best Short Film.

Wright's debut feature, *For Those in Peril* (2013), employs a
visual style that will be familiar to anyone who has seen his short
films. It tells the story of a lone survivor of a fishing accident who
has to live among the families and friends of the dead. Unable
to cope with the loss of his brother, Aaron becomes increasingly withdrawn from society, further alienating himself from the
people who resent his respite from death. Finding a balance between myth and reality, Wright's film is a remarkably assured
drama, aided in no small part by George MacKay's breakthrough
performance and the director's eye for stunning imagery.

What was the genesis of For Those in Peril?

I graduated from the NFTS and was fortunate enough for my
short films to have done pretty well. The BFI, Film4 and Creative
Scotland were aware of my work, as were Warp Films. I was
pretty lucky in terms of timing, because as I was embarking on
the idea of a feature, Warp had a scheme called Warp X. They
thought I might be a good fit for it and so, having liked my short
films, they put together a deal really quickly.

As for the idea itself, I grew up in similar surroundings – a
small fishing village on the Scottish coast. I lived about fifty yards

from the sea. It was always present on a sensory level. If you couldn't see it, you could always hear it everywhere you went. I spent so much time on the beach, playing with friends, no matter the weather – but especially in bad weather. There were always stories concerning the sea, with the inherent dangers and myths surrounding it. The mystery of it really interested me.

That fascination increased when I started to take an interest in photography and film. There wasn't any kind of film culture up there, so it was mostly me, with a camera, down on the beach filming some abstract images of the water.

I also lost my father when I was young. I was old enough to know about death but I guess I was too young to completely accept it. That was where the grief element comes into the narrative.

Were you inspired by actual events, or did it emerge from your experience of that world and an attempt to capture the nuances of life there?

It was more a desire to explore a drama in this small community than any reference to actual events. There were always fishing accidents happening all around the east coast of Scotland – it's one of the most dangerous jobs in the world. I wasn't touched by any specific incident as a young boy though.

I was also fascinated with the idea of the one person who survived and came back, and the mixed emotions of being a survivor – not only for that person but also the friends and relatives of those who died, who he was going to have to live among. That was really the catalyst for the film.

The texture of the sea plays an incredibly important role in the film. So much so that it feels as important a character as any of the people in the narrative.

It was always the idea to have the sea as a character in itself and to have it change throughout. We not only wanted to play with the way it looked, but to alter the sound of it, depending on the mood of a scene. It adds to the psychology of the film and enhances Aaron's story.

You mentioned the myths that were evoked when you were growing up. The film blurs the lines between myth, folklore and reality, culminating in the film's final sequence.

I'm fascinated by film featuring fragments that leave you wondering what's real from what's imagined. Telling a story from such a subjective viewpoint gives you a palette to play with that magnifies those elements. There's also a blurring of memories and nightmares, as well as what's imagined and witnessed in the waking hours of the day. The place between all those things is what interests me. In a way, it's more true to life. You go about your day but memories or thoughts flood your mind all the time.

It's refreshing to watch a film about a small community that doesn't imbue it with some supernatural quality. We're a long way from The Wicker Man *here.*

Absolutely. I love *The Wicker Man* but I wanted to find some grounding in reality, so that when you take a step out of that the effect is more powerful.

So much of the film is comprised of fragments: did the writing develop that way or was it written with a sense of linearity?

I started at the end. The image of Aaron on the boat and the scene on the beach were what came to me first. Once I had those, I began to question how these came into being and sort of worked backwards. It might not be the usual way of doing things but it worked in this case.

I had a list of so many moments, and it was a case of figuring out in what order these should go so that I would end up with a rounded story that featured a recognisable beginning, middle and end.

I wonder if this approach is what reinforces the sense throughout the film that Aaron's fate is already sealed.

If this were a Disney film, I guess it would be along the lines of 'The Boy Who Turned into a Fish.' My challenge was to ground a story in reality that would somehow, eventually, reach that point. It's odd that something so outlandish should allow me to work out how I could engage with the character of Aaron and the villagers in a realistic way.

George MacKay is stunning as Aaron.

He is. George sent in a tape to us. We had already seen a lot of potential Aarons, but as soon as we saw him on film we became really excited. He got what I was aiming for straightaway. We clicked instantly and were fortunate enough to have a few days before we began filming to go through the script scene by scene, discussing what we wanted to achieve and mapping the character's journey throughout. That was invaluable, because when it came to shooting we didn't have much time. However, by that point we had developed this shorthand and George got a sense of what I was looking for each time we began to film. George made Aaron his own, and as a result I think Aaron became something far stronger than he was on the page.

At its heart, the film seems to be about the bond between Aaron and his brother.

It's a strange love story in a way – between the brothers. But it's a love story in which one of the players is pretty much absent for the whole of the film. It's only with their coming together at the end that we see this bond. At the same time, we get a sense from what other people say that they didn't always get along, so we begin to see a darker side to that relationship, albeit tempered by Aaron's unconditional love.

This also extends into an exploration of a particular kind of masculinity. This is a tough industry populated by men's men. So it's interesting to see someone in that environment who doesn't quite fit in.

You challenge any kind of stereotyping of masculinity in this community. There's the man Aaron speaks to in the pub, who is outraged that all he's doing is asking for a job and not enquiring how he and his wife have been since the death of their son. And Michael Smiley's character might be a bruiser, but at the same time we can understand his concerns about Aaron seeing his daughter.

Knowing a community like this – they're the best people in the world – it was always about dealing with the impact of the accident and the way that Aaron behaves. In both those scenes it's Aaron who provokes them and they fight back. But in doing so, we see the pain they feel and what they will do to protect their families.

Like the visuals, the sound design of the film is incredibly complex.

A lot of the sound ideas were in the early drafts, and as I went along I developed it. When I first began studying film at the first film school I attended, in Glasgow, my initial role was as an editor. I've always been fascinated by the interaction between images and sound, and how they can be manipulated in tandem to draw out an emotion from the audience.

There was always something on every second or third line of the script that described how the sound should be. The way that we employed different kinds of film, affecting the graininess of the film or the different format that allowed certain images to be more expressionistic, more dreamlike, that's also what we did with the sound – to enhance that effect. It goes for the way that we employed the music too. It builds towards a crescendo towards the end of the film, but it's important from the beginning.

The songs in the film, from Kate Dickie's performance to the communal singing, echo the early films of Terence Davies, who would employ songs and people singing them to emphasise the notion of community and a shared spirit in hard times.

That sense of community spirit was what we were looking for. Also, the heightened nature of some of the music was something that helped blur the line between reality and an otherworldliness. It hinted at something more. Erik [Enocksson, the composer] was great, because his music has a sense of familiarity while also elevating certain moments to an almost spiritual level. That was something we wanted to achieve throughout the whole film.

Director filmographies (features only)

Lenny Abrahamson

Adam & Paul
Ireland 2004, 83 mins
Writer: Mark O'Halloran. Producer: Jonny Speers. Director of Photography: James Mather. Editor: Isobel Stephenson. Music: Stephen Rennicks.
Starring: Tom Murphy, Mark O'Halloran, Mary Murray, Anthony Morris.

Garage
Ireland 2007, 85 mins
Writer: Mark O'Halloran. Producer: Ed Guiney. Director of Photography: Peter Robertson. Editor: Isobel Stephenson. Music: Stephen Rennicks.
Starring: Pat Shortt, John Keogh, George Costigan, Anne-Marie Duff, Conor Ryan.

What Richard Did
Ireland 2012, 88 mins
Writer: Malcolm Campbell (based on the novel *Bad Day in Blackrock* by Kevin Power). Producer: Ed Guiney. Director of Photography: David Grennan. Editor: Nathan Nugent. Music: Stephen Rennicks.
Starring: Jack Reynor, Róisín Murphy, Sam Keeley, Lars Mikkelsen, Fionn Walton.

Frank
UK, Ireland 2014, 95 mins
Writers: Jon Ronson, Peter Straughan. Producers: David Barron, Ed Guiney, Stevie Lee, Andrew Lowe. Director of Photography: James Mather. Editor: Nathan Nugent. Music: Stephen Rennicks.
Starring: Domhnall Gleeson, Michael Fassbender, Maggie Gyllenhaal, Scoot McNairy, François Civil, Carla Azar.

Hossein Amini

The Two Faces of January
UK, France, US 2014, 96 mins
Writer: Hossein Amini (based on Patricia Highsmith's novel). Producers:
Tim Bevan, Eric Fellner, Robyn Slovo, Tom Sternberg. Director of
Photography: Marcel Zyskind. Editors: Nicolas Chaudeurge, Jon
Harris. Music: Alberto Iglesias.
Starring: Viggo Mortensen, Kirsten Dunst, Oscar Isaac, Daisy Bevan.

Amma Asante

A Way of Life
UK 2004, 91 mins
Writer: Amma Asante. Producers: Patrick Cassavetti, Peter Edwards,
Charlie Hanson. Director of Photography: Ian Wilson. Editors: Clare
Douglas, Steve Singleton. Music: David Gray.
Starring: Stephanie James, Brenda Blethyn, Gary Sheppeard, Oliver
Haden, Nathan Jones.

Belle
UK 2013, 104 mins
Writers: Misan Sagay, Amma Asante. Producers: Damian Jones, Robert
Norris, Jane Robertson. Director of Photography: Ben Smithard.
Editors: Victoria Boydell, Pia Di Ciaula. Music: Rachel Portman.
Starring: Gugu Mbatha-Raw, Tom Wilkinson, Sarah Gadon, Sam Reid,
Emily Watson.

Richard Ayoade

Submarine
UK, US 2010, 97 mins
Writer: Richard Ayoade (based on Joe Dunthorne's novel). Producers:
Mary Burke, Mark Herbert, Andy Stebbing. Director of Photography:
Erik Wilson. Editors: Chris Dickens, Nick Fenton. Music: Andrew
Hewitt.
Starring: Craig Roberts, Yasmin Paige, Noah Taylor, Sally Hawkins,
Paddy Considine.

The Double
UK 2013, 93 mins

Writers: Richard Ayoade, Avi Korine (based on Fyodor Dostoevsky's novel). Producers: Amina Dasmal, Robin C. Fox, Andy Stebbing. Director of Photography: Erik Wilson. Editors: Chris Dickens, Nick Fenton. Music: Andrew Hewitt.
Starring: Jesse Eisenberg, Mia Wasikowska, Wallace Shawn, Yasmin Paige.

Clio Barnard

The Arbor
UK 2010, 94 mins
Writer: Clio Barnard. Producer: Tracy O'Riordan. Director of Photography: Ole Bratt Birkeland. Editors: Nick Fenton, Daniel Goddard. Music: Harry Escott, Molly Nyman.
Starring: Manjinder Virk, Christine Bottomley, Monica Dolan, Neil Dudgeon.

The Selfish Giant
UK 2013, 87 mins
Writer: Clio Barnard. Producer: Tracy O'Riordan. Director of Photography: Mike Eley. Editor: Nick Fenton. Music: Harry Escott.
Starring: Conner Chapman, Shaun Thomas, Sean Gilder, Steve Evets, Lorraine Ashbourne.

Yann Demange

'71
UK 2014, 99 mins
Writer: Gregory Burke. Producers: Robin Gutch, Angus Lamont. Director of Photography: Tat Radcliffe. Editor: Chris Wyatt. Music: David Holmes.
Starring: Jack O'Connell, Sean Harris, Sam Reid, Charlie Murphy, Killian Scott, David Wilmot.

Iain Forsyth and Jane Pollard

20,000 Days on Earth
UK 2014, 97 mins
Writers: Nick Cave, Iain Forsyth, Jane Pollard. Producer: James Wilson. Director of Photography: Erik Wilson. Editor: Jonathan Amos. Music: Nick Cave and Warren Ellis.
Starring: Nick Cave, Warren Ellis, Ray Winstone, Kylie Minogue.

Alex Garland

Ex Machina

UK 2015, 108 mins

Writer: Alex Garland. Producers: Andrew Macdonald, Allon Reich. Executive Producers: Scott Rudin, Eli Bush, Tessa Ross. Associate Producers: Jason Sack, Joanne Smith. Line Producer: Caroline Levy. Director of Photography: Rob Hardy. Editor: Mark Day. Production Designer: Mark Digby. Music: Geoff Barrow, Ben Salisbury.
Starring: Oscar Isaac, Domhnall Gleeson, Alicia Vikander.

Jonathan Glazer

Sexy Beast

UK 2000, 89 mins

Writers: Louis Mellis, David Scinto. Producer: Jeremy Thomas. Director of Photography: Ivan Bird. Editors: John Scott, Sam Sneade. Music: Roque Baños.
Starring: Ray Winstone, Ben Kingsley, Ian McShane, Amanda Redman.

Birth

UK 2004, 100 mins

Writers: Jean-Claude Carrière, Milo Addica, Jonathan Glazer. Producers: Lizie Gower, Nick Morris, Jean-Louis Piel. Director of Photography: Harris Savides. Editors: Sam Sneade, Claus Wehlisch. Music: Alexandre Desplat.
Starring: Nicole Kidman, Cameron Bright, Lauren Bacall, Danny Huston.

Under the Skin

UK 2013, 108 mins

Writers: Walter Campbell, Jonathan Glazer (based on the novel by Michel Faber). Producers: Nick Wechsler, James Wilson. Director of Photography: Daniel Landin. Editor: Paul Watts. Music: Mica Levi.
Starring: Scarlett Johansson, Andrew Gorman, Dougie McConnell, Kevin McAlinden.

Joanna Hogg

Unrelated

UK 2007, 100 mins

Writer: Joanna Hogg. Producer: Barbara Stone. Director of Photography: Oliver Curtis. Editor: Helle le Fevre.
Starring: Kathryn Worth, Tom Hiddleston, Harry Kershaw, Emma Hiddleston.

Archipelago
UK 2010, 114 mins
Writer: Joanna Hogg. Producer: Gayle Griffiths. Director of Photography: Ed Rutherford. Editor: Helle le Fevre.
Starring: Tom Hiddleston, Christopher Baker, Kate Fahy, Lydia Leonard.

Exhibition
UK 2013, 101 mins
Writer: Joanna Hogg. Producer: Gayle Griffiths. Director of Photography: Ed Rutherford. Editor: Helle le Fevre.
Starring: Viv Albertine, Liam Gillick, Tom Hiddleston, Harry Kershaw.

D. R. Hood

Wreckers
UK 2011, 85 mins
Writer: D. R. Hood. Producer: Simon Onwurah. Director of Photography: Annemarie Lean-Vercoe. Editor: Claire Pringle. Music: Andrew Lovett.
Starring: Benedict Cumberbatch, Claire Foy, Shaun Evans, Peter McDonald.

Sally El Hosaini

My Brother the Devil
UK 2012, 111 mins
Writer: Sally El Hosaini. Producers: Julia Godzinskaya, Gayle Griffiths, Michael Sackler. Director of Photography: David Raedeker. Editor: Iain Kitching. Music: Stuart Earl.
Starring: James Floyd, Fady Elsayed, Saïd Taghmaoui, Anthony Welsh, Amira Ghazalla.

Asif Kapadia

The Warrior
UK, France, Germany, India 2001, 86 mins
Writers: Asif Kapadia, Tim Miller. Producer: Bertrand Faivre. Director

of Photography: Roman Osin. Editor: Ewa J. Lind. Music: Dario Marianelli.
Starring: Irrfan Khan, Puru Chibber, Aino Annuddin, Sunita Sharma.

The Return
US 2006, 85 mins
Writer: Adam Sussman. Producers: Aaron Ryder, Jeffrey Silver. Director of Photography: Roman Osin. Editor: Claire Simpson. Music: Dario Marianelli.
Starring: Sarah Michelle Gellar, Sam Shepard, Peter O'Brien, Adam Scott.

Far North
UK 2007, 89 mins
Writers: Asif Kapadia, Tim Miller. Producer: Bertrand Faivre. Director of Photography: Roman Osin. Editor: Ewa J. Lind. Music: Dario Marianelli.
Starring: Sean Bean, Michelle Yeoh, Michelle Krusiec.

Senna
UK, France 2010, 106 mins
Writer: Manish Pandey. Producers: Tim Bevan, Eric Fellner, James Gay-Rees. Director of Photography: Jake Polonsky. Editors: Chris King, Gregers Sall. Music: Antonio Pinto.
Starring: Ayrton Senna, Alain Prost, Frank Williams.

Hong Khaou

Lilting
UK 2014, 91 mins
Writer: Hong Khaou. Producer: Dominic Buchanan. Director of Photography: Ula Pontikos. Editor: Mark Towns. Music: Stuart Earl.
Starring: Ben Whishaw, Pei-pei Cheng, Andrew Leung, Morven Christie.

Andrew Kötting

Gallivant
UK 1996, 100 mins
Writer: Andrew Kötting. Producers: Ben Gibson, Ben Woolford. Director of Photography: Nick Gordon Smith. Editor: Cliff West. Music: David Burnand.
Starring: Eden Kötting, Gladys Morris, Andrew Kötting.

This Filthy Earth
UK 2001, 111 mins
Writers: Andrew Kötting, Sean Lock. Producer: Ben Woolford. Director of Photography: Nick Gordon Smith. Editor: Cliff West. Music: David Burnand.
Starring: Shane Attwooll, Dudley Sutton, Xavier Tchili, Ina Clough.

Ivul
France 2009, 100 mins
Writers: John Cheetham, Andrew Mitchell, Andrew Kötting. Producer: Émilie Blézat. Directors of Photography: Nick Gordon Smith, Gary Parker. Editors: David Dusa, Baptiste Evrard. Music: Christian Garcí.
Starring: Jacob Auzanneau, Jean-Luc Bideau, Aurélia Petit, Xavier Tchili.

Louyre: This Our Still Life
UK 2011, 58 mins
Writer, Producer, Director of Photography and Editor: Andrew Kötting. Music: Robin Rimbaud.
Starring: Eden Kötting, Andrew Kötting, Leila McMillan.

Swandown
UK 2012, 98 mins
Writers: Andrew Kötting, Iain Sinclair. Producer: Lisa Marie Russo. Director of Photography: Nick Gordon Smith. Editor: Cliff West. Music: Jem Finer.
Starring: Iain Sinclair, Andrew Kötting.

Gideon Koppel

Sleep Furiously
UK 2008, 94 mins
Writer, Editor: Gideon Koppel. Producers: Margaret Matheson, Gideon Koppel. Director of Photography: Gideon Koppel. Music: Aphex Twin.

John Maclean

Slow West
UK 2015, 84 minutes
Writer: John Maclean. Producers: Iain Canning, Rachel Gardiner,

Conor McCaughan, Emile Sherman. Associate Producer: Geraldine O'Flynn. Line Producer: Angela Littlejohn. Executive Producer: Michael Fassbender. Director of Photography: Robbie Ryan. Editors: Roland Gallois, Jon Gregory. Music: Jed Kurzel.
Starring: Michael Fassbender, Kodi Smit-McPhee, Caren Pistorious, Ben Mendelsohn.

Harry Macqueen

Hinterland
UK 2014, 79 mins
Writer, Producer and Editor: Harry Macqueen. Director of Photography: Ben Hecking. Music: Graham Hadfield.
Starring: Harry Macqueen, Lori Campbell.

Steve McQueen

Hunger
UK, Ireland 2008, 96 mins
Writers: Enda Walsh, Steve McQueen. Producers: Robin Gutch, Laura Hastings-Smith. Director of Photography: Sean Bobbitt. Editor: Joe Walker. Music: Leo Abrahams, David Holmes.
Starring: Michael Fassbender, Liam Cunningham, Stuart Graham, Brian Milligan, Liam McMahon.

Shame
UK 2011, 101 mins
Writers: Steve McQueen, Abi Morgan. Producers: Iain Canning, Emile Sherman. Director of Photography: Sean Bobbitt. Editor: Joe Walker. Music: Harry Escott.
Starring: Michael Fassbender, Carey Mulligan, James Badge Dale, Nicole Beharie.

12 Years a Slave
US, UK 2013, 134 mins
Writer: John Ridley (based on Solomon Northup's memoir). Producers: Dede Gardner, Anthony Katagas, Jeremy Kleiner, Steve McQueen, Arnon Milchan, Brad Pitt, Bill Pohlad. Director of Photography: Sean Bobbitt. Editor: Joe Walker. Music: Hans Zimmer.
Starring: Chiwetel Ejiofor, Michael Fassbender, Lupita Nyong'o, Benedict Cumberbatch, Brad Pitt, Alfre Woodard.

Christine Molloy and Joe Lawlor

Helen

UK 2008, 79 mins

Writers: Joe Lawlor, Christine Molloy. Producers: Joe Lawlor, Christine Molloy. Director of Photography: Ole Bratt Birkeland. Editor: Christine Molloy. Music: Dennis McNulty.

Starring: Annie Townsend, Sonia Saville, Sandie Malia, Dennis Jobling.

Mister John

Singapore, UK 2013, 95 mins

Writers: Joe Lawlor, Christine Molloy. Producers: Fran Borgia, David Collins, Joe Lawlor. Director of Photography: Ole Bratt Birkeland. Editors: Joe Lawlor, Christine Molloy. Music: Stephen McKeon.

Starring: Aidan Gillen, Zoe Tay, Molly Rose Lawlor, Michael Thomas.

Carol Morley

The Alcohol Years

UK 2000, 50 mins

Writer: Carol Morley. Producer: Cairo Cannon. Director of Photography: Peter Bathurst. Editor: Maggie Choyce. Music: Russell Churney, Vini Reilly.

Starring: Stella Grundy, Alan Wise, Pete Shelley, Dave Haslam.

Edge

UK 2010, 93 mins

Writer: Carol Morley. Producers: Cairo Cannon, James Mitchell. Director of Photography: Mary Farbrother. Editor: Fiona DeSouza.

Starring: Maxine Peake, Marjorie Yates, Joe Dempsie, Nichola Burley, Julie T. Wallace.

Dreams of a Life

UK, Ireland 2011, 95 mins

Writer: Carol Morley. Producers: Cairo Cannon, James Mitchell. Directors of Photography: Mary Farbrother, Lynda Hall. Editor: Chris Wyatt. Music: Barry Adamson.

Starring: Zawe Ashton, Alix Luka-Cain.

The Falling

UK 2014, 102 mins

Writer: Carol Morley. Producers: Cairo Cannon, Luc Roeg. Director of Photography: Agnès Godard. Editor: Chris Wyatt. Music: Tracey Thorn.

Starring: Greta Scacchi, Maisie Williams, Monica Dolan, Maxine Peake, Florence Pugh.

Ben Rivers

Two Years at Sea
UK 2011, 88 mins
Writer, Producer: Ben Rivers.
Starring: Jake Williams.

A Spell to Ward Off the Darkness (co-directed with Ben Russell)
UK 2013, 98 mins
Writers: Ben Rivers, Ben Russell. Producers: Julie Gayet, Indrek Kasela, Nadia Turincev. Directors of Photography: Ben Rivers, Ben Russell. Editors: Ben Rivers, Ben Russell. Music: Robert A. A. Lowe.
Starring: Robert A. A. Lowe.

Peter Strickland

Katalin Varga
UK 2009, 82 mins
Writer: Peter Strickland. Producer: Peter Strickland. Director of Photography: Márk Györi. Editor: Matyas Fekete. Music: Nurse with Wound.
Starring: Hilda Péter, Norbert Tankó, László Mátray, Tibor Pálffy.

Berberian Sound Studio
UK 2012, 92 mins
Writer: Peter Strickland. Producers: Mary Burke, Keith Griffiths. Director of Photography: Nicholas D. Knowland. Editor: Chris Dickens. Music: Broadcast.
Starring: Toby Jones, Cosimo Fusco, Antonio Mancino, Jozef Cseres.

Björk: Biophilia Live (co-directed with Nick Fenton)
UK 2014, 92 mins
Producer: Jacqui Edenbrow. Director of Photography: Brett Turnbull. Editor: Nick Fenton. Music: Björk.
Starring: Björk.

The Duke of Burgundy

UK 2014, 101 mins

Writer: Peter Strickland. Producer: Andrew Starke. Director of Photography: Nicholas D. Knowland. Editor: Matyas Fekete. Music: Cat's Eyes.

Starring: Sidse Babett Knudsen, Chiara D'Anna, Eugenia Caruso, Monica Swinn.

Ben Wheatley

Down Terrace

UK 2009, 89 mins

Writers: Robin Hill, Ben Wheatley. Producer: Andrew Starke. Director of Photography: Laurie Rose. Editors: Robin Hill, Ben Wheatley. Music: Jim Williams.

Starring: Robert Hill, Robin Hill, Julia Deakin, Michael Smiley.

Kill List

UK 2011, 95 mins

Writers: Amy Jump, Ben Wheatley. Producers: Claire Jones, Andrew Starke. Director of Photography: Laurie Rose. Editors: Robin Hill, Amy Jump, Ben Wheatley. Music: Jim Williams.

Starring: Neil Maskell, Michael Smiley, MyAnna Buring, Struan Rodger.

Sightseers

UK 2012, 88 mins

Writers: Alice Lowe, Steve Oram, Amy Jump. Producers: Andrew Starke, Claire Jones, Nira Park. Director of Photography: Laurie Rose. Editors: Robin Hill, Amy Jump, Ben Wheatley. Music: Jim Williams.

Starring: Alice Lowe, Steve Oram, Eileen Davies, Seamus O'Neill.

A Field in England

UK 2013, 90 mins

Writers: Amy Jump, Ben Wheatley. Producers: Claire Jones, Andrew Starke. Director of Photography: Laurie Rose. Editors: Amy Jump, Ben Wheatley. Music: Jim Williams.

Starring: Reece Shearsmith, Michael Smiley, Peter Ferdinando, Ryan Pope.

Paul Wright

For Those in Peril
UK 2013, 92 mins
Writer: Paul Wright. Producers: Mary Burke, Polly Stokes. Director of Photography: Benjamin Kracun. Editor: Michael Aaglund. Music: Erik Enocksson.
Starring: George MacKay, Kate Dickie, Michael Smiley, Nichola Burley, Brian McCardie.